Pra
Animal Liberation and Atheism

This is the first and only book that I know of that consciously connects atheism to animal liberation. Socha has written a powerful, enormously important, and truly ambitious book that goes to the heart of the tensions between organized religion and animal liberation. This book will make some people uncomfortable, but will be a breath of fresh air to many others. *Animal Liberation and Atheism* boldly initiates the kind of difficult conversations we must have in order to confront the myriad borders that divide and oppress us, both within the human species and between humans and the more-than-human world.

— David Naguib Pellow, Don A. Martindale professor of
  Sociology, University of Minnesota

This is an important book as it continues in more detail the movement toward vegan living among secular people of all stripes. As freethinking humans set aside divine privilege they should be able to show empathy towards non-human animals. Religious readers will enjoy the show as Socha takes to task many atheist heroes for their missteps and evasions on the ethical ideals of veganism.

— Jason Torpy, president of the Military Association of Atheists
  & Freethinkers

Animal Liberation and Atheism: Dismantling the Procrustean Bed is a remarkable text, one which affirms Kim Socha's deserved reputation as one of the most important and original scholar-activists writing at the present time. . . . Written with admirable rigor, eloquence, and verve, it is a book that deserves to be read widely across both religious and free-thinking communities. At the very least, it will inspire deeper personal reflections, and conversations that problematize religion and atheism against the needless suffering of other animals in this world. At best, the book provides incentive and encouragement for the reader to find ways to actively contribute to the animal liberation movement. This, as Socha reminds us, is a liberation movement which carries with it the hope of realizing a kinder, more just and peaceful future for all animals, humans included.

— Richard J. White, senior lecturer in Human Geography,
  Sheffield Hallam University, UK

The link between animal rights and atheism is apparent once we bring evolution into the conversation and abandon all supernatural religious beliefs about the nature of human nature, which is that we are connected to all other species. With that foundation in place the expansion of the moral sphere to include primates and marine mammals, then all mammals, and finally all sentient beings, follows logically, as Kim Socha demonstrates in this cogently argued treatise that science and reason, not religion and faith, are the primary drivers of moral progress. Socha lays out the arguments for animal rights so well that I predict you will abandon your speciesism by the end.

—Michael Shermer, publisher of *Skeptic* magazine, author of *The Moral Arc: How Science and Reason Bend Humanity Toward Truth, Justice, and Freedom*

If you are willing to read this thoughtful and well-documented book with an open mind, if you are willing to put aside the myths you have accepted to feel entitled to the flesh of non-human animals, then I guarantee that you will never think of food consumption in the same way again. Thank you Kim, for exploring the false teachings of animal consumption, especially the religious ones, that have led us, as animals, to embrace human exceptionalism and to inflict irreparable harm upon the non-human animals with whom we share the Earth.

—annalise fonza, Ph.D., independent writer, educator, blogger and humanist celebrant with the American Humanist Society

Animal Liberation and Atheism is not satisfied to merely celebrate a kinship between ideas but is a critical reflection on vegan practice and atheism which does great service to both. It constitutes the first explicit attempt to consider a path toward a new vegan atheology.

—Dr. Richard Twine, sociologist, author of *Animals as Biotechnology: Ethics, Sustainability and Critical Animal Studies*

Animal Liberation
and Atheism

Animal Liberation and Atheism

Dismantling the Procrustean Bed

Kim Socha

Minneapolis–St. Paul

To Patrick, the atheist in the other room

&

To those who have suffered and continue to suffer under
justifications based on myth, tradition, and whimsy

Library of Congress Control Number: 2014949051

Cover and interior design by Robaire Ream

ISBN: 978-0-9884938-1-0

Table of Contents

Foreword ix

Acknowledgements xiii

Introduction: Dismantling the Procrustean Bed 1

Chapter 1: Hotel Procrustes 29

Chapter 2: Animals Minus Myth 87

Chapter 3: No More Room at the Inn 141

Afterword 191

Bibliography 195

Index 207

Foreword

Al Nowatzki

Famed author Alice Walker is often quoted as saying, "The animals of the world exist for their own reasons. They were not made for humans any more than black people were made for white, or women created for men." What many people who use this quote don't know, however, is that it comes from a foreword that Walker wrote for Marjorie Spiegel's book, *The Dreaded Comparison: Human and Animal Slavery.* With these words, Walker was simply summing up Spiegel's argument.

While it's technically accurate to say that Walker wrote those words, to say that she believes in them is just plain intellectually dishonest. Yet an online image search of the quote shows numerous photos of Walker alongside the words. It's a quote that has graced uncountable vegans' email signature lines. In their haste to claim anyone with name recognition as one of their own, animal activists took a couple of sentences and exploited them, thus deceiving others into thinking that Alice Walker fit into their preferred, preformed box—a Procrustean bed, if you will. (Don't worry, Kim defines "Procrustean bed" in the first couple paragraphs of her introduction.)

I first met Kim Socha at a vegan dine-out in 2010. Everyone at the table was taking turns introducing themselves. Some were going to school, one was a full-time activist for animals, one was a vegan caterer. I was, and still am, a stay-at-home dad, atheist, and vegan. And then came Kim: She was finishing up her doctoral dissertation titled *Women, Destruction and the Avant-Garde: A Paradigm for Animal Liberation.* I think I was the only person at the table to squeal a little and ask her for more information. She sent me a rough draft of the book, and I read the introduction. A couple years later, I won the now-published book at a vegan potluck. It's now a couple years later, and I still have not read the rest of the book. Sorry, Kim. It's thick stuff. Academic, complicated, immensely important stuff. And did I mention thick?

The book you hold in your hands, however, is not thick. It's immensely important, but it's neither academic nor complicated. At times, it will seem like the most common sense thing you could possibly read. But the *sense* that this book makes is sadly uncommon, for if logic—trusted friend of the vegan atheist—were common sense, we would live in an unrecognizable world.

I'm a vegan atheist, unlike my parents before me and their parents before them. Most of us come from a long lineage of people who fit nicely into their surroundings in most ways. But we were fortunate enough to find a newfangled hammer in the form of veganism and atheism. And with that hammer, we pried old nails and pounded new nails and made a different sort of home for ourselves. It's newer. Relatively untested. It's damn near experimental. So, coming from long lines of conformers like we do, it's only natural that we try to convince those still living in the old houses that we are, all evidence to the contrary, still like them and that they are, unbeknownst to them, more like us than they know.

But try as we might to argue otherwise, a geodesic dome is not a log cabin. The fact that we have our special hammer does not make everything a nail; some things are worms and some things are clouds. Our hammer doesn't apply to them. And besides, worms and clouds are horrible things for making sturdy houses.

So perhaps you're vegan. You know what alienation feels like. You know how it feels to be a single voice surrounded by a vast, omnipresent majority who disagrees with your arguments for animal rights, or more often, just disregards them as some fringe position not worth worrying about because, really, what's the difference. Maybe you appeal to religious tradition in order to make your argument more palatable to the mainstream. This book is for you. Kim's going to help you understand how the persistent current of religion that's never far beneath the river of history is what keeps propelling humanity further and further away from ever respecting the right of animals to live free from unnecessary harm and death at our hands.

Perhaps you're an atheist. You beat your head against the desk daily, wondering how in the world people believe the stuff they believe. You have friends and family who don't care as much about the "here and now" because they think that there's an "up there and later." You see public policy corrupted by millennia-old superstition and dogma that has no relevance to current society. This book is for you. Because when that classic epithet of "baby eater" is hurled your way by a vegan activist, it's actually true! You eat nonhuman babies. And your inconsistent application of logic is making us vegan atheists beat *our* heads against *our* desks.

Side rant: We know that animals are suffering and being killed by humans every second of every day. There's no debate there. Arguing that religion causes more harm than good while ignoring and even participating in the harm inflicted upon other sentient animals is like a freethinker opposing religion while supporting slavery. And that's barely even an analogy when you think about it.

We all have unopened doors in our ostensibly open minds that we're not even aware of. Even the shiniest geodesic dome has a cellar door the tenant didn't realize was there. With this book, Kim throws daylight on these unopened ideas and shows us just how much useless and unusable crap we have laying around. A deep cleaning is in order.

It's time to stop putting animal exploitation and religious belief in the recycling bin of history. They belong instead on the trash heap. And the trash heap needs to be lit afire. Then, and only then, can we move forward.

That's a snappy condensation of the argument Kim makes in this book. Feel free to spread that quote far and wide. Also, please note that my last name is spelled with a "z" and not an "s," and I'll take a vegan mint on my Procrustean pillow.

Acknowledgements

I am forever and always in awe of my parents Ed and Lois Socha, for they have shown me levels of love and forgiveness beyond that which I deserve. Thank you for being constants in my somewhat erratic life. *You* are proof that infinite kindness and compassion exist. I am also grateful to my closest companions Patrick and Siouxsie. Although one of you is not with me by choice, I am so fortunate to share a home with two loving people with whom I can experience life's joys, sorrows, and prized moments of even-keeled contentment.

This book existed in my brain for quite a while. I felt a counterpoint to the many religious books promoting animal liberation was sorely needed. However, the text you now hold may have been delayed further or never written if not for the urging of Bill Lehto of Freethought House. I thank Bill for being open to the inclusion of animal liberation within the growing field of secular literature and for creating a publishing company focused on freethought perspectives. Along with Bill, Al Nowatzki and Dr. Scott Hurley served as my readers, and to them I am grateful as well. As a religious studies scholar, Scott helped me historicize, contextualize, and understand the nuances of religion. I needed his expertise to circumvent my proclivity to paint religions in the broadest of strokes. As to Al, my fellow vegan atheist, his commentary, counsel, and source recommendations were vital to this book's development. As an unexpected bonus, his marginal comments made me laugh almost as often as they made me ponder.

I never knew peer review could be so enlightening *and* amusing. I must also thank another fellow vegan atheist, Rohit Ravindran, for alerting me to some key resources and presenting on animal liberation and secularism with me at the 2013 Minnesota Atheists/ American Atheists Regional Conference, as well as for writing about animal issues in the anthology *Atheist Voices of Minnesota*.

Finally, I thank the many activists, scholars, and scholar-activists who inspire me to continue speaking on behalf of those whose voices the masses refuse to hear. You fight for justice and peace with no promise of reward. That is the height of compassion, morality, and ethics to which religion need not apply.

Introduction

Dismantling the Procrustean Bed

> The philosophy of Atheism represents a concept of life without any metaphysical Beyond or Divine Regulator. It is the concept of an actual, real world with its liberating, expanding and beautifying possibilities, as against an unreal world, which, with its spirits, oracles, and mean contentment has kept humanity in helpless degradation.
>
> —Emma Goldman

Greek mythology (a religious belief system no longer in vogue) tells the story of Procrustes, a smith, thief, and torturer. When not roaming the paths between Athens and Eleusis looking for people to rob, Procrustes would invite travelers into his home to rest for the evening. He would then proceed to fit them to his bed. If one was too short for the bed, he would stretch him out (the name Procrustes means "the stretcher" or "he who stretches"). If one was too tall, he would hack away at her limbs until she fit properly. And lest we think anyone could ever survive the "the subduer," Procrustes actually had two beds. If an unsuspecting traveler fit one bed, his tormenter would move him to the other and stretch or hack as the situation demanded.

The idea of the "Procrustean bed" has been adopted and adapted into contemporary vernacular with slightly different meanings depending on the context. The idea of the Procrustean bed is most often used to signify (and I go no further than the online *Free Dictionary* here) "[a]n arbitrary standard to which exact

1

conformity is forced." I will show that religious arguments for animal rights, emancipation, and advocacy, despite the compassion behind them, merely hack away at or stretch the parameters of religion to make animal liberation fit what is essentially an anthropocentric, speciesist, hierarchical belief system that fails to speak to the liberation of nonhuman animals.

I do not address each individual religion throughout human history to explain why it is ultimately not animal-friendly, although I will take specific religions to task. Rather, my purpose is to explore how the very concept of religion—the belief in a higher power, in whatever form it may take—is antithetical to liberating nonhumans from the human perception that other species are ours to do with as we please. Of course, some religions are considerably kinder to animals than others, but there is not one that claims nonhuman animals and human animals have an equal claim to personhood or parity. Similarly, the secular community has been slow to acknowledge what a lack of human exceptionalism means to how we treat other animals. When that association is made by atheist luminaries such as Richard Dawkins (see his essay "Gaps in the Mind," to which I will later refer), they do not follow up with appropriate action such as going vegan or vegetarian, or becoming advocates for nonhuman animals. Thus, a further purpose of this book is to explore the lack of interest in animal concerns within the secular world and to inspire freethinkers to think more seriously about the other animals with whom we share the Earth.

Before getting too far into the purpose of this text, I want to define religion. This seems simple, but not so upon further investigation. Entire books have been written about what religion is without coming to any definitive conclusions! It all depends on whom you ask: the believer, the non-believer, the sociologist, the anthropologist, the scientist, the priest, the shaman, or the rabbi. I have selected a few definitions that set the tone for this book. The first comes from sociologist Émile Durkheim: "A religion is a unified system of beliefs and practices relative to sacred things, that is to say, things set apart and forbidden, beliefs and practices which unite into one single unity called a church, all those who adhere to them" (46). Anthropologist Clifford Geertz offers a more academic but concise five-point overview of religion:

(1) a set of symbols which acts to (2) establish powerful, pervasive, and long-lasting moods, and motivations in men (sic) by (3) formulating conceptions of a general order of existence and (4) clothing these conceptions with such an aura of factuality that (5) the moods and motivations seem uniquely realistic. (208)

Why human beings from pre-history to the modern era feel the need to create these beliefs and practices, these symbols that determine moods and motivations is far outside this book's purview. (See scientist and philosopher Daniel C. Dennett's *Breaking the Spell: Religion as a Natural Phenomena* or the scholarship of Andrew B. Newberg, a neuroscientist interviewed in comedian Bill Maher's film *Religulous*, for more on that topic.) Regardless, the world's myriad religions self-evidently demonstrate Durkheim and Geertz's definitions. Dennett adds another key element to religion: "I propose to define religion as *social systems whose participants avow beliefs in a supernatural agent or agents whose approval is to be sought*" (9).

From these definitions, I draw upon the concepts of unity and order as fundamental human attributes, something we all seek for security and meaning in different ways. Religion is a way to meet those human needs in what can seem like a chaotic world outside of our control: "Understanding the human predicament and the origin and destiny of the world is a powerful incentive for people to convert [. . .] The myths, rituals, and symbols of religion can infuse life with intensity, drama, and significance, offering many people a deep sense of affective gratification" (Rambo, *Understanding* 82–83). This desire for answers and fulfillment is understandable and likely endemic to the human condition. It is the only final aspect of supernatural beings that some humans have abandoned.

Books that regard animal liberation from religious perspectives are common in the movement. From the Abrahamic religions, to Buddhism, to Wicca, to tribal religions of indigenous peoples, individuals from the most recognized belief systems have argued that their respective faiths foster a compassionate view of nonhuman animals. Books regarding animal liberation from a deliberately secular perspective, however, are virtually nonexistent. While there are many books about animal liberation written by those without religious affiliations or agendas, there is a dearth of arguments for animal liberation that are consciously and blatantly grounded in atheism. Some interesting textual and virtual media resources connect atheism with animal liberation, but these are not enough to develop a body of literature that articulates those connections, perhaps because the movements are moderately new.

Both the atheist and animal rights movements are in their relative infancies. Contemporary animal advocacy began in the 1970s with the release of utilitarian philosopher Peter Singer's *Animal Liberation*; however, arguments against animal cruelty have existed throughout documented history. And while non-believers have existed likely as long as the concept of god(s), atheism as an area of scholarship and political momentum is a relatively new initiative.

In *Atheist Manifesto*, philosopher Michel Onfray argues that such a secular oeuvre has yet to materialize because even Western philosophers who are considered to be non-believers never completely removed the shackles of religious ideology. This caused Onfray to search for atheism's "missing link, a precursor, an inventor, milestone from which we may proclaim: this was the first atheist, the one who denied [without equivocation] the existence of God" (27). After an interesting trek through history's forgotten semi-atheists, Onfray appears to conclude Friedrich Nietzsche is that "missing link" (32).[1] Thus, one could arguably suggest

---

1. This idea is not without its detractors. For example, Christopher Cox argues Nietzsche's declaration that "god is dead" was not a "personal confession of atheism or loss of faith"; rather, he was noting the destruction of European systems of thought and value (16–17). Further, Gavin Hyman counts eighteenth-century French philosopher Denis Diderot as "the first explicit and self-confessedly atheist philosopher."

atheism (or an "atheology," as Onfray calls it) is only about one hundred or so years old, which is not to discount the works of Nietzsche's predecessors. Singer proposes that it was not until the 1960s that the study of ethics was more formally disengaged from theology, and he cites the work of Derek Parfit which emphasizes that "[b]elief in God, or in many gods, prevented the free development of moral reasoning" (*How Are We to Live?* 15). In the interim, atheists have been forced to defend the idea that they can be good without God, faced with questions more suited for evolutionary psychologists than the average non-believer.

This book attempts to unite these nascent areas of thought: animal liberation and atheism. I chose the subtitle "Dismantling the Procrustean Bed" because that is just what I propose to do: take apart religious arguments for nonhuman animal welfare and liberation and offer new ideas for liberation that need not be squeezed into an unsustainable position. Initially, I had thought about "destroying" the Procrustean bed, but that seemed excessive. The bed wasn't the problem for Procrustes' victims; Procrustes was the problem. The bed was only a tool used to deceive and torture a cruel man's victims. I see religion in the same way, as something that humans created because it serves a purpose. For the masses, religion gives life meaning. Religion gives reason to be good, hopeful, and kind. However, we mustn't forget Steven Weinberg's classic quip that "good people can behave well and bad people can do evil; but for good people to do evil, that takes religion." As animals who can contemplate death, it further gives humans solace that we will escape mortality through divine will. These are pleasant ideas, and I personally have no problem with their existence as long as such beliefs are kept to the individual and not forced, either subtly or overtly, upon others. But religions are not, of course, all sweetness and light.

For those with religious authority, religion-as-tool is an avenue for the domination of animal-kind, humans included, and the Earth's resources. Like Procrustes' bed, religion is a device that has been repeatedly used to harm others. Any time religion has been used to deceive, violate, and discriminate, it is violence. And as one who believes that gods, goddesses, demons, spirits, divine mandates, and other supernatural concepts are made up and often abused by humans in power, I argue that religion is in a perpetual state of deception. It is up to the individual to decide whether to use religion. Thus, my intentions herein are to dismantle the bed and expose it as a dangerous apparatus, but one on which you need not lie. And if you do find solace there, I ask that you critically analyze its foundation. The pillows and blankets may feel comforting, but you are prostrate, meaning both lying down and powerless. The other-than-human animals upon which Western civilization is built are prostrate and slaughtered by the billions every year. Religion allows, even sanctions and demands, this avoidable butchery.

At this point, perhaps you are wondering what became of Procrustes. The answer to that will extend the metaphor and clarify the purposes of this book. He was killed by the Greek hero Theseus upon the very bed on which he had mutilated countless victims. Fritz Graf notes that Theseus represented a new kind of hero in ancient Greece, one more progressive than brutes such as Hercules; indeed, Graf calls Theseus a "civilizer" (137). Procrustes, and by extension his tortuous bed, was destroyed by a civilizing and enlightening force. Theseus "made the road from Troezen to Athens safe for travelers. He is shown clearing the road of all sorts of bandits" and other malicious men who threw people off cliffs, crushed them, tore at them (Graf 137). To me, that is what atheism does. It clears the road through and to secular enlightenment so that, for example, people of the same gender (or no iden-tifiable gender) can live without fear of social exclusion; it al-lows women education and influence; it negates the need for human children to have their genitals mutilated; and it chal-lenges any of the other myriad atrocities enacted in the name of an imperceptible deity. At this point, however, atheism does not adequately speak for other-than-human animals. They too need the path cleared so they can go about their business, even if that business is killing other animals for survival, without the human interference that so often manifests as abuse. The purpose of this text is to begin that conversation, which should be of interest to animal advocates and those in the secular community. Ideally, it will interest anyone who wishes to live in a less violent and more just world.

The Making of a Vegan Atheist (or an Atheist Vegan)[2]

I enjoy hearing stories of those who have adopted and fight for unpopular yet righteous perspectives. Within my interactions with ethical vegans and atheists, stories of "How did you get here?" naturally arise. In a sense, we are really asking the following questions: How did you get to be like me in this way? What caused you to take on a viewpoint that may make you an object of suspicion, ridicule, and scorn amongst the mainstream public? Whether you are an atheist, vegan, or an atheist vegan, you comprise a theological and ethical alternative. According to most recent surveys, atheists and agnostics account for about twelve to fifteen percent of the US population (Stenger 23; A. Sullivan[3]), and although reports vary slightly, vegans—those who avoid animal products and byproducts as much as is practically possible—encompass about 1.5 percent of Americans (Singer and Mason 5). I am part of these percentages, and my best and most principled thinking has led me to identify as an atheist and an ethical vegan, as opposed to one who chooses veganism for health reasons but has no quarrel with other types of animal utilization. Over the past few years, I have realized these identifiers are not distinct. Rather, they are closely allied, making me not just an atheist and a vegan, but an atheist

---

2. This section is closely adapted from my chapter "Why I Am Not Religious . . . And What That Has to Do with Being Vegan" published in *Atheist Voices of Minnesota: An Anthology of Personal Stories* (Freethought House, 2012).

3. Citations that do not provide page numbers both here and throughout the text indicate material accessed through Internet resources without pagination or electronic books.

vegan and vegan atheist. What follows is a brief recap of how that identity came to pass.

I was raised a Catholic meat eater. I come from a loving family, but they do not value nonhuman animals except, in the case of my mother, as canine companions in the home. While growing up, my father insisted that my brother and I attend church with him on Sunday mornings. As we went off to church, my mother slept in. She did not go to mass, but she occasionally prays to the saints. (Eventually, my father too would stop going to mass. The child abuse scandals turned him off to Catholicism, and then God.) At age sixteen, I was allowed to make my own decision about continuing in the faith.

Once sixteen came and went, I continued believing in God, though my attendance at mass was sporadic. A quintessential troubled teen without ready access to or interest in drugs, alcohol, or sex, I used religion—specifically, the image of the loving, fair-haired, blue-eyed Christ—to support me, just as I did Metallica's *Ride the Lightening* cassette and my own dour poetry. The latter two ironically caused my peers to accuse me of being a Satanist. I would spend my lunch hour in my high school's chapel because I had ostracized my friends and didn't want to spend that social time being alone or scorned. I asked my mother to help me find a convent school because I hated my high school and wanted to leave. Once we found out that such schools didn't exist anymore for teenage girls, my desire to become a nun quickly faded. What I was really seeking through religion was escape, not to become a bride of Christ. I would have to just wait out the high school angst. Soon, it was time to think of college, and there I finally began to question God's existence and the human right to appropriate animal bodies at will.

Ironically, my path to atheism began in a world religions class at a Catholic women's college. There I learned about Buddhism, a vegetarian-friendly, questionably atheistic religion. Buddha was not a big-bellied Eastern Santa Claus who ruled from a perfect realm as I had thought. Rather, he was a man who taught self-reliance and the idea that we are all potential Buddhas ("enlightened ones"). The historical Buddha did not teach reincarnation as we commonly understand it today.[4] Instead, he taught his followers to value the only thing we can be sure of—our awareness of now. As fascinating as I found Buddhism to be, the class didn't make me Buddhist; the result was more important than that, for it made me question Catholicism. Having attended Catholic school for twelve years, and attending a Catholic college for my last two years as an undergraduate, I had grown up with the belief that non-Christians were evil and destined to burn in Hell. I still remember being at my brother's little league baseball game as a child and hearing adults talk disdainfully about Judaism. I was shocked to learn there were some individuals who didn't believe Jesus was God. In this class on world religions, however, I began to question why a righteous God would damn a Buddhist to Hell simply because she did not believe in Jesus Christ as God's son. Other things didn't cohere anymore either, such as damning unbaptized babies to Hell (which the Catholic Church has since reconsidered, I believe; does it really matter?) and damning people who were never told about Jesus Christ for not accepting him. None of it made ethical, moral, or rational sense.

I read Charles Darwin, and I came to accept that humans are animals just as animals are animals. We all feel pain and joy and seek survival upon threat of danger. With this in mind, it seemed less ethical to eat other animals, so I went vegetarian, though eggs and dairy were still part of my diet. In a philosophy class, wearing my "Against Animal Testing" T-shirt from a store I now know uses animal byproducts in their make-up and lotions—words are tricky; just because a product wasn't tested on animals does not mean it is free of products taken from animals—I offered an argument against animal experimentation, explaining to the audience of young Catholic women that mice and rabbits feel pain just as humans do. I explained that humans are animals, and just as we

---

4. Some strains of Buddhist thought would argue both this assertion and that Buddhism is an atheistic theology. This gets back to the nature of religion, a point to which I return below.

have no moral right to claim the bodies of other humans as our own, we must question the supposed right to appropriate animal bodies for use as science experiments. I received an "A" on the assignment, but no one in the class asked questions or showed much interest, though I overheard two classmates giggling and saying "You're such a wild animal!" to each other as I returned to my seat. I think the idea that humans are animals was new to some of my classmates (or at least acceptance of the idea was new). I don't blame them for ignoring my message, as my own transition to veganism was not as immediate as my acceptance of atheism. In fact, I would not go vegan until fourteen years later.

In retrospect, the God I was taught to worship was fairly easy to renounce because he never existed, which is not to say I wasn't giving anything up by becoming atheist. I was letting go of eternal life, of seeing dead loved ones again, of a celestial protector, and more. However, those ideas had always existed in the abstract. These days, I am more apt to see atheism in the vein of the late iconoclast Christopher Hitchens, as detailed in *The Portable Atheist*:

> There are, after all, atheists who say they wish the fable were true but are unable to suspend the requisite disbelief, or who have relinquished belief only with regret. To this I reply: who wishes there was a permanent, unalterable celestial despotism that subjected us to continual surveillance and could convict us of thought-crime, and who regarded us as private property even after we died? How happy we ought to be, at the reflection that there exists not a shred of respectable evidence to support such a terrible hypothesis. (xxii)

And though it even sounds glib to my non-believing ears, letting go of God really *was* like letting go of the Easter Bunny. It was just another cultural myth set to waste by knowledge and reason. But while religion kept me focused on death, food kept me alive and content, which is why I found certain food items difficult to forgo. It was the tangible gratification I got from eating animal products such as ice cream and cheese that kept me vegetarian for so long, even backsliding into meat eating for a brief time, although I knew the dairy and meat industries are interconnected and that egg production is particularly abhorrent. Just as I had once set aside my misgivings about a higher power, I also ignored nagging questions about where my food came from. The answers to both seemed too upsetting and inconvenient. Eventually, I would come to see those answers as blessings, in the most secular way possible.

While Buddha and Darwin led me to atheism in my early adulthood, a 2006 documentary called *Behind the Mask: The Story of People Who Risk Everything to Save Animals* led me to veganism years later. This documentary by Shannon Keith helped me see, rather than just know, that all animals suffer immensely in the cages humans force them into, both those with whom we share almost 100 percent of our DNA and those we have declared our food, clothing, entertainment, and research. My transition to veganism was dawdling, but I have now come to accept without reservation that I am a primate, and as an animal with moral agency and the privilege of making choices that severely limit other animals' exploitation and death, I see no justification for using animal products.

Indeed, just as Darwin's work gave scientific credence to the nullification of a higher power, sending church leaders into a panic, it too has led progressive thinkers to question human dominance over nonhumans. Darwin undoubtedly saw associations between humans and animals, as acknowledged in *The Descent of Man*:

> All have the same senses, intuitions, and sensations,—similar passions, affections, and emotions, even the more complex ones, such as jealousy, suspicion, emulation, gratitude, and magnanimity; they practice deceit and are revengeful; they are sometimes susceptible to ridicule, and even have a sense of humor; they feel wonder and curiosity; they possess the same faculties of imitation, attention, deliberation, choice, memory, imagination, the association of ideas, and reason, though in very different degrees.

Sadly, knowledge of our similarities to other species has not always resulted in respect, but in their continued victimization in research experiments. Shaking off the assumption of human supremacy and species-specific natural rights is indeed a hard row to hoe. Nevertheless, challenges employed by the animal rights movement spring from Darwin's work, as does the challenge his work poses to theological explanations for humankind's existence. Indeed, corporate interest groups of the animal industrial complex blame "Darwin's publication of *The Descent of Man* [. . .] [and] the voyage of the Beagle [as charting] a course that lead to the Animal Welfare Act [1966]" and radical animal rights groups (Potter 127). Culturally established institutions—in this case, animal industries and religion—fear alternative viewpoints when their power is premised upon false claims such as our need to eat animals to live healthfully and our need to worship God to be moral. Regardless of his personal beliefs, Darwin is undoubtedly a founding theorist of both atheism and animal liberation, allowing me to unite those seemingly disparate ideologies. With that said, Darwin and Buddha are certainly not the only connecting threads.

A superficial point of similarity resulting from my atheism and veganism are what I call the "I gotcha questions": queries people ask that they are sure will zing me into belief in God or meat eating. The "I gotchya questions" are almost always asked with a sense of self-satisfaction as if I have never been asked them before, and I will be taken aback by their profoundness or humor. Some of the atheism queries include:

> "Are you sure you aren't just *angry* at God?"
> "Isn't atheism simply another religion?"
> "How do you explain people going to Heaven and coming back?"
> "There might be a God, so isn't it better to worship him just in case?"

To which I respond, respectively, "No," "No," "Ask a neurologist," and "If you are worshipping God 'just in case,' you'll be in Hell with me come Judgment Day." Of course, there are also questions that are so absurd they nearly silence me, but they also speak to the public relations work still needed to help people understand atheism.

For example, I was out with a group of graduate school friends a few years back. One of them dropped his cigarette butt on the ground; I picked it up and threw it away. One of my companions questioned why I did that, saying something akin to this: "You're an atheist. What do you care about littering or the environment?" At first, I was more puzzled than irritated by his question. Once I found my bearings, I asked him if he only does good things because of the promise of a reward in the afterlife, and if this is so, what does that say of his moral compass? I then explained that my disbelief in a higher power makes me value the world that we actually live in, which must involve respect for all living creatures and the environment. Although I do not claim to be a paragon of virtue, I do my best to be kind and respectful, knowing there is no promise of recompense in this life, and surely not in a next one.

As annoying as the atheism "I gotchya questions" are, they pale in comparison to the ones I get as a vegan. Interestingly, people have responded more acerbically and rudely to my refusal to eat, wear, and use animal products than to my disbelief in God. An acquaintance of mine told me that her Catholic father was more upset by her going vegan than by her coming out as a lesbian. As some see it, heresy and same sex relationships are one thing, but not eating nonhuman animals or their byproducts is absurd![5] Although they vary greatly, the vegan "I gotchya questions" usually revolve around plant sentience, protein, and the fear that cows will take over the world unless we kill and eat them.

Sometimes, the questions are sincere, especially the protein one. Incidentally, nearly everything we eat has protein, and vegans would have to try really hard to not get enough. The plant sentience question is usually asked by one who thinks he is hysterically funny or has found a fissure in vegan ethics; it is rarely, if ever, asked by someone who is concerned about plant pain. When I explain that plants have no central nervous system or fight-or-flight response mechanism that most pain-feeling organisms have, I am usually met with "Yeah, but how do you know for sure?"

---

5. To add another ripple to this issue, Victor Stenger notes that atheists "fall below homosexuals in the esteem of a majority of Americans" (23).

thereby echoing those who question my disbelief in God. I usually respond by saying, "If you are worried about eating plants because they possibly feel pain, then stop eating meat because animals irrefutably feel pain. Further, meat eaters are responsible for exponentially more plant death in their lifetimes because of the amount of plant foods so-called 'food animals' eat before slaughter and ingestion by humans."[6] I then usually explain that veganism is not a claim of perfection, but a decision to do the least amount of harm while still taking care of oneself (humans are animals too, after all). Until my conscience will no longer allow me to eat fruits and vegetables, I will continue to eat living organisms from the plant world.

As to cows or other "food" animals taking over the world, the very reason they exist in such vast numbers is humans keep forcing them to reproduce so they can be slaughtered and eaten. This reproduction is by human design; indeed, farmers have developed what is known both within and outside the industry as "rape racks" that forcibly impregnate cows. If humans stopped doing this, the population problem would rapidly diminish, and the planet would be saved from environmental devastation resulting from factory farms. Many animals used for food have also been genetically altered to such an extent that they would not be able to live long, let alone reproduce, if actually freed from their places of confinement. For instance, chickens are grown to have unnaturally large breasts because Americans enjoy white meat. This massive enlargement puts such pressure on their bones that they cannot stand very long and must stop to rest after taking only a few steps (*Food, Inc.*).

Inevitably, the issues of atheism and veganism align in my life via the standard comments I hear at vegan outreach events, such as, "Animals are ours to eat because God says so in the Bible." My response depends on my mood. If I'm feeling flip, I might explain that the Bible also says people who eat shellfish or wear blended fibers are an abomination, and questioning if the person believes

---

6. I briefly address plants again in the second chapter.

that is true. Invariably, she will say no, to which I respond, "See how easy it is to disregard lessons from the Bible?" If I'm in an especially combative mood, or just plain tired, I'll acknowledge that Christianity is *not compatible* with *real* compassion for animals—hence the purpose of this book.

People never actively interrogated my ethics and morals until I became an atheist vegan. I find this somewhat ironic because I maintain that atheism and veganism have made me a more principled person as well as one who is more critical of widely accepted cultural norms. When I was religious, I was self-centered, reward seeking, intolerant, and sanctimonious. When my perimeter of empathy was confined to humans alone, and mainly just included me, I was being disingenuous, thinking hierarchically, and limiting my compassion. Through atheism and ethical veganism, I have challenged the dangers of dichotomous (good versus evil) and stratified thinking (God, angels, man, woman, animals, plants, minerals). In this process, my disbelief in God and my belief in respect for all life has allowed me to progress from a diffident Catholic girl to an atheist vegan woman who feels an ethical imperative to defend her views because the alternatives—faith in man-made Gods and the presumption that other animals exist for human use—bring so much preventable suffering into the world.

As an academic and activist, my primary (but not exclusive) focus has been upon nonhuman animals, for I feel they are the most ignored and abused among us. Within my scholarship and activism, I have tried to position animal liberation as a political movement with social relevance not limited to nonhumans, and I encourage those who term themselves "animal activists" to consider other ways in which oppression manifests. Being an atheist activist is a little different and, up to this point, I can't say I've been much of one. On the surface, atheism appears to be little more than disbelief in a higher power. It is a lack, rather than an indicator, of something. For some atheists, that is an appropriate definition (the term for this is "apatheism," indicating apathetic atheism). Even my vegan animal activist comrades, many of whom are atheist or agnostic, have teased me about attending atheist functions, wondering what we could possibly have to do or talk about.

They and others do not acknowledge atheism as anything other than a lack. In contrast, I pose my atheism as a political marker.

When I rally against the unfair treatment of those in the LGBTQIA community by a government that claims separation between church and state, I do so as an atheist. Atheism underpins my sadness and palpable rage when hearing that a Pakistani teen was shot by the Taliban for championing education for girls. When I show support for the legalization of traditionally shunned topics such as marijuana and prostitution, I am being an atheist. Atheism as a political act happens, ceases to be a lack, whenever I or anyone questions outdated and unreasonable cultural institutions perpetuated by religious beliefs—and so many of them do.

I am most surely an atheist when professing that any type of animal slaughter for human sustenance in the Global North (halal, kosher, or otherwise) is unethical. I am an atheist when I say even if the law protects the practice, sacrificing animals for any religious purpose is a moral indignation. And then I am an atheist vegan/ vegan atheist when I point out the hypocrisy of the Westerner who will eat a slaughtered chicken bought at the grocery store but finds barbaric the Santero who kills a chicken for his God and then eats her afterwards. Just as I argue that ethical veganism is a political act against oppression, so is atheism, and more often than one might expect, those perspectives can powerfully unite in the face of ignorance, cruelty, and hierarchy.

The Making of an Atheist Animal Liberation Book

The seeds of this book were planted when I was publishing my doctoral dissertation in 2010. Although the book series editors accepted the manuscript, I had to go through a typical anonymous peer review process. That book is about a lot of things, but atheism really isn't one of them. However, within an overview of animal rights history, I made some comments about the Christian Bible's views on nonhumans that were eventually edited out of the text, as cited here from the initial manuscript:

The Holy Bible, within both the Old and New Testaments, gives mankind free rein over lesser beings not made in God's divine image. While [Peter] Singer does see some "flickers of concern" for animal suffering in the Judaic Old Testament, the Christian New Testament "is completely lacking in any injunction against cruelty to animals, or any recommendation to consider their interests" (Singer 191). Like all things biblical, a book crammed with contradictions and "divine" laws that contemporary readers neglect to put in historical context, one can find permission to eat animals, while another can find proof that God wants us to be caretakers of nonhuman animals, which cannot include their consumption. Interpretation aside, *sine qua non* Christianity is not a religion that advocates vegetarianism, and its profound influence over the years since its inception hardly needs defending. Most profoundly, Christianity "spread the idea that every human life—and only human life—is sacred [. . . a] doctrine [that] served to confirm and further depress the lowly position nonhumans had in the Old Testament" (Singer 191). (Socha, "Dumb Animals" 29–30)

One of my reviewers (who I will call Reader X) took umbrage with this sweeping diatribe against Christianity. Although I do not know who Reader X is, he is most likely a Christian for whom my commentary had tripped a wire. The reviewer said I was making uncritical generalizations against a religion and a God (Jesus Christ) who is animal-friendly. In sum, I was misreading the Bible, and to include such material in my book, I would have a lot of defending and further research to do.

Specifically, the reviewer focused on John 2:13–17, the scene in which Jesus gets angry in the Temple, overturning tables, and driving out merchants. The story goes like this:

When it was almost time for the Jewish Passover, Jesus went up to Jerusalem. In the temple courts he found people selling cattle, sheep and doves, and others sitting at tables exchanging money. So he made a whip out of cords, and drove all from the temple courts, both sheep and cattle; he scattered the coins of the money changers and overturned their tables. To those who sold doves he said, "Get these out of here! Stop turning my Father's house into a market!" His disciples remembered that it is written: "Zeal for your house will consume me." (NIV[7])

Reader X interpreted this scene as Jesus being angry that the animals were going to be sold for slaughter or sacrifice. While I have no doubt this person is thoughtful and erudite, such a reading of that biblical passage both amused and angered me. For me to pretend to know why Jesus was mad is, perhaps, as pompous as any other reading of the passage. However, both my Catholic upbringing and common sense lead to a clear determination that Jesus was mad that the Jerusalemites had turned a holy house into a place of commerce. He does not remove the doves because they are in cages but because they are being sold in his father's house. And he actually makes a whip to drive out the sheep and cattle! Jesus is blatantly thrashing animals and this person read the passage as one of Christ-like care and compassion.

I did not want to argue with my anonymous reviewer, and since the passage wasn't integral to my book, I omitted it entirely because the way in which Reader X wanted me to consider John 2:13–17 was, and I don't choose this word lightly, ridiculous. Even though this person gave me other fine suggestions, I still viewed him as ridiculous for a long time. In retrospect, that wasn't fair. I imagine that Reader X saw his values under attack. I imagine a person who worships Jesus Christ as a supreme, all-loving deity while also believing that nonhumans should be free from human use as food, clothing, entertainment, and research. If I was that person, I too would want my God to have my back, along with the animals'. Further, I would likely seek proof in holy books that

7. All biblical passages in this text are taken from the *New International Version* accessible via *BibleGateway.com*.

God's ideas of a just world align with mine. In a sense, Reader X had to read John 2:13–17 in that "ridiculous" way or face some disturbing conclusions about his supposedly loving God.

Reader X in not alone in his assessment of John 2:13–17. In *The Slaughter of Terrified Beasts: A Biblical Basis for the Humane Treatment of Animals*, evangelical minister J.R. Hyland offers a similar interpretation. Against the typical explanation for that biblical passage, Hyland avers that Jesus wasn't overly concerned with the economic system of his era (56–57); rather, his anger was directed at the potential slaughter of animals. But even giving Hyland and Reader X the benefit of doubt, the former also states that Jesus was enraged "[b]ecause this slaughter of the innocent was *idolatrous worship* [the animals were being sold for sacrifice], Isaiah and the other Latter Prophets had called for the end of sacrificial religion" (56, emphasis added). Animal sacrifice was associated with non-Christian religions at a time when Christianity was attempting to gain momentum and power. The "slaughter of the innocent" broke the first commandment to not worship false idols, and considering other biblical passages that will later be discussed, the Bible is blatantly anthropocentric and speciesist with no instruction to cease slaughtering animals except in the case of idolatrous sacrificial offerings.

Hyland provides another example to reinforce this need to interpret the Bible as animal-friendly. She cites a passage from Luke in which an angel of God appears to shepherds telling them not to fear, for good news is afoot! There will be a sign, and they will come across an infant in a manger (Luke 2:9–12). Hyland goes on to explain: "So it was that those chosen to be the first to know the good news of Christ's coming were men who cared for animals" (48). From ancient origins until now, sheep have been kept for their wool, milk, and meat. The men of whom Hyland writes were caring for sheep only until they would be sheared, have their milk stolen from their bucks or ewes, and then slaughtered. This end game of shepherding gets nary a mention in Hyland's creation of an animal-friendly Christianity.

Another event that prompted me to write about atheism and animal liberation occurred within my local Twin Cities freethought

community. I attended a group discussion about animal intelligence, which is more complex amongst different species than
most might imagine, prompted by a documentary on our local
Public Broadcasting Service channel. The very idea that an atheist
organizer would arrange an event to discuss how humans should
treat nonhumans in light of scientific research offered promise
that the atheist movement might be a locus of progress for animal
liberation. At the same time, the tenor of the talk was still highly
anthropocentric, demonstrating what I see as fallout from earlier
religious indoctrination.

   With all of this anti-religious sentiment in mind, I should
acknowledge that religious texts and traditions do offer some
passages and ontological conceptions that advocate kinder consideration of nonhumans while challenging humans to think of them
as more than property. For example, native "traditions recognize
animals [human and nonhuman] as fundamentally the same under
the skin" (Kemmerer 48). The Quran states: "There is not a creature (that lives) on earth [. . .] that is not (a member of) nations
(and groups) like unto yourselves. Nothing have We omitted from
the Book, and they (all) shall be gathered unto their Lord in the
end" (6.38). The Holy Bible also contains injunctions not to be
total jerks to animals; to wit, don't eat animals if they are still alive
(Deut. 12:23). These ideas allow people to use their holy manu-
scripts and traditions of choice as proof that humans ought to be
kind to nonhumans, and I would be remiss if I did not acknowledge that religious beliefs can motivate individuals to compassionate practices. However, the concept of "kindness to animals" can
mean many things, and herein lies my need to explain the place
from which I write and to offer my own definitions of kindness
and atheism as they are used in the milieu of this book.

   As noted above, *Animal Liberation and Atheism* is more concerned with religion proper than it is with particular religions; this
is partly because even specific religions are not monolithic entities. One cannot really speak of Buddhism, Hinduism, Judaism,
or Christianity writ large. Lisa Kemmerer notes in *Animals and
World Religions* that "[t]here is no *one* Buddhism, and there is no
one Christianity [. . .]. Religions are notoriously complicated" (5).

The same can be said of animal advocacy. There is no catch-all concept of an animal activist; in contrast, animal advocacy is an expansive spectrum of ideas and strategies. There are those who work for welfare, protection, or rights, working within the legal system or with animal industries to change laws and attitudes so that animals are not egregiously harmed. In kind, one can theoretically claim to be an advocate for animals while believing humans should be able to use them as food and in research as long as restrictions are in place. Others vehemently argue that if animals are no longer seen as legal property, we can abolish their abuse and exploitation. Still others use direct action, which includes illegal acts that literally release nonhumans from their cages or cause economic damage to a particular institution or industry. This list of positions could go on and on, but that story is another book entirely.

I write this book as an advocate for unconditional animal liberation, the idea of which is effectively explained here within the mission statement of the Animal Rights Coalition, a Minneapolis-based group of which I am a member as of this writing:

> We believe that animals matter for their own reasons and that they should not be used by human beings for profit, pleasure, amusement, or simply because it is our habit to do so. We seek to abolish the use and exploitation of animals for human interests, rather than simply reforming or improving the conditions under which animals are used and exploited. We believe that animals are morally entitled to pursue their lives free of human violence according to the needs of their species and should be free from coerced physical and psychological suffering.

As an adherent to this position, I will only rarely refer to what is commonly called the "animal *rights* movement," which I think promotes a specific strategy and end game: legal reform and attainment of government issued rights for nonhumans, respectively. I prefer the term "animal liberation movement" because liberation, as noted by pattrice jones, "has only positive associations within an array of movements while still communicating commitment to ending of ownership and exploitation of animals

by people" (276). This is also why I use terminology such as
"nonhuman animal" and "other-than-human animal"; it is my attempt to bridge the culturally ingrained binary that sets humans
apart from other species. Other times, either for stylistic flow or
when referencing how *others* perceive nonhumans, I will simply
use the word "animal."

As to my position as a member of the secular community, I am
an atheist, indicating one without belief in a god or gods. Again,
when deciding on a title for this book, my publisher and I wavered
on terminology. Questions arose: Will "atheism" exclude others
from the secular community? What about those who identify as
freethinkers, agnostics, non-believers, humanists, et cetera? As
with my choice of the term "animal liberation," "atheism" is the
most honest and liberating to me. To claim there is no God is as
portentous as claiming to know there is a God. In a sense, we are
all agnostic. We do not know if there is a God. However, to paraphrase the title of Richard Dawkins's fourth chapter in *The God
Delusion*, I am almost certain there is no God, and I say this without the learned philosophical explanation with which Dawkins
follows his assertion. Despite indoctrination into Catholicism as a
child, I do not believe there is a God because I have no reason to
believe otherwise. This is the same reason that I and most other
people, even religious ones, don't believe in vampires. In fact, the
inconsistent, unkind, haphazard nature of reality—notwithstand-
ing life's many positive aspects—has led me to the conclusion
that there is no God, and if there is, he, she, or it is certainly not
benevolent but rather somewhere between insensible and wicked.

I believe religions arose to explain the world's mysteries and
because the thought of our own mortality is frightening. In subsequent years, religion gained momentum as a source of political
and cultural capital. It now exists as a worldwide deception that
brings more harm than good to modern civilizations. As much
as I believe animal exploitation to be an evil, I see religions in
somewhat the same way, as they all promote the idea of human
exceptionalism, which is adverse to animal liberation. However,
I do not hope or act for the end of religion as I do for the end
of animal exploitation. For more in-depth explanation of why

religion is dangerous, one should read Christopher Hitchens's *God Is Not Great: How Religion Poisons Everything*. My purposes herein are different, for in the ensuing three chapters, I also want to consider how religion poisons nonhuman animal lives as well as human ones.

In the first chapter, I appraise animal rights literature that looks at the liberation of nonhumans from religious perspectives. Then, I defend in greater depth a position stated in this introduction: the notion of a higher power perpetuates hierarchy, speciesism, and anthropocentrism[8], consequently, no religion can speak to animal liberation in the way I have previously defined it. At most, religions can foster a more compassionate view of nonhumans while still condoning their exploitation. To argue that any religion promotes true animal liberation is to engage in a form of scholarly gymnastics that will not fare well when held up against the actual texts and positions of religious institutions. Although my arguments are against the concept of religion, I home in on Christianity for a few reasons. First, I am most familiar with Christianity, write from a Christian nation, and my worldview has been shaped by Western, Christian perspectives. Further, Christianity is, inarguably, the most influential religion in the world. A 2010 demographic study from the Pew Charitable Trusts reveals that 32% of the world's population, or 2.2 billion people, are Christian.[9] Christianity has

---

8. While "anthropocentrism" is the word I will use throughout this book to indicate human-centric thinking, in reality, most religious views about animals are anthropomonic, meaning humans are God's only concern, as opposed to being his primary concern, with other aspects of creation on the periphery of relevance (Clough xix). I rely on the former term because it is more commonly used and understood.

9. The study also revealed that there are "1.6 billion Muslims (23%), 1 billion Hindus (15%), nearly 500 million Buddhists (7%) and 14 million Jews (0.2%) around the world as of 2010. In addition, more than 400 million people (6%) practice various folk or traditional religions, including African traditional religions, Chinese folk religions, Native American religions and Australian aboriginal religions. An estimated 58 million people—slightly less than 1% of the global population—belong to other religions, including the Baha'i faith, Jainism, Sikhism, Shintoism, Taoism, Tenrikyo, Wicca and Zoroastrianism, to mention just a few."

historically been more focused on conversion than other religions (Rambo, *Understanding* 68), which likely explains such high rates of adherents. Finally, the first chapter—and the book as a whole— is most focused on Christianity for a reason best stated by Emma Goldman: "Much as I am opposed to every religion [. . .] I yet feel that no other religion has done so much harm or has helped so much in the enslavement of man [sic] as the religion of Christ" (389). Despite this overarching analysis of Christianity, I also investigate Eastern religions such as Buddhism, Hinduism, and Jainism. I had a personal interest in investigating religions of the East because I have formally studied Buddhism after becoming an atheist and many view Eastern religions as innately animal-friendly. With these arguments made, I also explore the unintentional vilification of nonhumans that arises from those who engage in progressive revelation and liberation theology, which are attempts to make problematic religious texts into social justice guidebooks.

The corpus of secular thought lacks much direct reflection on the connections between animal liberation from humans and human liberation from god(s). Within that body of work, one can find glimmers of thought, sometimes unintended, about the animal question. Therein, I primarily focus on New Atheism as an area of both promise and problems. The reverse can be said about animal liberation theory. While little is yet written to explicitly unite secularism with the animal liberation movement, there is some material available—mainly book chapters, blogs, articles, and videos—through which those ideas have coalesced. I expand upon these passages in the second chapter to make a distinct case for animal emancipation from an atheist standpoint.

The purpose of the third and final chapter is to consider the unique role of ethical veganism in Western culture. First, I address the expected accusation that I am merely making an atheist Procrustean bed to advance the lot of other-than-human animals. I then explore the tendency of some in the animal rights movement to both directly and indirectly pose their veganism as a religion and/or use religion as a conversion device. There are a few sound reasons for doing so, but ultimately I argue against that mode of rhetoric and outreach by exposing the dangers of posing veganism as a moral stance parallel to religion while offering ideas for how ethical veganism can be culturally situated and respected. Next, I consider the ways in which past and current social justice movements have critiqued religion as a cause and tool of oppression, considering how those ideas pertain to animal liberation. Ultimately, I propose a union of atheism and animal liberation, presenting ideas for what an atheist animal liberation philosophy can mean for the future of the animal liberation movement, the secular movement, and, perhaps, a distinct association of the two that can become its own progressive faction for peace and justice.

I end this introduction with honest admittance that this was a difficult book to write. While I am a scholar, I am not a philosopher or a religious authority. But as an activist of about six years, and as one who has researched and written about topics outside of my specialized academic area of English literature, the drive to expand disciplinary boundaries feels natural. However, my intrusion into other disciplines is only a minor difficulty. The more complex dilemma is my unapologetic intrusion upon culturally ingrained standards: nonhuman animal usage and religion. For the majority of the world, as they were in my own life for quite some time, both of these cultural mainstays are as ordinary and *true* as are breathing air and a setting sun. As such, there is a tendency to believe these constructions are natural and permanent.

While I don't believe this or any other book will destroy religion and animal exploitation in one fell swoop, I do hope that both of those human practices will cease as more people embrace compassion as a *reasonable, rational* response to animal exploitation (which can include emotion). In an introduction to a book about anarchism, Noam Chomsky makes the following commentary about the historic progress of humankind:

> [A]t every stage of history our concern must be to dismantle those forms of authority and oppression that survive from an era when they might have been justified in terms of the need for security or survival or economic development, but that now contribute to—rather than alleviate—material and cultural deficit. (viii)

I do not know what the world would be like, better or worse, if humans had not utilized other animals and created god(s) and religion throughout the course of our history. Perhaps, as Chomsky states of things outside this book's parameters, they were once necessary for "security or survival or economic development." As I see it, their (possible) needful use then results in "material and cultural deficit" now. One can also look at this issue epistemologically. On one hand, some believe in "mind-independent" concepts resulting in ultimate truths accessible only to certain privileged humans (Lackey 4). In contrast, Michael Lackey discusses an alternative through which ideas are considered "extremely valuable but albeit provisional 'forms' of meaning that shift in relation to the ever-changing resources, needs and desires of various language communities. The idea that there is such thing as true Religion, true Morality, or true Faith is simply incomprehensible to those who subscribe to this second theory of 'knowledge'" (4). In sum, needs and morality can be modified by any culture that reconsiders its past. Things once seen as truth beyond doubt can be questioned and, in the case of unjust and violent practices, hopefully abolished. Looking at knowledge and morality as malleable is pertinent to understanding atheism as an avenue for social progress. And herein lays the difficulty for an author such as myself who wishes to enlighten, not offend. To take on the topics of atheism and animal liberation in the way I propose is to critique core epistemological concepts seen by many as static truths.

In Will Potter's *Green is the New Red*, an exposé on governmental and corporate wars against animal and environmental activists, he insightfully asserts that although such activists have been pegged as terrorists—as were Communists (and freethinking persons) in 1950s America—they are not feared in the same way as Islamic suicide bombers. Rather, radical animal advocates pose a threat to the American way of life. Potter states: "This cultural threat was perceived by many as an unholy war for the very heart of America, *and often framed in biblical terms*" (242, emphasis added). The rise of atheism in America poses a similar cultural threat.

In a presentation at the 2013 Minnesota Atheists and American Atheists Regional Conference, LGBTQIA activist Greta Christina explored the similarities and differences between coming out as an atheist and coming out as gay in a way relating to this book's focus. She explained that when one reveals a non-heteronormative sexual identity, there is no implication that heterosexuality is wrong in any way. Thus, heterosexual friends or family members can hear of one's coming out and not feel their sexuality is under attack (which doesn't exclude other types of negative responses, of course). In contrast, coming out as atheist to a believer tacitly implies that the believer is erroneous in his/her beliefs. The same can surely be said about revealing one's ethical veganism. Such revelations are perceived as assaults on omnivores' ethics.

Both atheism and animal liberation philosophies tell people they are been doing things incorrectly and, more importantly, immorally and unethically. Traditions seen as wholesome and healthy—God and meat—are violent and oppressive. The truth does hurt sometimes in an abstract way best seen as an assault on tradition. It is exigent to mess with people's mythologies, myths they cling to out of custom, fear, and pleasure. However, as Carol Adams argues, "that is what consciousness raising does. It argues with the mythologies we are taught to live by until suddenly we are able to see the same thing differently. At that moment a fact becomes a contradiction" (*Sexual Politics* 16). And when messing with mythologies, albeit in the name of raising consciousness, it is difficult not to sound arrogant or dismissive of what others hold dear. But I find it morally imperative to muddle with these mythologies—human supremacy and the existence of a higher power—because they are violent, unjust, and tyrannical tactics of a bygone era. Thus, this book is grounded in my desire for a more peaceful planet with exponentially less suffering and slaughter. I see promise for those things in the vegan atheology that I offer within the rest of this book. I hope you will too.

Chapter 1

Hotel Procrustes

What have you done, O skies,
That the millions should kneel to you?
Why should they lift wet eyes,
Grateful with human dew?

—Voltairine de Cleyre, "The Gods and the People"

Have not all theists painted their Deity as the god of love and goodness? Yet after thousands of years of such preachments the gods remain deaf to the agony of the human race. Confucius cares not for the poverty, squalor and misery of people of China. Buddha remains undisturbed in his philosophical indifference to the famine and starvation of outraged Hindoos; Jahve continues deaf to the bitter cry of Israel; while Jesus refuses to rise from the dead against his Christians who are butchering each other.

—Emma Goldman

This chapter's title, in keeping with the book's metaphor, asks you to imagine a hotel in which each room is furnished with a bed representing a different religion or strain of religious thought. Each guest is a proponent of a particular otherworldly perspective and argues that his or her belief system promotes the end of animal exploitation. As they make those arguments, they are forced to extend some doctrines and chop off (or completely ignore) others;

even those from the same religious traditions will argue against each other. At Hotel Procrustes, one Christian argues Jesus was vegan; another states that even though he ate fish, he would promote veganism if alive today (at the very least, he would oppose factory farms); still another Christian contradictorily declares that Jesus was vegan even though he ate fish! Similar debates arise about Buddha—some are sure he was vegan while others say since he avoided ascetic extremes, meat was likely a small part of his diet. No matter what religion one is promoting at Hotel Procrustes, all guests are doing the same thing: seeking proof that *one* particular man, *one* particular text, or *one* particular spiritual path encourages animal liberation. In practice, however, most religions have very little to say about veganism or nonhuman animals and, in fact, continue to serve the human-centric status quo.

This procrustean problem is not unique to the animal advocacy movement. Religious texts are regularly used to support wildly contrasting views. Westboro Baptist Church finds biblical support (Leviticus 20:23) to underpin its odious "God Hates Fags" campaign. In contrast, many within the gay community argue that such vitriol is incompatible with the loving God they see manifest in the Bible. It is an old practice to cull passages from religious books, decontextualize them, and then use them to support or defame everything from slavery, to abortion, to corporal punishment, to war, to women's rights.

Returning to the animal question, in *Dominion: The Power of Man, the Suffering of Animals, and the Call to Mercy*, Matthew Scully eloquently critiques this practice of biblical procrusteanism: "To stretch the text any further, enlarging the place of animals in the biblical narrative, would be as egregious and presumptuous as the 'conservation' hirelings at Safari Club with their camouflage-covered Bibles and idolatrous deer head beneath the cross" (98). Despite this cautionary comment by one who writes from a religious perspective, the stretching of religious texts continues on as audaciously as ever.

The easiest retort to this continued search is to question why it should matter what Jesus, Buddha, Mohammed, or any other purportedly divine being ate. Who cares what one person ate thousands of years ago when there are billions of nonhuman animals suffering today because billions of people are exploiting and eating them today? Who cares about some semi-animal-friendly passage cherry picked from a religious text? Why should that one passage amidst thousands of others that ignore or defame animals be of any interest to those who care about animal liberation?

In *The Dominion of Love: Animal Rights According to the Bible*, Norm Phelps includes a list of about 200 Bible verses that mention nonhuman animals. At best, some of these passages are passably animal-friendly. Other passages read as injunctions against blatant cruelty to animals. However, there is not one passage that demands full respect and compassion for nonhumans. Finally, 200 out of about 30,000 total Bible verses shows that animal concerns are so unimportant that they make up less than one percent of total biblical subject matter. When animals are mentioned, their exploitation is often ignored or encouraged. (Consider the story noted in this book's Introduction of Jesus thrashing animals to drive them out of the temple.) So, why this continued search for divine proof that nonhumans matter?

The answer is evident: numbers. If all the religious people in the world saw nonhumans the way religious vegan animal advocates do, the exploitation, torture, and slaughter of animals would vastly diminish. Religion is a powerful cultural force; thus, it appears strategically sound to use it to modify people's views of other-than-human animals. This is not to say that religious arguments for animals are only made to advance animal rights, as many who make them are genuine believers in godly things. In fact, sometimes those believers are left scratching their heads in wonderment as to why more religious folk don't care about nonhumans. In her introduction to *Animals and World Religions*, Lisa Kemmerer acknowledges this predicament:

Though this book highlights animal-friendly teachings, it is important to note that the discrepancy between religious teachings and actual practice is often disappointing [. . .] *Therefore, this book can make no claim about actual behavior* [. . .] *This book is about what religions teach, not about how*

religious people live. In truth, there appears to be embarrass-
ingly little correlation between the two. (10)

This incongruity is similarly acknowledged by others making religious arguments for animal rights and liberation. From an animal
advocacy perspective, I see why religion could be used tactically to
win the hearts and minds of a speciesist culture.[10] Even as an atheist, I would be remiss if I didn't recognize the potential of religion
as a strategic conversion device in the animal liberation movement.
However, I think religious arguments for animal liberation are
dead ends if one is to actually pursue them fully rather than just
choose select passages to come to conclusions they already hope
to find. And to those questioning why more religious people don't
care about nonhumans, I ask them to consider that religion itself,
in whatever form it takes, might be the problem.

Indeed, there is much cause to believe that atheism and agnosticism do more to foster compassion toward animals than does
religion. There have been quite a few studies correlating non-
religiosity with lower rates of racial prejudice and higher rates of
political liberalism and radicalism (Beit-Hallahmi). Thus, the associations between animal advocacy and freethought should not
be too surprising. In Harold Guither's history of the animal rights
movement, he notes a 1984 survey in *Animals' Agenda* magazine
in which 65 percent of respondents reported being agnostic or
atheist (67). Of the twenty-three animal rights activists Harold
Herzog studied in 1993, only two of them credited "traditional
religion" for their interest in animal issues, thereby confirming
his earlier 1992 findings, published with Shelley Galvin, that the
majority of animal activists are not traditionally religious (117). In
2000, Wesley Jamison, Casper Wenk, and James Parker note the
following that confirms these and other earlier findings: "Social
science data indicate that most animal rights activists are not
members of traditional churches; indeed, they think of themselves

10. Speciesism is founded on the presumption of human supremacy; it
devalues other species' needs, desires, and integrity in deference to human needs and desires.

as atheist or agnostic" (306). More recently, in a 2012 study, Kara Gabriel, Brook Rutledge, and Cynthia Barkley from Central Washington University determined that individuals identifying as nonreligious (atheist or agnostic) are more supportive of nonhuman animal rights than those with religious beliefs.

There is also anecdotal evidence. Renowned law professor and abolitionist animal advocate Gary Francione states on his popular blog, if only as an aside, "Many animal advocates claim to be atheists" ("New Atheism, Moral Realism, and Animal Rights"). Further, a recent article in the *New York Times* defines animal rights activists as "a mostly secular lot" (Oppenheimer). I too have found that to be the case within the small activist community I frequent in the Twin Cities and within larger, national contexts. Despite these linkages, religious arguments for animal liberation far outweigh *consciously* secular ones, which is not to say that atheists and agnostics have not written books about animal issues. The lack of texts connecting animal issues to secular thought may exist because, as discussed in the Introduction, some non-believers do not consider their lack of faith to be an ethical indicator, as do those with belief in a higher power. Also, religious people are forced to conform their beliefs to match their animal advocacy. With atheists, such accord is not necessary. My purpose in this chapter is to demonstrate the ways in which religion is actually detrimental to animals.

In the ensuing sections, I first pose religious arguments for animal liberation as secular thought dressed in religious rhetoric, albeit unknown to the rhetorician. This isn't a unique tendency. The New Atheists, Richard Dawkins in particular, have come to similar conclusions. As newly reported in *The Telegraph*, many self-identified Christians actually hold secular views on issues such as gay rights and the role of religion in affairs of the state, leading Dawkins to conclude that such Christians are "not really Christian at all" (qtd. in Pollard). A 2005 Baylor University study similarly reported that many self-identified Christians disagree with core Christian principles (Stenger 24). However, they will not surrender their beliefs in an almighty overseer, even when those beliefs contradict both the Bible and those who claim themselves God's henchmen. Out of fear, tradition, or a sense of cultural identity, religion keeps an iron grip on the hearts and minds of many otherwise progressive people.

When considering a recent survey by the American Bible Society, one can't help but wonder if there would be even more Christians with secular views if they actually read the Bible. An article called "Americans Love the Bible but Don't Read It Much, Poll Shows," reports that only 26 percent of Americans regularly read the Bible. However, this survey does not report on how many Christians have read the Bible in its entirety. Many also just read passages or sections selected by their pastor or other spiritual leader, so there is no balanced or representative selection indicating what most people are reading. Indeed, I often wonder what Christians make of God's demand for blood for both capricious and political reasons. For a bizarre example, see 2 Kings 2:23–24, in which the Lord allows forty children to be mauled by bears for making fun of the prophet Elisha's bald head. Getting political, consider Joshua 8:1–2:

> Then the Lord said to Joshua, "Do not be afraid; do not be discouraged. Take the whole army with you, and go up and attack Ai [a Canaanite city]. For I have delivered into your hands the king of Ai, his people, his city and his land. You shall do to Ai and its king as you did to Jericho and its king, except that you may carry off their plunder and livestock for yourselves. Set an ambush behind the city."

Here, God's encouraging words support bloodlust and theft, notably enforcing ownership of animals as well. As the famous suffragist Elizabeth Cady Stanton said of biblical passages demoting women to low cultural status: "No symbols or metaphors can twist honor or dignity out of such sentiments" (125). That comment applies here as well. Both of these passages exemplify the biblical content Christians must regularly ignore if they are to claim God is loving and compassionate. In the introduction to his intriguing book *Fighting Words: The Origins of Religious Violence*, Hector Avalos, Professor of Religious Studies at Iowa State University, illustrates this disparity: "Religious violence has preoccupied me ever since I began to ask myself how I could hold sacred the Bible, a book with so much violence. I then expanded the question to how anyone today can deem sacred those books that endorse any level of violence" (17). The only way, it appears, is to ignore unpleasing passages or to only focus on biblical elements endorsed by one's spiritual leader.

As an atheist concerned with nonhumans, I think that human beings in their great imperfection created god(s). Therefore, it is not surprising that humans keep recreating those belief systems to fit their purposes, stubbornly refusing to let go of the anthropocentric traditions that gave animals their low cultural status to begin with. Until these recreations (that use the same speciesist materials) cease, we will only get more bloody Procrustean beds. I defend this position by focusing on the inescapable foundation upon which all religions are built: hierarchy. With hierarchy—and, concomitantly, human supremacy—as a base, religious arguments for animal liberation will always crumble when interrogated.

For reasons explained in the Introduction, my primary focus in this book is Christian views on nonhuman animals. In addition to those reasons, there is currently an influx of Christian animal rights scholarship. Historically, there has been regular theological commentary on animals, but up until recently, few theologians have made other-than-human beings the primary focus of their scholarship (Clough 173). This academic field is in such vogue that it has garnered recent mention in *The New York Times*. But even within that article itself, one notices the hedging, qualifying, and intellectual gymnastics I explore in this chapter, especially regarding aquatic animals. Before continuing, I must stress that fish do feel pain. In "The Fiercest Predators of the Sea," the title being an apt reference to human beings, Heather Moore cites the work of successive scientists who have determined that the pain- and stress-feeling abilities of birds and mammals are the same in fish (97), yet for many Christian animal advocates, sea creatures are acceptable human fare.

In "Scholars Explore Christian Perspectives on Animal Rights," Mark Oppenheimer notes the work of scholars such as David Clough and Charles Camosy. Camosy "still eats fish, 'half because Jesus Christ ate fish, and half because I am too weak to give up my grandmother's tuna spaghetti sauce'" (qtd. in Oppenheimer). Catholic conservative Mary Eberstadt, who reviewed Camosy's work, also declares she eats fish (Oppenheimer). Fish consumption amongst animal advocates frequently goes uncritiqued, especially within mainstream publications such as *The New York Times*. It is disconcerting how nonchalantly animal advocates put aside concern for fish, 90 to 100 billion tons of whom are killed each year by humans (Animal Liberation Victoria), with other sources claiming the true number to be incalculable ("Report"). But as will be seen below, the fish question is regularly dismissed by Christians promoting animal welfare and rights, likely because no amount of intellectual gymnastics can negate that Jesus eats fish in the Bible.

Along with the Abrahamic traditions, I devote a section of this chapter to Eastern religions, as well as provide some commentary on the spiritual traditions of indigenous peoples because they are often romanticized in the West as being animal-friendly and immune to critiques leveled against Euro-American anthropocentric and theocentric religions. But while other-than-human animals may fare better in some of these traditions, they still do not speak to the liberation of animals in the encompassing way described in this book's Introduction. They are still built upon hierarchical foundations with humans at the top as the most important species or as being completely outside the animal realm.

Finally, I report on a disconcerting trend I unexpectedly found while reviewing religious pleas for animals: the vilification of nonhuman animal natures. This maligning of animals, along with the assertion that they willingly give their lives to humans, is a thread that religious animal advocates have unintentionally woven into their treatises on nonhumans' behalves. To be clear, I don't think most of these negative animal conceptions are purposeful, but their existence within the writing of animal advocates speaks strongly to why religion is not an effective mechanism for ending the exploitation, torture, and slaughter of other animal species.

Progressive Revelation, Intellectual Gymnastics, and Secularism in Disguise

Religious texts are sacred, as most of them propose collaboration between a divine being and a human or humans who write down that divine being's thoughts. The rest of the world, those not of this partnership, are to use the sacred text as both a guidebook for living morally and as a source of solace during troubling times. So, with animal concerns garnering less than one percent of mention in the Bible and a slightly better three percent in the Quran, what is a religious animal advocate to do?[11] *Make stuff up!* Or, more properly, foster progressive revelation, "a concept accepted by theologians of diverse backgrounds and loyalties. [Progressive revelation] has to do with the belief that although God's self-revelation does not change, the human capacity to receive that revelation does change" (Hyland 1). I consider this concept as part of liberation theology, a mode of religious discourse that arose in the US during the 1960s and '70s to challenge and offer alternatives to racism and other types of oppressive ideologies in Christianity (fonza 189–90). In a recent study using systematic theology, David Clough admits that when it comes to arguing for animal rights from a "theological context, there is [. . .] very little ground to stand on [. . .] which means that the foundations necessary to construct a [animal-friendly] theological ethic are largely absent" (xiv). Consequently, we see religious animal advocates getting so creative with biblical content that their resulting scholarship is often as confounding as it is fascinating.[12]

Other religious theorists may not use that exact term, but they are engaging in progressive revelation within their attempts

---

11. Of course, these are only mentions. None of the verses advocate for the total animal liberation that many religious advocates seek.

12. Clough's *On Animals* exemplifies this outcome.

to enmesh animal advocacy with religious doctrine. Ecofeminist Carol Adams calls this "[r]evisioning," or "looking again, 'in order to improve or correct'" ("Introduction" 5). While eco-feminism is, at its core, about connecting feminism and ecological concerns, many of its proponents have added a spiritual element to the theoretical perspective. Sallie McFague integrates ecofemi-nism into the recent move toward liberation theologies, explain-ing that the "encompassing agenda would be to deconstruct and reconstruct the central symbols of the Jewish and Christian tradi-tion in favor of life and its fulfillment, keeping the liberation of the oppressed, including the earth and all its creatures, in central focus" (87). In sum, this means ignore all of the other stuff—the violent, Earth-destroying God; sanctioned slavery; holy wars; denigrating commentary on women, children, homosexuals, and animals—and reconstruct the Bible into a loving tome. This is not possible with what the Bible has given us to work with, for "[n]ever can Christianity, under whatever mask it may appear—be it New Liberalism, Spiritualism, Christian Science, New Thought, or a thousand and one other forms of hysteria and neurasthenia—bring us relief from the terrible pressure of conditions, the weight of poverty, the horrors of our iniquitous system" (Goldman 390). But this does not keep people from trying to palliate Christianity.

Adams and Margorie Procter-Smith state: "To recognize ani-mals as Others requires that we stop colluding with structures of domination" (299). However, their use of theology is a direct collusion with one of the most dominating institutions in world history—religion. Rather than recognize this innate theologi-cal quality, feminists who do not renounce religion attempt "to significantly reconceptualize God, the divine, and the spiritual, thereby retaining their feminism without (or so they think) being compelled to declare themselves atheists" (Overall). These revi-sions of holy texts continue without consideration that religion does not promote a world of harmony and parity, most especially for nonhumans. Ecofeminists are not alone in their attempts to reconstruct holy texts into something amenable to their visions of a just world, and some proponents of religious animal advocacy seem aware of the intellectual gymnastics required in such pursuits.

In *Creatures of the Same God: Explorations of Animal Theology*, the Rev. Dr. Andrew Linzey[13] jokingly states that because there is so little thought given to animals in his Church of England, he considered starting the Linzey Church comprised of those who share his worldviews (xviii). More seriously, he calls for an Animal Bible that gathers animal-friendly passages from the Bible while acknowledging the book is not always friendly to animals or humans (103). Thus, the Linzey Church isn't a joke; rather, he is creating it by recreating God through a secular view of nonhuman animals with little to no basis in Christian theology. This is a specific type of secularism: through progressive revelation and liberation theology, religious animal advocates, sometimes unwittingly, use moral codes not grounded in religious dogma; they are rooted instead in non-religious ethical considerations.

Linzey admits that "although Christianity has a poor record on animals [. . .] it is also the case that Christian theology, when *creatively* and critically handled, can provide a strong basis for animal rights" (xii, emphasis added). I cannot help but pose my critique of Linzey as a series of questions: If the Bible is inspired by an almighty, all knowing deity who rules the world from a perfect, celestial realm, why would we have to get creative with it? Wouldn't God's expectations of us be clearly stated (he is perfect after all) rather than contradictory and confounding? If God inspired a text purposely meant to confuse and frustrate humans, what does that say of this great being's character? And if, as Linzey and others admit, the Bible was penned by fallible humans thousands of years ago, why are we still looking to it for how we should live today? When it comes to the animal question, the answer of theocratic promoters will always be more religion, albeit morphed into something new.

---

13. Unless otherwise noted, all attributions to Linzey are from this book.

To be fair, for some people, religious traditions are meaningful even if they do not attach much metaphysical belief to them. Thus, they have found a way to keep those traditions while still promoting social and ethical progress, which is admirable. Liberation theology and progressive revelation are complex and have raised questions within the secular world. Should we join with progressive believers on issues upon which we agree, such as gay rights? Or should we criticize them because we think their foundation is faulty even if they are in agreement with us on a particular issue? Ultimately, I don't think this has to be an either/or situation for everyone, even for me, yet I still feel an ethical imperative to problematize the role of religion in human domination of other species.

Removing this quandary from the Abrahamic traditions for a moment, even Diane Sylvan, a Wiccan spiritualist, poses religion as the answer to animal exploitation when writing that "[s]ometimes [. . .] change comes from within established religions, and other times, entirely new religious ways provide alternatives" (226). Even non-religious proponents of ethical veganism raise the ghost of religion to sway readers to a more compassionate lifestyle. Will Tuttle opines: "A moderately open mind and a willingness to make connections are all that are needed to apprehend these [vegan] principles, and to see that they never contradict our deeper religious teachings or our spiritual yearnings, but always fulfill and illuminate them" (xvii). But considering the intellectual gymnastics animal-friendly theologians must use to sweeten religion's bitter treatment of nonhumans, it would seem that religious teachings dissuade followers from understanding the principles needed to make the world less violent toward nonhumans. At the very least, they provide conflicting arguments using the same materials, never coming to a spiritual consensus on animals.

Thomas Aquinas, thirteenth century Catholic theologian (and later saint), provides an apt case study for why religious arguments for animal liberation are tenuous, even desperate, and to demonstrate the rifts amongst theorists asserting that religion is the pathway to animal salvation. Aquinas is the most prominent Catholic philosopher since Catholicism's inception in the first century of the Common Era. His work still influences those entering the priesthood of the world's largest Christian institution. Of the 2.2 billion Christians mentioned in the introduction, 1.2 billion of them are Catholic, according to Vatican figures ["How Many"][14]. Philosophy professor Judith Barad, in "Catholic Exemplars: Recent Popes, Medieval Saints, and Animal Liberation," claims that modern popes John Paul II and Benedict XVI and medieval saints Aquinas and Francis of Assisi should "enlighten and inspire contemporary Christians" to love animals (127). When it comes to Francis, an argument can be made that he encouraged kindness to animals, but he is only one of many Catholic saints,[15] and his affection for animals and nature was certainly not influential enough to have any effect on Catholicism's official stance on nonhumans. I also argue that Francis's love of animals was secular, the ideas of one man whose compassion toward other-than-human animals was in defiance of his Church, not in collusion with it. On Aquinas and the popes, however, there is little room for debate.

Barad premises Aquinas as an "exemplar" because he concluded that animals and plants have souls, although they are not the same as human souls; he also acknowledged that animals have feelings (128–129). To counter such a depiction of Aquinas who, I assert, helped embed speciesism more deeply into Catholicism that it had been before, I need go no further than other Christian animal advocates. As Linzey explains, Aquinas declared "by divine province that non-rational beings should serve the higher species" (11); he further notes: "We may recall that Aquinas regarded animals as non-rational, and that idea has in turn influenced centuries of Christian thought" (15). Phelps agrees with Linzey: "St. Thomas Aquinas [. . .] denied not only that animals are our neighbors, but [he said] that we do not have any direct obligation to show

---

14. Of course, this number does not indicate those actually practicing Catholicism according to Church law. In fact, as one baptized in the faith, I am likely counted amongst those 1.2 billion.

15. I use the vague phrase "many Catholic saints" because there are no clear numbers. For an explanation of why the answer ranges from 45 to 810, see Stephen Beale's October 30, 2012 article "Saints 101: How Many Saints Are There?" on *Catholicexchange.com*.

them kindness" (41). If Aquinas is one of the best "exemplars" Catholicism has to offer, there is no hope for nonhuman animals through the Catholic approach. Even other Christians can see that.

As to the popes, Barad cites John Paul II's 1990 speech stating "'animals possess a soul and men must love and feel solidarity with' other animals" (127). In 2002, Benedict XVI, then Cardinal Ratzinger, said that "we can see that they [animals] are given to our care, that we cannot just do whatever we want to them" (qtd. in Barad 135). He then condemns some of the most egregious forms of "food" animal cruelties, such as foie gras production (force feeding ducks to the point of liver disease and then slaughter). These are fine positions to take, but at most they condemn extreme instances of animal mistreatment; no pope has ever argued against the use of animals to serve human ends.

Rather than select those one or two statements in which animals garner a sensitive nod, it is more useful to look at the official position of the Catholic Church. In 1982, this is what John Paul II said about scientific experimentation to Members of the Pontifical Academy of Sciences, a stance that never changed during his lifetime:

> Consequently, I have no reason to be apprehensive for those *experiments in biology* that are performed by scientists who, like you, have a profound respect for the human person [. . .] On the other hand, I condemn, in the most explicit and formal way, experimental manipulations of the human embryo, since the human being, from conception to death, cannot be exploited for any purpose whatsoever. Indeed, as the Second Vatican Council teaches, man is "the only creature on earth which God willed for itself" (*Gaudium et Spes*, 24) [. . .] *It is certain that animals are at the service of man and can hence be the object of experimentation.* (Second emphasis added.)

This is a clear directive, an executive statement. Somehow, an infallible man, a direct conduit of God, can maintain this sentiment while also declaring we humans must love and feel solidarity with animals. Likewise, in the official *Catechism of the Catholic Church*, the Holy See (or papal court/Vatican government) concludes about other uses of animals: "God entrusted animals to the stewardship of those whom he created in his own image. Hence it is legitimate to use animals for food and clothing. They may be domesticated to help man in his work and leisure" (Catholic Church 640).

At the beginning of this section, I defined progressive revelation. After considering how animals fare in the Catholic Church, I cannot help but wonder how many nonhumans have to suffer and die under the researchers' and scientists' knives before revelation would ever progress enough to countermand positions such as the Vatican's. At what point do otherwise kindhearted and intelligent people stop looking to God and his mouthpieces to foster a compassionate view of other-than-human animals? I also used the word "desperate" above, for that is what I find progressive revelation and liberation theology to be, bleak attempts for advocates of specific religions to find advocacy for animals within those institutions. Such desperation is prevalent in other areas as well, as in continued investigation into what Jesus Christ ate.

Printer cartridges have run dry at the fingertips of those who want to create an animal-friendly Jesus, often resulting in texts that are as contradictory as the Bible itself. In *The Dominion of Love*, Norm Phelps admits that "[w]e do not know, on the basis of direct evidence, whether Jesus was a vegetarian" (125). At the beginning of the book's twelfth chapter, Phelps states the following: "[W]e have seen that—with the exception of fish—the Bible provides no evidence that Jesus or his disciples ate or drank animal products" (137). He ends that paragraph with the assertion that "[b]y any reasonable standard of historical evidence, the claim that Jesus was a vegan has to be taken seriously" (137). But this claim cannot be taken seriously with contradiction of it stated by the author himself within the same paragraph.

The Christian Vegetarian Association (CVA) also paints the image of an almost-vegan Jesus: "Luke 24:43 describes Jesus eating fish after the Resurrection. However, Jesus' diet 2,000 years ago in a Mediterranean community, where many people struggled to get adequate nutrition, does not tell us what Christians should eat today" (8). Surely, things were different 2000 years ago in the Mediterranean, *but this is Jesus Christ we are talking about—the son of God.* He was clear about a lot of things. If consuming animal flesh was an abomination to such a holy being, one would think it would merit a mention. Assuming that Jesus of Nazareth was a real historical figure, one should consider what this person said (or didn't say) while he was alive. Thomas Jefferson's *The Life and Morals of Jesus of Nazareth,* also known as *The Jefferson Bible,* is a valuable resource for it includes only verses directly relating Christ's words and activities, taking out all reference to the supernatural.[16] This leaves modern readers with 69 passages to consider, none of which admonish humans against using non-human animals for their own purposes. *The Five Gospels: What Did Jesus Really Say?* is a more recent project taken on by about 100 religious scholars (collective authorship known as The Jesus Seminar) which ultimately determined that only about eighteen percent of Jesus' biblical sayings are historical. Like Jefferson, the scholars differentiate the "Jesus from history from the Christ of faith" (7), so they remove anything he is purported to have said after the resurrection. Predictably, the historical Jesus said nothing of significance about animals.

When putting the supernatural back into the mix, Jesus Christ doesn't fare well either for those concerned with compassion toward animals. The case of the Gadarene swine often arises to prove this. Luke 8:26–39 describes Jesus coming upon a man possessed by many demons, known collectively as Legion. Legion asks Jesus not to send them to the Abyss, but rather to send them into a large herd of nearby pigs. Jesus obliges, and the demons, now in pig bodies, run into a nearby lake to drown themselves. Jesus Christ, loving son of God, cared more for the fate of demons,

---

16. Of course, we should not forget or excuse one of the nefarious reasons for this text, which was to convert to Christianity native peoples not seen to be as intelligent as Euro-Americans, and therefore less able to understand the Bible.

beings whose sole purpose is to torment humankind and defy the almighty God, than he did for nonhumans harmlessly eating on a hillside. Christ gave into the demons' request, showing more respect for pure evil than he did for animals. As Bertrand Russell observes in his 1927 essay "Why I Am Not a Christian," "[I]t certainly was not very kind to the pigs to put the devils into them and make them rush down the hill to the sea. [. . .] He could have made the devils simply go away; but He chose to send them into the pigs" (19). This manifestation of indifference bordering on detestation toward animals seems indefensible, but defenders there are.

Phelps goes into a quite impressive explication to excuse Jesus' actions and to discount the story as a whole (139–142). He notes that there are many different versions of the legend, pigs would not have been around in a heavily Jewish area during Christ's era, and it is unlikely that such a vast number of swine would have been gathered on a free-range farm in the first century C.E. He further argues that "Jesus' action would have cost him a sizable fortune [that he would have to pay back to the pigs' "owner"]. More importantly, the drowning of pigs would have been taken as a political act of aggression," and Jesus would have been arrested by Roman authorities (140). In effect, Phelps is attempting to historically discount the story of the Gadarene swine, never questioning the absurdity of there being a demon-possessed man to begin with. But whatever the historical or mystical reality is, even if this story is just a fable, a legend with absolutely no claim to historical fact, even if the pigs are used metaphorically, it demonstrates complete apathy to the plight of nonhuman animals in a book that purports to teach moral action. Even as metaphor, animals can be denigrated and exploited.

The tale of the Gadarene swine is not the only example of Christian pit-hating. In *Pig*, Brett Mizelle writes that Christians were historically ambivalent about the species. Pigs were good in that association with them could help "distinguish Christians from Jews"; however, they were also associated "with all that was unclean and disgusting" (35). Mizelle also remarks that in Christ's

tale of the Prodigal Son, the young man who wasted his father's
inheritance resorted to becoming a lowly swineherd, quite an
indecorous job for the times (35). Even the "animal-loving" St.
Francis of Assisi displayed pig-hating behavior. When one of his
Brothers (in the holy sense) cut off a pig's foot because yet another
Brother craved boiled pig's feet, Francis was more concerned with
appeasing the peasant who "owned" the pig than he was with the
violent act. In fact, Francis explained to the peasant that "pigs are
made for man's use, for his nourishment and food, that everything
belonged equally to all men" (Jørgensen 112). Obviously, the
Christian view of Jews, as noted in this very paragraph, negates the
idea that all things equally belong to all people. Christians have a
long history of persecuting those of the Jewish faith. And again
we see that the best icon of compassion for animals the Catholics
can muster up is a saint who aligns with the Church on the proper
role of nonhuman animals in God's sacred agenda.[17]

Of the Gadarene swine and Jesus' fish eating, Linzey foregoes
the intellectual gymnastics and admits that "[t]here is no simple
way of answering all the problems that arise from biblical accounts,
still less of harmonizing them [. . .] What Jesus offers us is paradigm of inclusive moral generosity that extends to the poor, the
disadvantaged, and the outcast" (17). A similar sentiment arises
in Tuttle's comment that "Jesus' exhortation that we love one
another and not do to others what we wouldn't want done to us
is the essence of the vegan ethic, which is a boundless compassion
that includes all who can suffer" (209). In the New Testament,
there are passages to support this "paradigm" of kindness to the
poor and outcast, to prostitutes and beggars, but they are all human. Jesus Christ does not offer a sufficient paradigm for how we
are to treat other-than-human animals. He unambiguously does
not embody the vegan ethic.

---

17. Indeed, just days before I reviewed this part of my book, I attended a protest against pig wrestling at St. Patrick's Catholic Church
in Stephensville, WI. Disdain for pigs—and for those who would protest their abuse—was painfully evident through the townfolks' verbal
and physical abuse of the animals and the activists.

As to the God of the Old Testament—often used in angry contrast to the supposedly loving Christ—Phelps[18] finds an argument for veganism on the basis that there is no direct instruction for humans to eat meat; God merely allows it to happen (95). There are two ways to look at this assertion. The first is to consider the biblical passage that addresses the matter:

> The fear and dread of you [man] will fall on all the beasts of the earth, and on all the birds in the sky, on every creature that moves along the ground, and on all the fish in the sea; they are given into your hands. Everything that lives and moves about will be food for you. Just as I gave you the green plants, I now give you everything. (Gen. 9:2–3)

Clearly, God gives humans permission to eat other animals, along with plants. Biblical context aside (but later addressed), God, who is aggressively clear about a lot of things—such as not worshipping false idols—is, at the very least, unconcerned that the many animal species he has created will be slaughtered and eaten by the one created in his image. Second, just because he isn't forcing animal flesh down human throats does not show him to be a God who cares about the fate of his nonhuman creations. Indeed, his only caveat is that "you must not eat meat that has its lifeblood still in it" (Gen. 9:4). This is a request not to eat live animals; kill them first.

Similar sentiments arise in Islam, the monotheistic belief system whose influence continues to rise, for, as Lewis Rambo states, it has "captured the hearts and minds of many who desire to transform the world's economic and political realities—especially those living in places around the globe encumbered by the legacies of Western colonial oppression, military domination, and economic exploitation" ("Anthropology" 211). Despite the anti-imperialist religious alternative Islam ostensibly offers, Muslim traditions offer much the same view of nonhumans as does colonial Christianity.

---

18. This argument is not unique to Phelps. I am merely using his book as an example of similar polemics. For example, see Kemmerer (278).

Of her Muslim upbringing, Ruby Hamad explains that vegetarianism is not common since Allah, through the words of the
Prophet Mohammed, sanctions meat eating as "permissible" as
long as the "right" animals (i.e. clean cows, not filthy pigs) are
slaughtered (7). Hamad explains that halal slaughter "proscribes
strict conditions designed to minimize animal distress [. . .] 'If
you must kill,' the Prophet Mohammed said, 'kill without torture'" (12–13). If I was to be eaten, I would prefer that someone
kill me first as well, as opposed to being eaten alive or tortured
to death and then eaten. However, my ultimate wish is not to
be killed for food at all; and I believe that being raised as a food
source is torture. All other-than-human animals, whether reared
on a small family farm or in a large factory facility, share a common
end. They can sense and smell the fear of their fellow creatures
struggling against the eventual knife to the throat, a fate they too
will face. That, as I see it, *is* torture, whether the Christian God
or the Prophet Mohammed permits it. But as the Abrahamic religions are intrinsically anthropocentric, viewpoints such as mine
simply have no place.

Another instrument in the progressive revelation toolbox is the
use of apocryphal texts to create an animal-loving Jesus. These
are stories about Christ's time on Earth that did not make it into
the certified biblical canon. For example, in *The Lost Religion of
Jesus Christ: Simple Living and Nonviolence in Early Christianity*,
Keith Akers argues that the earliest conception of Christianity, as
practiced by Jewish Christians, was about "simple living, pacifism,
and vegetarianism," making the apostle Paul the culprit who portrayed early Jewish Christians as "narrow minded [. . .] heretics"
(3). Akers explores the contrasting messages articulated by Jesus
and Paul, with focus on Paul's support for meat eating and denigration of vegetarianism (157). While these are interesting works
from a historical perspective, they ultimately just add to this end-
less cycle of revisioning meant to show what one man ate, as if
that is something we will ever know for sure, and that if we did, it
should determine what all individuals should eat. In response, to
quote Scully again,

[I]t is best not to try fitting Him into our own categories, be it Jesus the Gamekeeper or Jesus the Vegetarian, and the point in any case only cuts both ways [. . .] I could hardly care less whether any formal doctrine or theory can be adduced for these creatures. There are moments when you don't need doctrines, when even rights become irrelevant, when life demands some basic response of fellow-feeling and mercy and love. (94; 287)

In sum, the monotheistic religions explored in this section do not promote sufficient compassion toward other-than-human animals. They are theocentric and androcentric, and that is all they will ever be, despite the intellectual gymnastics of Hotel Procrustes's guests. As to Christianity, which is my primary focus in this section, God did not show concern for animals and neither did his son. Attempts to make Christian doctrine animal-friendly is secularism in the guise of pre-established deities and dogmas. These progressive revelations, as well-meaning as they are, need to forgo the dogma and advocate for animals without seeking divine authorization that simply does not exist. Further, the continued pursuit of doctrine and dogma that will make religion animal-friendly, whether official or apocryphal, speaks to the authoritarianism and hierarchy that renders religion an ineffective means of advocating for nonhumans, as I now address.

Hierarchy
The Inexorable Hitch

Within social justice movements and scholarship, critique of hierarchy proliferates, for it is the basis by which one group is given greater consideration than another. As such, it is the cause of many of society's inequities: sexism, heterosexism, racism, ableism, classism. Quite often, patriarchy—rule by men, specifically white, heterosexual, moneyed, Euro-American, Christian men—causes this inequity. Scholar and activist Riane Eisler provides a succinct definition of what she terms "domination hierarchy" that explains how I use it in this section:

[Hierarchy] refers to systems of human rankings based on force or the threat of force [. . .] [D]omination hierarchies characteristically inhibit the actualization of higher functions, not only in the social system, but also in the individual human. This is a major reason that a gylanic model of social organization opens up far greater evolutionary possibilities for our future than an androcratic one. (105–106)

In other words, Eisler is arguing that domination hierarchy fosters male-centered (androcratic) rather than male-and-female-centered (gylanic) political and social systems. Herein, I go beyond a critique of hierarchy as it relates to men and women (and if this was a different book, I would critique the rigid gender categories of man and woman) with focus on nonhuman animals. Domination hierarchy, of course, also limits full parity in regard to the other "isms" mentioned above. Even within other oppressed groups such as the poor and people of color, patriarchy, as a form of domination hierarchy, flourishes.

Animal advocates, as most succinctly theorized by ecofeminists, contend that patriarchy is the cause of women's, animals', and environmental degradation. Greta Gaard frames all oppressions as interconnected, indicating ecofeminism as "the framework that authorizes these forms of oppression as patriarchy, an ideology whose fundamental self/other distinction is based on a sense of self that is separate, atomistic" (2). In an early ecofeminist text, Carol Adams explains hierarchy, which imposes false binaries (culturally determined social divides) as well, in a way that defined the course of history for millennia: "Women serve men; nature serves culture; animals serve humans; people of color serve white people" ("Introduction" 2). In religious traditions of the Western world, the "self/other distinction" and false binaries are found within the concept of a chosen people beloved by God, much to the detriment of those not chosen, as framed here in a violent, speciesist biblical passage: "But these people blaspheme in matters they do not understand. They are like unreasoning animals, creatures of instinct, born only to be caught and destroyed, and like animals they too will perish" (2 Peter 2:12).

Returning to Aquinas, his worldview, as detailed in *Summa Theologica*, is grounded in hierarchical thought demarcating the arrangement of God's creations on Earth:

> Now the most necessary use would seem to consist in the fact that animals use plants, and men use animals, for food, and this cannot be done unless these be deprived of life: wherefore it is lawful both to take life from plants for the use of animals, and from animals for the use of men [. . .] Dumb animals and plants are devoid of the life of reason whereby to set themselves in motion; they are moved, as it were by another, by a kind of natural impulse, a sign of which is that they are naturally enslaved and accommodated to the uses of others.

Of women, Aquinas concluded it "was necessary for woman to be made, as the Scripture says, as a 'helper' to man" in the work of childbirth. In sum, all living organisms, from plants to women, are for men's use, and man is to serve God. This is hierarchy, and it sets the tone for cultures well beyond that of Euro-American Christianity. Hierarchy is best imaged as a ladder or pyramid, with patriarchy (men) on the highest human rung. Feminism has been one of the most advantageous critical avenues for exposing and subverting hierarchy in social and political realms.

In *Getting Off: Pornography and the End of Masculinity*, feminist scholar Robert Jensen asks a question that echoes those of religious animal advocates confused as to why others of their faith don't care about nonhumans: "How do we explain the fact that most people's stated philosophical and theological systems are rooted in concepts of justice, equality, and the inherent dignity of all people, yet we allow violence, exploitation, and oppression to flourish?" (30). His answer: hierarchy. This is how the system works: we live in hierarchical "systems and structures" that bring "privileges, pleasures, and material benefits" to those in dominant positions who resist giving up those dispensations; however, these

benefits come at the cost of subordinated people; to thrive, hierarchy must be made invisible, as existing for reasons beyond "crass
self-interest"; resultantly, hierarchy is proposed as "natural and,
therefore, beyond modification" (30–31).

Jensen goes on to state that the monotheistic religions—
Judaism, Christianity, and Islam—bolster hierarchical oppression
by posing it as natural (32). When reviewing the course of human history, Victor Stenger concludes that religious cultures did
not win out over areligious alternatives because spiritual practices
better human behavior; in contrast, religion won out because
it benefited those few in power (228). The hierarchy found in
human affairs mirrors "divine hierarchy," with its "rituals and
consolations" comforting those low on the hierarchical latter
with the "promise of eternal bliss" (Hyman). In kind, Michael
Lackey, in relation to race in America (a topic addressed again in
the final chapter), argues that "God-based systems of knowledge
and subjectivity" lead to a stratification of humans that is posed as
"so natural that questioning or challenging it would not even be
considered a possibility" (5). Religion has been vital in proffering
politically and culturally motivated conceptions of normalcy in the
guise of truth.

I detour into feminist and racial critiques of hierarchy because
a response I often hear when advocating for animals is that hierarchy and human use of animals are natural and, to borrow Jensen's
verbiage, "beyond modification." If theorists from social justice
movements can pinpoint hierarchy as the founding problem
within their communities, so should animal advocates. To avoid
the role of religion within hierarchical oppression is to ignore the
metaphorical (though sometimes literal, if protesting a circus)
elephant in the room.

Although the assertion is debated amongst academics, Will
Tuttle, citing the work of Eisler, argues that "[v]iolent conflict,
competition, oppression of women, and class strife [. . .] need not
characterize human nature but are relatively recent products of
social pressure and conditioning brought by invading herding culture whose dominator values we have inherited" (20). Sociologist
David Nibert similarly asserts that "systemic human exploitation

and social stratification can be traced to the advent of agricultural society roughly 10,000 years ago," including the confinement and utilization of the skin, flesh, fur, and fluids of other-than-human animals (ix). The development of agricultural societies had a correspondingly negative impact on women. In *Gender in World History*, Peter Stearns notes that the movement from hunter/gatherer societies to agricultural effectively ended an egalitarian arrangement between the sexes (10).

Even if aggression and competition have prevailed in human cultures since time immemorial, I cannot accept that these attributes must remain as such. Indeed, if all who fight for justice felt this way, well, there would be no reason to demand change. We would give up as slaves to our biological, racial, and socioeconomic lots. Once again, Jensen asks pointed questions that agreeably mirror my challenges to existing conditions: "If such behavior [in Jensen's case, aggressive male dominance] has consequences that violate our most fundamental sense of justice, would we still not want to do everything in our power to prevent it? Would we not in fact work especially hard to overcome that unfortunate reality of our evolutionary history" (178)? Indeed, we should feel compelled to fight against subjugating behaviors since evolution has given us the ability to ask such questions and strive for justice.

Murray Bookchin, founder of social ecology, which presumes that our social problems arise from our destruction of the ecological sphere, defends the position that hierarchy is not natural; rather, it is a long established social institution with a foundation in patriarchy: "We have good reason to believe that as biological factors such as kin lineage, gender distinctions, and age differences were slowly institutionalized, their uniquely social dimension was initially quite egalitarian. Later this development acquired an oppressive hierarchical and then an exploitative class form" (31). Hierarchy, binaries, and domination are not innate to our existence and can be subverted. Indeed, Ralph Acampora argues that those who wish to free animals from their cultural bondage have a moral imperative to "shed anthropocentric hierarchy altogether" as the only way to appreciate the corporeal integrity of other-than-human animals (132). This is difficult to do, even for the most hardcore vegan activist, but it is possible with continued critical self-reflection and a felt duty to expose speciesism in the myriad ways it manifests. Annie Laurie Gaylor asserts that "[f]eminism and other human rights cannot be argued by authority, much less by divine authority" ("Introduction" 10), and the same applies to animal rights. Thus, challenges to religions which claim divine power are far more promising for animal liberation than is using religion as a tool to subvert religious views of other species.

There is a celebrated saying within anarchist communities: "No Gods, No Masters." This rallying cry springs from late nineteenth century France via a libertarian manifesto acknowledging that until we stop looking to centralized authorities, both human and divine, to tell us what to do and how to do it, we will never be free. Alexandre Flandin initially instituted the dictum with the statement that "[a]narchists strive to implement the motto Neither God nor Master" (qtd. in Guérin 2). Yet one need not be an anarchist to accept that looking heavenward (or sideways, or downward, or all around us) for an outside authority to command us is hierarchical, be it an unseen deity, spirit cabal, or promise of reaching a higher plane of existence. As Bob Torres concludes in his social anarchist critique of the animal rights movement, if "we are to challenge hierarchy and domination across the spectrum of society, we must question *all* hierarchy" (106), and that includes the domination of nonhumans. In kind, we must expose the intrinsic hierarchy of religion and the unquestioning acceptance of how stratified thinking fortifies the low cultural value humans have placed on other animals.

Sallie McFague, in "An Earthly Theological Agenda," states "that theology should [not] reject theocentrism" (87). However, placing religion/God at the center of all existence *is* building a chain of command with God at the top (or in the center). She goes on to argue that the Earth "is not a 'realm' belonging to a king [. . .]. Rather than viewing God as an external, separate being ruling over the world, it is appropriate to see God as in, with, and under the entire revolutionary process" (93). Here is yet another Procrustean bed, secularism disguised as liberation theology. Christ is called "king" enough times in scripture that the Catholic and many Protestant churches celebrate an event called the Feast of Christ the King (and as shown above, Christ did not feast, nor did he demand others to feast, on vegan delicacies).

Hierarchy thrives in other religious animal advocacy texts as well. The following passages are taken from J.R. Hyland's *The Slaughter of Terrified Beasts: A Biblical Basis for the Humane Treatment of Animals*: "Because humans were their *leaders*, the animals reflected their fall from a higher estate" (21, emphasis added); "Abraham was able to substitute a ram for his son [to be sacrificed]" (35); "[p]et-companions [. . .] [make] an important contribution to the physical, mental, and emotional health of their *owners* [. . .]. Animals have also become eyes for the blind and ears for the deaf—trusted companions whose love and *service* are irreplaceable" (73, emphases added). Of the final passage from Hyland, one sees a sincere but misguided attempt to show that animals have worth on the basis that they can serve human beings. This removes the value they have as entities distinct from the human animal.

As an illustration of sensitivity toward nonhumans in Judaism, Lisa Kemmerer offers the following example:

> "Jewish law requires that anymals (sic) be allowed to rest (*yanuah*) on Sabbath." This is included in the Ten Commandments: "the seventh day is a Sabbath of the LORD your God; you shall not do any work—you, your son or your daughter, your male or female slave, your ox or your ass, or any of your cattle" (Deut. 5:14, Exod. 20:10 and 23:12). The ox, ass and cattle are mentioned along with human members of an extended, working household: All are granted a day of rest. (184)

Jewish law comes from "the LORD your God" and trickles down to the head of the household, the patriarch. Thus, at God's command, the male rests and allows his children, slaves, and animal workers to rest as well. They are all to rest in fealty to the great being who created them. In what way is this passage animal- *or* human-friendly? In what way is it not the epitome of hierarchy? Are the slaves, ox, ass, and cattle to make merry because they get one day of rest from being someone's property? To argue that any beings forced into labor should ever be thankful to their masters is disconcerting at best. The Sabbath is set aside for God's creations to honor him, including the husband, wife, their children, and their slaves. As far as we know, nonhuman animals do not have gods in the human sense, so the only reason they get a day of rest is because there are no humans to work them in the field, for the animals' masters are too busy worshiping their master.

Mastery also manifests in less obvious ways that religious animal advocates appear unaware of. Christian Vegetarian Association asserts that "Adam named the animals, which we believe shows concern and friendship. We don't name the animals we eat" (6). Stephen R. Kaufman makes a similar assertion that Adam didn't merely name species; rather, he gave every animal an individual name (203). Both of these interpretations are of the following passage:

> Now the Lord God had formed out of the ground all the wild animals and all the birds in the sky. He brought them to the man to see what he would name them; and whatever the man called each living creature, that was its name. So the man gave names to all the livestock, the birds in the sky and all the wild animals. (Gen. 2:19–20)

First, CVA's claim is patently false. So-called humane farms proudly declare that they care for and name the individual animals they will eventually slaughter for profit. Further, Kaufman's biblical exegesis is highly questionable, as he implies that Adam gave individual creatures distinct names as one would a feline or canine house companion. But even giving Kaufman the benefit of the doubt, such naming rights still manifest domination. In a lecture by English Professor Thomas J. Gasque called "The Power of Naming," he observes that "the relationship among name, namer, and named is a complicated one involving privilege, ownership, and freedom." Gasque also identifies naming as the first action taken by a human (Adam) upon God's command. This is the human's first act of power and privilege and also his first act of deference to a greater being. God granted Adam the authority to name the species—either individually or as species—with which he would share an earthly paradise (and eventually eat and force into labor after the flood); this is an act of dominance, not "concern and friendship," as CVA declares.

It is not viable to extricate hierarchy, anthropocentrism, and speciesism from religion, which is why it shows up so often within religious animal rights literature. Returning to Norm Phelps, he asserts that Jesus flipped the Greek tradition of hierarchy's upward flow, thereby supporting a "Hierarchy of Service, in which the powerful and privileged have a moral obligation to nurture and protect the weak and vulnerable. *Jesus made the Hierarchy of Service the theme of his gospel*" (149). Once again, when Jesus Christ spoke of doing unto others as you would have done unto you, he was referring to human beings; there is nothing in scripture that includes nonhuman animals in this concept. More importantly, Phelps argues that Jesus Christ made hierarchy the central focus of his ministry, as opposed to preaching *against* the concept of hierarchy. While one could argue that Jesus was just being practical considering the culture he had to work with, wouldn't a God who promotes true parity and harmony critique hierarchy rather than make it a "theme of his gospel"? How could the son of an almighty God not see what Bookchin did thousands of years later, "that the hierarchical mentality and class relationships that so thoroughly permeate society are what has given rise to the very idea of dominating the world" (20)?

Even when scholars make seemingly strong cases against hierarchy, as David Clough does in *On Animals*, the problem intrinsically remains. Using the work of fourth century theologian Basil of Caesarea and contemporary systematic theologian Colin Gunton as a foundation, Clough claims to have determined "a radical and distinctive Christian insight that the affirmation of God as creator of all things means the subversion of all human attempts to create hierarchy among creatures" (27). Yet Clough misses a key point that including God as a creator with all other creatures under his dominion maintains the stratified thinking he feels has been abolished. At the very least, the dualism of God and all other beings remains. And even with impressive application of systematic theology on behalf of animals, Clough *must* conclude the following when using the Bible as a scholarly base: "The only aspect of hierarchy amongst creatures that seems to have a biblical basis is a much simpler one than the grade scales of beings we have so far surveyed[19]: that human beings stand above the rest of the created order" (64). With religion as a foundation, hierarchy and human ascendency simply cannot be subverted.

As I argued previously, at most, religion will give us a smattering of passages that admonish cruelty for the sake of cruelty. Religious texts are also obliged to state that nothing God creates is worthless; if God created something, by its very essence, it matters (even Satan and his minions). So animals do matter in religion, but their importance is on the lowest rungs of the hierarchical ladder. As in Christianity, all Muslims are servants of their creator: "O you people! Worship (and pray to) your Guardian-Lord, Who created you, and those who came before you, that you might have the chance to learn righteousness" (Quran 2.21). And as in the Bible, there are verses (*ayahs*) in the Quran that encourage compassion toward nonhumans. Sura 3.108 reads: "These are the Signs of Allah: We recite them to you in Truth: And Allah does not mean injustice to any of His creatures." Kemmerer explains the "Prophet encouraged kindness and compassion, and taught his followers that how we treat anymals (sic) [. . .] are noted by Allah and will be a matter of considerable importance on the day of judgment" (245). But again, Islam is a hierarchical religion in which all are to serve Allah and in which using animals for food and other purposes is sanctioned without equivocation.

In Ruby Hamad's "Halal," she narrates her experiences growing up as a Muslim woman who at an early age became critical of the sexism and speciesism of her faith. She describes being a five-year-old child witnessing her friend, a chicken, held in her father's "big hands and, invoking the name of God, [he] slice[d] her little head clean off her neck" (6). Hamad further narrates:

---

19. Here Clough refers to the Great Chain of Being. See Chapter 2 for more on that topic.

The [Islamic] animal sacrifice is a long-standing religious tradition, with the meat to be distributed among the poor. I, however, couldn't reconcile the blood rushing from the animal's limp body with the concept of "charity" [. . .] This is when I announced my intention to go vegetarian for the first time, a declaration that was met with a mixture of amusement and horror by my Muslim parents: "*But God made animals for us to eat!*" (7)

The assertion that "Allah does not mean injustice to any of His creatures" and that how humans treat animals will be of importance on judgment day is at odds with Islamic acceptance of animal slaughter. In an odd twist on hierarchy, Islam also vilifies the pig as inedible, as opposed to other animals who are clean. So, while this saves pigs from slaughter in the Islamic community, the religion's commentary on pigs lacks any sense of compassion for this particular animal genus.

Echoing Christ's treatment of the Gadarene swine, pigs are maligned in Islam. These creatures do not fare well in the Abrahamic religions, which is, not surprisingly, at odds with current science. Natalie Angier reports recent studies on pig intelligence and cognition, noting that researchers are finding them to be some of the most "self-aware" and "brilliant" amongst nonhumans.[20] Yet Rashid Shamsi states in *The Muslim World League Journal* that the "pig is naturally lazy and indulgent in sex, it is dirty, greedy and gluttonous [. . .] It is for this reason that its flesh is not suitable for consumption [. . .] [Y]ou can't change its nature. It is still a pig and will always stay so." To paraphrase Bertrand Russell, that is not a very kind thing to say about pigs. Such a view makes one wonder why God created pigs at all.

---

20. Intelligence aside, pig sentience—the ability to feel pain and emotion—is more important than their ability to recognize themselves in a mirror, which maintains an anthropocentric view of rights arguing that nonhumans only have value when they emulate humans in some arbitrary way.

Even in Matthew Scully's *Dominion,* a text I have favorably cited many times thus far, he states: "Kindness to animals is not our most important duty as human beings, nor is it our least important" (398). This leads me to ask: What about equal importance? Why not an equal consideration that can only arise through a critique of hierarchy both within the culture we live and within our own actions? In concluding this segment, much of what I have argued can be summed up in this concise comment from Joan Dunayer: "Extremely human-centered and hierarchical, Christian doctrine is incompatible with animal equality" (11). The same can be said of the other monotheistic religions. But what of non-Abrahamic belief systems? They are often posed as welcoming of all living beings and of challenging the hierarchical/dualistic nature of Western theology. While there is some reasoning for that assumption, that is not the whole truth about religions of the East.

Eastern Religions
Better Doesn't Mean Good Enough[21]

In terms of compassion for other-than-human animals, Eastern religious traditions are touted as superior to Western. Indeed, veganism and vegetarianism are more common in Buddhism and Hinduism than they are in the Abrahamic traditions. In Jainism, veganism (or what Jains call *ahimsa,* non-violence) is seemingly taken to its ultimate expression, with Jains wearing cloths over their mouths and sweeping brooms as they walk to avoid killing living organisms so small as to be unseen. If one wants a spiritual path and animal liberation too, Eastern religions appear the way

---

21. In this section, I explore Buddhism, Hinduism, and Jainism. After consideration, I left out Daoism, as any commentary on it would reveal nothing of significance and a lot of repetition about what I say of other Eastern religions. I will leave what little comment I have to another author, Louis Komjathy: "Daoist commitments to a vegetarian diet, more often than not, derive from anthropocentric, cosmocentric, or theocentric views, and are most frequently understood through a prism of personal benefit and communal requirements, whether ritual purity, immortality, soteriological import, or monastic conformity" (98).

to go. Nonhumans undoubtedly fare better in most Eastern traditions than they do in the West (and interestingly these religions are arguably atheistic [Martin]). Close investigation into these belief systems again reveals speciesism, hierarchy, and anthropocentrism, albeit less violent and explicit than in monotheism. Ultimately, Buddhism, Jainism, and other Eastern religions do not foster a revolution in the way humans perceive their fellow animals. Thus, they are better for animals, but still not good enough.

Religious studies scholar Dawne McCance asserts that "idealized" versions of Eastern religions have made their way to the West, as manifest in the scholarship of animal advocates.[22] However, she notes there are "studies indicating that generalizing statements about 'Eastern' traditions [. . .] obscure the complexity and diversity of their philosophical and ethical teachings, some of which are speciesist and anthropocentric [. . .] and not all of which endorse vegetarianism" (109). For example, in Paul Waldau's *The Specter of Speciesism: Buddhist and Christian Views of Animals*, he concludes, as one might surmise from his book's title, that Classical Buddhism is speciesist because it depicts nonhuman animal existence in less agreeable terms than human existence (94–95) and allows animals to be used as a means to human ends without much dispute (155).

In an interesting critique of Waldau's conclusions, Colette Sciberras asserts his arguments are unsuccessful because he filters Buddhist teachings through Western conceptions of rationality that do not consider the time in which specific Buddhist texts were written (she specifically references the Pāli texts), a time in which animal use may have been necessary for human survival (225). Her analysis, however, fails to invalidate Waldau's findings. As happens within arguments for animals from Western religious perspectives, Sciberras asserts that just because Buddhist texts do not condemn the use of animals does not mean they condone them

---

22. There is a similar tendency amongst Westerners to fetishize indigenous spiritualities, which I will briefly touch on at the end of this section.

(217). Once again, I disagree, trusting that lack of commentary indicates lack of interest in the lives of other-than-human beings. While one could arguably accuse me of appealing to ignorance here, since no such confusion exists when it comes to humans, there is a clear presence of speciesism at play in Buddhism.

Sciberras then makes the following statement with the caveat that Buddhism does not condone human slavery: "The conclusion that Buddhism is speciesist will only follow if it is shown that the Buddhist texts allow some morally considerable beings to be used as means, yet prohibit it for humans. The Pāli texts, however, contain references to the utilization of humans, too" (217). My response to this assertion mirrors what I say about slavery in the Bible: just because a sacred text advocates for or tacitly accepts one type of oppression does not make it immune to accusations of egregious acceptance of other forms of oppression. In the case of the Bible and the Pāli texts, mention of human slavery does not in any way negate the works' clear interests in human ascendency. Scibberas herself is forced to admit this when acknowledging that humans are "better able" to follow Buddha's teachings, thereby validating Waldau's charge of speciesism (218). Ultimately, even within her noteworthy critique of Waldau, the problem of hierarchy remains, for Scibberas claims that "although a human life is better than one as an animal, life as a god is valued even more highly" (228).

Moving from Classical Buddhism, there are many schools of thought springing from that tradition, some of which promote vegetarianism. As Joe Gaziano and Jacquie Lewis write in "All Beings Are Equal but Some Are More Equal than Others," assessing Buddhist principles is complex because there are numerous suttas and sūtras that have been interpreted differently, making it hard to determine what the Buddha considered ethical, especially within the vegetarian/meat eating debate (63). Nevertheless, Buddhism as a whole is not a vegetarian spiritual practice (hence, it is surely not vegan). Gaziano and Lewis, who argue in favor of vegetarianism as a Buddhist moral baseline, note that Buddhist teachers in the U.S. will rarely, if ever, even address the topic of vegetarianism (59). In *How Are We to Live?*, Peter Singer declares

Buddhism "a failure" for not following through on its first precept to refrain from taking the lives of sentient creatures. He details a trip to a Japanese Buddhist temple that printed that very precept on the admission ticket while also noting the absence of vegetarian Buddhists in that country (190).

Buddha, as the historical man Siddhārtha Gautama, gave more thought to the meaning of animal slaughter and ingestion than Jesus Christ or the Prophet Mohammed. That said, his counsel on dietary habits, mainly intended for monks, is inconsistent and capricious. To wit, he permitted meat eating as long as the animal eaten was not slaughtered for the specific person eating the animal's flesh (this fully sanctions about 99.9% of the situations in which people eat meat today in the United States); he acknowledged that one who kills an animal is tapping into cruel and unsympathetic natures; and he proffered a very specific list of animals whose meat should not be eaten (Keown 77). However, Buddha did eat meat himself (and while the assertion is contentious, some stories claim he died of food poisoning from eating pork). Lisa Kemmerer argues that "[b]ased on Buddhist philosophy and practice, the Dalai Lama's Government of Tibet in Exile provides teachings on the Buddhist doctrine, which simultaneously provides a Buddhist rationale for anymal (sic) liberation" (120). Yet the current embodiment of Buddha nature—the 14th Dalai Lama Tenzin Gyatso—eats animal flesh. That hardly provides a platform for liberation. The take away here is if the personification of compassion (the Dalai Lama) eats meat, how unethical could meat eating really be?

Despite these inconsistencies, *The Lankavatara Sutra: A Mahayana Text* is a remarkable example of Buddhism's sympathetic consideration of nonhuman animals. Written between 350 and 400 C.E., this work details Buddha's teachings to Mahāmati, a bodhisattva (enlightened being). Chapter Eight makes strong admonishments against meat eating in response to the early Buddhists who engaged in the practice. Buddha clearly advises that "the Boddhisattva (sic), whose nature is compassion, is not to eat any meat" (212). In case that is not lucid enough, he later states the following: "But in the present sutra all [meat-eating] in any form, in any manner, and in any place, is unconditionally and once for all, prohibited for all" (219).

With such overt disdain for meat eating, one wonders why Buddhism is not a wholly vegetarian religion. One reason might be that the eighth chapter is a later addition to *The Lankavatara Sutra*. Further, it is generally agreed amongst scholars and historians that the historical Buddha, Siddhārtha Gautama, lived about 500 years B.C.E. This means that up to 700 years passed between Buddha's death and development of text. Much as Jesus' teachings were penned long after his death by those with social, political, and personal agendas, there is no reason to think the same did not happen in the case of Buddhism. So, while the animal advocate may give kudos to those inspired to write the chapter, Buddhism remains an anthropocentric religion.

Still, it *is* pleasant to see such ideas from a sacred text. Parts of it even appear to advise against meat eating for the sake of the animals themselves, not just for human benefit. The bodhisattva is to avoid meat because it causes "terror to living beings" (213). In the end, however, Chapter Eight of *The Lankavatara Sutra* is about human beings and the ways "they will discipline themselves [. . .] and be awakened in supreme enlightenment" (211). Buddha warns Mahāmati that eating nonhuman meat may cause one to "fall into the wombs of [. . .] excessive flesh devouring creatures," making it more difficult to fall into a human womb, which will makes attainment of Nirvana (freedom from suffering) more arduous (217). To be born nonhuman is to inhabit a lower state of being. In sum, the majority of the text is not concerned with the lives of nonhumans as beings with innate value. Rather, karma concerns are afoot.

High rates of vegetarianism in Eastern religions have a lot to do with karma, as explained by Vidushi Sharma:

Vegetarianism accompanied traditional Hindu-Buddhist philosophical values on life and nonviolence—known as ahimsa. Human actions had karmic consequences; by inflicting pain and suffering upon other beings, we would ensure reciprocity. By ingesting animal bodies, we would concur-

rently ingest their fear and anguish prior to slaughter, block-
ing ourselves from higher consciousness. (158)

Here is the speciesism, anthropocentrism, and egotism to which
Waldau was referring. The Hindu-Buddhist concept of samsara
(the transmigration of human and nonhuman souls) is very hierarchical, for those who do not bear their karmic burden are
downgraded to nonhuman animal states (Linzey, "Is Religion
Bad for Animals?"). As Tibetan scholar Robert Thurman explains
of Buddha's six-sectioned "Wheel of Life," living in "delusion
and stupidity and stupefaction" will cause humans to be reborn
as animals. Such beliefs do not foster a positive view of other
animal species as beings with inherent worth. Similarly, karma is
about human self-concern (i.e. becoming enlightened or reborn
as a higher being) not respect for the lives of other animals. Yes,
there is at least implicit acknowledgement that animals experience terror and pain, but the nonhuman's experience is of value
mainly for the impact it will have (or not have) on the human's
experience.

Foreseeing such critiques, Kemmerer notes that "[s]ome might
argue that karma turns ahimsa into a selfish act, but [. . .] from
the anymal's (sic) point of view, it matters little why freedom is
granted, why their life *is* spared, so long as it is spared and freedom
granted" (82). This is a valid statement and testament as to why
Eastern religions are better than Western in terms of recognizing and limiting animal suffering. In fact, similar arguments are
made as to why small free-range farms are better for animals than
large factory farms. At least the animals get to live more natural,
less tortured lives on small farms before they are killed; and with
karma, there is no slaughter at all when life is spared in fear of
karmic consequences.

So, why is this still not good enough? Isn't animal activism
about limiting the number of animals tortured and killed? Yes,
but that is only part of the story. Animal liberation, as defined in
the Introduction, will only come about with a change in the human perception of other animals as less significant beings. Animal
liberation is a challenge to hierarchy, while Eastern dogmas such

as reincarnation, higher births, and karma only reinforce stratified thinking and the idea that animals are human stepping stones to ascension. Animals should matter for their own reasons, not for what they can do for humans on a material or spiritual level. An upheaval in the animal liberation movement should not be seen as an October Revolution type event, but as a radically fundamental change in how Homo sapiens view the purpose and worth of our fellow animal species. Karma does not challenge speciesism and neither do other religious practices of the East.

Kemmerer says of the Vedic/Hindu view of bovines: "Cows eat grass and produce milk; the people of India understood that *living* cows could carry them through famine much better than *dead* cows, especially in a land without freezers or refrigerators" (59). Again, a case is made that treating nonhumans kindly is good because it will benefit humans. In this case, a cow's milk will be taken from her young and given to humans to drink or make into food products. This is the same mentality one finds in the rhetoric, though surely not in the actions, of farmers. Consider the words of Wisconsin veterinarian Tony Bolen, who speaks in defense of "food" animal farms: "Most of the farmers, they're treating them [animals] right [. . .] And the animals are pretty much happy, or the farmers aren't making money" (qtd. in Kotz). This is a common, though never sufficiently proven, defense used by animal farmers—that their animals have to be treated well to ensure a quality "product" (I use Bolen merely because he is the latest person I've read reiterating that position). Neither of these views, Vedic or veterinarian, fosters a new conception of other-than-human animals. They are still things used to meet human ends, as opposed to being ends in and of themselves.

Jainism, often held up as a vegan ideal, is not an exception to this worldview, though on first look, the opposite appears true. In *An Introduction to Jainism*, Bharat S. Shah makes a statement about Jainism that appears to level the hierarchy of significance for all living beings: "The first Vrata [vow] is Non-Violence, or Ahinsa (sic). Since all living things are equal, and are interchange-able by rebirths, and since all are potentially capable of achieving the same Siddha status, a Shravak [Jain man; a Shravika is a Jain woman] respects life in all forms and shapes" (29). Shah then makes a solid case for veganism, explaining why consuming eggs and dairy is not in keeping with non-violence.

These significant tenets of Jainism have been eagerly appropriated by some individuals from the animal rights movement. In a guest blog post for *Faith in Memphis,* prominent animal advocate Gary Francione extols the virtues of early Jain practitioner Mahavir (599–527 B.C.E.). To be sure, Mahavir was quite a revolutionary for his time, having criticized sexism and the caste system. He is noted as "the first historical figure to regard all nonhuman animals as full members of the moral community. He was also the first historical figure to articulate the view that the planet itself, including air, water, and earth, consists of living systems. Mahavir was, indeed, the first ecologist" (Francione "Jainism's Greatest Gift"). With all of this said, Francione, as do others advocating for animals from religious perspectives, scratches his head in wonder that more Jains are not vegan, and he makes a case that this discrepancy goes against the concept of ahimsa ("Ahimsa and Veganism"). Perhaps if he dug more deeply into Jainism, he would understand the seeming contradiction between premise and practice.

To start, one must consider the origins of the ahimsa concept, which is well contextualized here by Nobel Peace Prize winning theologian and missionary Albert Schweitzer[23]:

> It did not develop, as one might think, from a feeling of compassion. The earliest Indian thinking knew hardly anything about sympathy with animal creation. It was, indeed, convinced of the homogeneity of all creatures through the Brahmanic idea of the universal soul. But this remained a purely theoretical conviction. [. . .]. [It arose] from the idea of remaining pure from the world. Originally, it belongs to the ethics of becoming perfect, not to ethics of action. (143–144)

---

23. Not wanting to misrepresent Schweitzer's thoughts on Jainism, he ultimately lauds the "ancient Indian thought [that] makes the tremendous discovery that ethics are boundless—and this at a time when ethics in other respects were not yet very far advanced!" (145).

Ahimsa, at its core, is about the human animal, which explains why Jainism is not activism in the way many conceive of the term. Further, Shah makes a notable concession at the end of an otherwise eloquent plea for what he calls vegetarianism, stating that one should attempt "not to eat these [eggs, chicken, fish, or meat] at least on some day(s) of the week, or of the month. And don't forget to be thankful to all those who died, so that you could live" (37). There is no such flexibility in terms of killing or abusing humans. This is likely because, as Christopher Chapple states, in Jainism human birth is seen as the "highest birth" (248).

Another problem with Francione's borrowing from Eastern traditions is well stated by atheist vegan author and blogger Al Nowatzki who notes that the term "ahimsa," while specific to certain Eastern practices, means the same as "non-violence" in the way Francione uses it in his work. Nowatzki continues: "[I]t's confusing as to why Francione, who has otherwise crafted a logical argument for animal rights, doesn't just take religious language out of [the] conversation and stick with the broadly appealing language of non-violence and justice" ("Religion"). Most likely, Francione is blanketing the market, so to speak. He is using the language of logic in one instance and religion in another to boost his chances of influencing a wider range of readers. While some may call this strategy, I call it disingenuous and akin to animal rights groups using analogies of race and genocide to further the cause for nonhumans.

For example, I have written in opposition to national groups that appropriate the histories of First Nations people, African Americans, and Holocaust victims and survivors to illuminate animal mistreatment, thereby "trading on tragic histories while also limiting those cultures to tragedy alone (Socha "'The Dreaded Comparisons'" 232). In this case, Francione is taking a concept with thousands of years of tradition and simplifying it through misrepresentation to suit his specific purposes. Perhaps he is aware of this misappropriation, for he ends his article "Ahimsa and Veganism" with the plea: "If I have offended anyone as a result of this essay, Micchami Dukkadam [a request for forgiveness]" (10).

Whether or not he will be forgiven is up to his Jain readers to decide. As I see it, he has both appropriated and simplified a religion that appears to promote animal liberation.

Charlotte Laws explains that "Jain ascetics often wear mouth shields in order to protect minute organisms in the air, gently sweep the ground as they walk so as to avoid inadvertently crushing insects, avoid sex (in part, because it kills sperm), and may eventually choose to starve themselves to death in a journey toward spiritual perfection" (50). Putting aside the impractical nature of such a lifestyle, Jainism is still a speciesist religion for their modes of action/non-action are ultimately about karma and ascension. Chapple explains that "Jainism, with few exceptions, avoids sentimentalizing animals. Ultimately, the reason one respects animals is not for the sake of the animal, but for the purpose of lightening the karmic burden that obscures the splendor of one's own soul" (248). Once again, nonhumans are not inherently precious beings; rather, they are obstacles to or pathways toward *human* enlightenment and positive karmic consequences.

As explored in the previous section, hierarchy prevents full recognition of the worth of all living beings, and as with other religions, Jainism is extremely hierarchical. In fact, they have a rather rigid taxonomy that ranks animals according to their sense perceptions. Living beings with only a sense of touch are on the lowest rung, building up to those with hearing and, of course, all the other senses in between (Chapple 241). Hence, humans, with all senses intact and capable of understanding (and creating) the concept of rebirth, top the taxonomy.

An example of anthropocentrism in Jainism arises in Laws's conversation with Gom, a Jain practitioner. Like vegan animal rights activists, Gom opposes zoos. However, while an animal advocate would protest a zoo because animals are taken out of their expansive natural environments, confined, and used for profit to entertain human gawkers, that is not the case with Gom. He explains: "A zoo is a commercial enterprise that causes animal suffering [. . .] Zoos do not value animals' lives. And Jains are against vivisection. We might find ourselves in an animal body in the next life" (qtd. in Laws 53). The differing perspectives are evident. Gom is concerned about animals in zoos and labs in part because he or others may someday be born into such an animal body. In contrast, animal activists protest zoos because they are concerned solely with the lives of those imprisoned in them, not because it may affect them, the activists, in a future life.

As with karma, one might here question what the problem is. For whatever reason, isn't it important to have as many people as possible against zoos? Yes, but only if one is willing to *actively* oppose them; this is not the case with Jainism. Jains, for all of their ostensible concern with nonhumans, are not activists, and the reason for this is quite unnerving. Laws explains: "In addition to practical difficulties, karma helps explain why Jains don't feel compelled to desperately strive to rescue every living being who is in need. In their view, those who suffer have brought misfortune upon themselves, in previous lives" (55). Animal advocates have heard many reasons for why nonhumans are at human disposal: God deems it so, it is the natural order of existence, the animals don't know the difference because they can't reason like humans. The Jain perspective, or at least Gom's, is that animals in zoos are imprisoned due to wicked behavior in a previous life. There is an underlying implication that one who suffers, be it in a sweatshop or on a farm, has it coming because of karma. This is why Jains are not activists.[24] Finally, as Andrew Linzey notes in "Is Religion Bad for Animals?", the Jains' "extreme emphasis on not killing means that in practice even terminally suffering animals are not allowed to be euthanized." Allowing a being to suffer unimaginable pain out of fear for one's personal ascension is not an act of compassion but an example of human selfishness.

It is important to now imagine a world without religion (cue John Lennon here). As an atheist who cares about nonhumans, I have faith in only one reality—the here and now. As such, I do not imagine that the animals suffering in human-made prisons earned

---

24. Here I write of Jainism proper. I'm sure there are many activists who claim to be Jains.

it through misdeeds in another life, nor do I imagine that maybe next time, again in another life, they will get it right. I believe in one life, a life force I cannot explain but won't chalk up to divine intervention or a cycle of rebirths. As such, I will fight for the end of abuse and violence in the lone world I know. With few exceptions, religion in its many manifestations keeps humans focused on another world or life when things will be better. This keeps us distanced from the reality, often violent, that surrounds us daily. And as seen through Jainism, it keeps compassionate humans in a state of inaction.

To conclude this section, I want to briefly touch on the spiritual traditions of native peoples who were displaced, converted to Christianity by force, and/or massacred by European invaders. I don't like to speak of indigenous traditions as religions because, even keeping just within the US, there are many tribes to consider, and they do not share common founders (Christ and Mohammed) or texts (the Bible and Quran). As such, they do not practice religion in the ways previously defined. As with Eastern religions, indigenous spiritualities are more respectful of nature, nonhuman animals included. Kemmerer explains that such "traditions teach people that we owe respect, responsibility, and compassion to our nonhuman kin," and "indigenous peoples believe that all beings are endowed with souls" (55).

This commentary makes me think of a casino nearby my home, owned and operated by the Shakopee Mdewakanton Sioux Community. A few years ago, they had a display about bison, which they call tatanka. At one time, bison roamed North America by the millions. After European arrival, they numbered fewer than 1,000. The Euro-Americans killed the bison indiscriminately, treating them as they did both the New World and non-white peoples—as free resources. While the native people killed limited bison for practical uses, about 100 uses per bison, Euro-Americans killed them for profit and as a way to exterminate the people themselves who were dependent on the tatanka for survival ("Tatanka"). Thus, there are stark differences between how diverse cultures have behaved toward each other, nonhuman animals, and nature in the past. And there are undoubtedly those groups who have offered a more compassionate ethical paradigm. Many Native American tribes respect(ed) nature and nonhuman animals in a distinct way that differentiates them from those who practice Western and Eastern religions. There is/was a respect for the inherent value of other species with whom they share(d) the Earth, but there is danger in positioning indigenous traditions as representative of a Edenic paradise to which we can return.

Foremost, it is an insult to Native Americans to first take their land and then their culture. A recent article in the *Tampa Bay Times* reports on the development of the Fraudulent Native American Task Force, aimed at those who want to claim Indian heritage and appropriate tribal customs. As Sal "White Horse" Serbin declares in the article, "The stealing and exploitation of the Native American culture [. . .] has become an epidemic" in the U.S. (qtd. in Anton). White people, ironically and perhaps well-meaningly, fetishize a time before white people, a time in which the land we now call North American was at peace. This is not the whole truth. As Will Tuttle frankly admits,

> primitive cultures are often not as we would romanticize them, and some American Indian cultures, for example, practiced cannibalism, genocidal warfare on other tribes, and horrific ritual torture on captives from other tribes [. . .]. [If] attending an American Indian gathering today, we would find dead animals being served as food [. . .] and we would find the participants at any of these events prepared to vehemently justify their meals. (235)

As with almost all cultures we can imagine today, indigenous ones evolve from a past in which using animals for food, clothing, and shelter may have been required for survival. Currently, there is not one such spiritual tradition that declares nonhumans as worthy of respect and compassion on par with human beings. Indigenous spiritualities are still anthropocentric. In sum, indigenous spiritualities, though evidently better than Western and even Eastern religions, do not lead to animal liberation, which starts with a revolution in human perception of other species.

Vilification of Animal Natures
in Progressive Revelation

Many religious traditions maintain belief in a time of peace on Earth when violence did not exist and all cohabitated in concord. This mythical era of peace amongst all beings is found in indigenous traditions as well as Christian ones: "Many indigenous creation stories tell of [. . .] a time when animals lived peacefully in community with one another [. . .] [in] a vegan world where all species consumed only plants and plant products, and shared space peacefully" (Kemmerer 29–31). Such a view makes one wonder why the religious, Christian or otherwise, would not, en masse, use God's (or gods') idea of a peaceful world and try to mirror it on the Earth today. If the right way of living excludes bloodshed, and there is no actual injunction against being vegan in any religious text or tradition of note, why not live as close to that era of peace as is humanly possible? Would that not please God?

I feel I have partially answered those questions above. First, there is no God of which humans have knowledge. Next, while no God is demanding that humans eat meat—although animal sacrifices were once common in both Western and Eastern religions—the *indifferent* way in which animals are treated (or completely ignored) in spiritual texts and traditions gives tacit permission to consume them. In current contexts, that leads to other uses of nonhumans for purposes of research, clothing, sport, and entertainment. Many religious advocates for animal rights and liberation home in on the idea that God, let's say the Christian God, never demanded that humans eat animal meat. But while this is true, I think the argument weak because it ignores the ways in which indifference can be a form of violence and permission. To quote Elie Wiesel, author and Holocaust survivor, in an aptly titled speech "The Perils of Indifference": "Indifference reduces the Other to an abstraction." And when animals are reduced to parts, they become abstractions, not real beings with interest in their own lives.

Looking ahead to the end times, as some religious folk like to do, Victor Stenger notes a vast array of religions that foresee an occasion when the world will end and this Eden in which our forebears lived will be ours once again. Christian sects such as Jehovah's Witnesses and Rastafarians believe this, as do advocates of "Islam, Zoroastrianism, Buddhism, Hinduism, the Baháh'í Faith, and the Hopi, Lakota, Mayan and other Native American religions" (Stenger 55). This paradise on Earth will be one of peace and harmony in which violence will have no part. The gist of all these perspectives is that existence was once serene, it is brutal now, but someday we will again live in bliss after some kind of cataclysmic event that will first end the world as we know it. That will be the time in which aggression will have no place, including violence amongst the many animal species.

In the meantime, all bets are off, and we have free rein to live sinfully—it is in our natures, after all—with the promise that someday a magical event will occur and all the bad stuff will go away. As many religious critics have argued before me, such dogma keeps the oppressed in line with the assurance that even though life is horrible now and we are all brutes, someday we will live in heaven with our God, everyone will be equal, the bad people will be punished in fiery pits for eternity, and all of the pain will have been worth it. Where does this leave nonhuman animals?

Those who argue for animal liberation through theological filters look to these fabled times as proof that humans and nonhumans should, and will one day again, dwell together. The lion will lie beside the lamb and humans will feast congenially on vegetation alone. To illustrate, consider this biblical passage (Isaiah: 6–9) noted by the Christian Vegetarian Association as promoting a hopeful future:

> The wolf will live with the lamb,
> the leopard will lie down with the goat,
> the calf and the lion and the yearling together;
> and a little child will lead them.[25]
> The cow will feed with the bear,

---

25. Here we see that even in paradise, humans will be in charge.

their young will lie down together,
and the lion will eat straw like the ox. The infant will play
near the cobra's den,
and the young child will put its hand into the viper's nest.
They will neither harm nor destroy
on all my holy mountain,
for the earth will be filled with the knowledge of the Lord
as the waters cover the sea.

In Judaism and Christianity, this was the way of the world before
the first woman, Eve, led Adam into sin. Norm Phelps notes that
this peaceful paradise lasted even longer: "According to the Bible,
at the time of giving humanity dominion over the animals, God
also instructed us to maintain not just a vegetarian but a vegan
diet, one that includes no animal products whatsoever, a command that Genesis tells us stayed in effect until after the flood"
(35). Once the flood came because of human misdeeds, the situation altered, and the supposedly all loving God decided that nonhumans would live in fear of men as both a food source and via
early sacrifices (see Gen.: 2–3, cited above). In other words, God
is punishing nonhumans because of human sin, and this is true
even when nonhumans are the victims of violent sexual cruelty.
Leviticus 20:15–16 advises: "If a man has sexual relations with an
animal, he is to be put to death, and you must kill the animal. If a
woman approaches an animal to have sexual relations with it, kill
both the woman and the animal."[26] The ethical implications of
these hallowed demands are decidedly unethical, as other species
are made to suffer for human sins.[27] Even in supposedly pro-ani-
mal religious studies, these conclusions abound: "It would make
sense to say that in some ways some animals other than humans

---

26. An interesting note about this passage: it appears as if men actually
have to have sex with animals to be put to death, but women only need
to attempt such an act.

27. And we must not forget that to this day, women under Islam can
be jailed (or worse) if they are victims of rape.

do manifest signs of sinfulness, whereas there are other modes of sinfulness that seem to be particular to humanity" (Clough 117).

Of course, in Christianity, especially Catholicism, other-than-human animals would become further maligned, manifesting as the bull horned, cloven hoofed, tail swinging devil. Not only would nonhumans become so unimportant as to be deemed food stuff for a sinful humanity, they would become the cause of fear due to associations with Satan. Will Tuttle aptly notes this paradox when commenting that the "devil is ironically represented as having the horns and hooves of a goat or cow—the very victims we relentlessly confine and attack for food!" (162). Pigs are especially maltreated as symbols of filth and evil.

In Christopher Hitchens's *God is Not Great*, in the amusingly titled chapter "A Short Digression on the Pig; or, Why Heaven Hates Ham," he notes that in the Quran, Jews and other non-believers are punished by being turned into pigs and monkeys, while commenting upon the simultaneous "reverence" and "disgust" early Semites felt toward pigs (37; 40). Not surprisingly considering what has already been said of pigs in this chapter, they get special (mis)treatment from religious leaders. In an extreme case that Hitchens deems "ancient stupidity" in the modern era, Muslim hardliners in Europe shield their children from Miss Piggy and literary classics such as "The Three Little Pigs" and *Winnie-the-Pooh* (re Piglet) because they offer agreeable images of porcine characters (41).

The maligning of pigs has become so commonplace in Western culture that it has even made its way into the animal rights movement. *Skinny Bitch* is a bestselling book, the first of a series, aimed at women who want to lose weight (a later book was written for men entitled *Skinny Bastard*). The authors Rory Freedman and Kim Barnouin are associated with People for the Ethical Treatment of Animals, and the book is a pitch for veganism disguised as a diet plan. Much like the Bible, *Skinny Bitch* is a pig-hating venture. Some of their commentary includes the following: "being a fat pig will hinder you [. . .]. And habitual drinking equals fat-pig syndrome" (12); if you follow the Atkins diet "you are a gluttonous pig who wants to believe you can eat cheeseburgers all day long and lose weight" (39); and the first line of their chapter "Use Your Head" advises readers not to be pigs anymore (184). The power of religious ideology is clearly visible here when even those who sincerely wish to liberate animals will resort to maligning them, refusing to critically analyze the source of our culture's hatred of a specific animal species that is not supposed to be skinny.

As we see, in Christian and Muslim traditions, and the animal rights movement, nonhuman animals can be both a source of fear and a source of nourishment. In the latter case, pigs are used to incite women's fear of being fat. That is a contradiction worthy of religious doctrine, but it also speaks to another trend in animal-friendly progressive revelation and liberation theology: vilifying nonhumans for being nonhuman. Not only are they punished for humankind's sins and made into mythical monsters, they are further maligned for their innate behaviors. To wit, Freedman and Barnouin demonize pigs for being fat when they are, in reality, just being pigs. That makes as much sense as criticizing giraffes for being too tall.

Without doubt, humans are the most violent and destructive animal in all of recorded history, and we indisputably do have something to learn about compassion and peacemaking. The oddity of progressive revelation is that nonhumans are presented in that same way. They are defamed because they kill other animals, and that they do so for survival—not profit, gluttony, entertainment, research, and plain old cruelty—is routinely ignored. J.R. Hyland reports that "both men and beasts were created with a nonviolent nature, that goodness was their innate characteristic [. . .]. And although all have fallen from a higher state, their innate goodness—their nonviolent nature—will be reactivated" (20). Similarly, Phelps states that Eden was "very good because there was no violence. No living soul harmed any other living soul. All of God's children lived together in peace" (91). Unintentionally or not, such posturing vilifies nonhumans for what they must do for survival, as if they have moral agency in the human sense (or the agency to grow vegetation or shop at co-ops).

Moral agency is "the ability to bring impartial reasons to one's decision making" (Regan 241); thus, humans are moral agents. In *The Case for Animal Rights*, Tom Regan explains that nonhuman animals, as are very young children and humans with impaired cognitive abilities, are better seen as moral patients. Although they are cognizant of their being and subject to emotions and physical pain, moral patients cannot properly be seen as committing right or wrong acts (154). In religious terms, this means that nonhuman animals are not capable of good and evil in the way humans have developed the concepts. This seems an acceptable premise from any sensible perspective, but again, religion rarely deals in sense.

There is an unspoken insinuation within progressive revelation and liberation theologies that, for example, the lion is evil and sinful for preying upon the gazelle. From my anthropocentric perspective, a lion killing a gazelle appears violent (and I can only assume the gazelle agrees), but to put that act of predation on the same level of human predation throughout the course of history, especially in modern contexts, is ludicrous. Such a perspective is concisely summarized and critiqued here by radical feminist Catherine MacKinnon:

> We justify it [eating animals] as necessary, but it is not. We do it because we enjoy it, and we can. We say they eat each other, too, which they do. But this does not exonerate us [. . .]. The place to look for the bottom line is in the farm, the stockyard, the slaughterhouse. I have yet to see one run by a nonhuman animal. (324)

In sum, nonhumans predominately eat other nonhumans for their continued existence, and perhaps at some time in history, as animals, this was necessary for humans to do as well.[28] However,

---

28. I say "predominately" because there seem to be cases where non-humans enjoy killing other species. To wit, I had a cat as a child, and although he had a never ending supply of food at home, he appeared to delight in "playing" with small animals such as mice and chipmunks before killing them and leaving their carcasses at my family's back door.

many in the Western world have moved past this evolutionary stage, and the vestiges of animal consumption by humans arise from, as MacKinnon states, human enjoyment of animal flesh. The theological tendency to claim that animals fell from grace when humans did opens up the door for the former's exploitation and punishment. Thus, as we wait for Eden to return, humans are permitted to eat the flesh of their fallen earthmates until that mythical day when the wolf, the lamb, the leopard, the calf, the human child, and the viper will all be as one, nestling together as would a family. But for those of us who don't buy the myths, for those who care about animal suffering *now*, the fantasy will stay just that, and holy books only perpetuate mythologies that demonize animals.

This sort of commentary also reinforces an image of the animal activist who thinks that with just enough love and compassion, all beings will live in harmony. At a recent conference I attended in Germany, an apolitical animal studies scholar stated the opinion, as fact, that animal advocates do not understand that nature is, to quote poet Alfred, Lord Tennyson, "red in tooth and claw." Another anti-vegan writer Lierre Keith explains that a "turning point" for her against veganism occurred when she went to an animal rights message board to read of a vegan's idea that a fence should be constructed down the middle of the Serengeti to keep predators away from prey; "[h]e knew that [carnivorous animals] would be okay because they didn't need to be carnivores," which is something the meat industry has made up (7). This representation of vegan activists is false.

I am sure there are some who think in the "head in the clouds" way exemplified above, but the majority of animal liberation activists are insightful, intelligent individuals who understand that for survival purposes, animals eat other animals (though you will never find a nonhuman overseeing a vivisection lab or training other animal species to jump through hoops of fire), and we acknowledge that there are true carnivores who must eat the flesh of other animals for optimal health. We fight against the use of nonhumans by human beings who have plentiful, less violent options for food, clothing, cosmetics, and entertainment. The critical activist knows that the nonhumans for whom we have respect

and compassion "are likely to flee as far away from us as possible
if they had a chance" (Pedersen and Stănescu x). In defiance of
the "animals are our friends" mentality, Al Nowatzki explains, in
an essay on vegan parenting, that he told his children these truths
as soon as they were old enough to comprehend: "Bees aren't
their friends [. . .]. A hungry tiger is not their friend" (94). When
contemplating where this "all animals are our friends" idea comes
from, religion is once again at least partly responsible.

In Judith Barad's essay, she tells the story of Saint Francis of
Assisi and a wolf who had been terrorizing a town. In response,
the people of Agobio wanted the wolf slain. St. Francis stepped in,
and with a sign of the cross and a few choice words, the wolf became a docile creature whom the townsfolk fed and adopted as a
kind of roving pet, even grieving his eventual death. Again noting
the "animal-friendly" Aquinas, Barad explains that some "find the
anecdote of the wolf to be so unbelievable that they view this story
as having no literal foundation. But those of us who, like Aquinas,
are aware of animal intelligence, are also aware that animals, when
treated with respect and love, are capable of responding much like
the wolf in this story" (133). *This is not true.* A free-living animal,
let's say a bear, may eat you if he is hungry enough, no matter
how much respect one offers, no matter how much one loves that
bear.[29]

Returning to the tale, the wolf retreated from his instincts,
which was not to kill indiscriminately, but for nourishment, and
he is then *de*wolfed, acceptable only when he was no longer a
threat to humans. Putting aside for a moment that the story is
silly, what does this have to do with the intelligence Aquinas supposedly imbued animals with? It doesn't matter how much respect
and love you give a hungry wolf; if she is hungry, she will eat you,
and she should not be vilified for it. This is no mere passing story
either, as wolves have been disparaged for centuries, leading up to

---

29. For painful evidence of this reality, see the documentary *Grizzly
Man* in which a bear-obsessed man named Timothy Treadwell and his
girlfriend are eaten by one of their supposed ursine brethren.

the present day. The Wolf Information Center reports that "[c]onflicts with humans and fears originating from *religious beliefs*, myths and folklore influenced human attitudes toward wolves and, as a result, wolves have been persecuted for hundreds of years" ("Wolves of the World," emphasis added). The false message from this Catholic tale is two-fold: wolves will respond warmly and obediently to human love and they are treacherous beasts only of importance when an agent of God does his magic so that people can pet and feed them.

To foster compassion toward animals amongst believers, Andrew Linzey tells a similarly absurd tale involving Jesus Christ and his mother Mary. Mary sees lions and panthers approaching, and she rationally responds with fear. The baby Jesus assures her that they mean no harm; rather, they are there to serve the infant and his mother, as the prophets foretold (Linzey 67). Hyland states that although animals "have adapted to a violent lifestyle, both animals and humans can readapt to their original peaceful natures" (20). The meaning is clear. Animals have "violent lifestyles" that can only be subdued by otherworldly forces. Putting aside the oddity of animals having "lifestyles" in the human sense, this is the best Christianity has to offer us about other-than-human animals. They exist to serve humans and should be castigated for their nonhuman animal natures. Unless they are domesticated as our pets, food, laborers—and, in the case of divine beings, adorers—they are to be vilified as violent beasts much like Satan and his demonic cronies. These ideas are propagated by those attempting to cultivate a more sensitive approach to nonhumans through religious fables.

Another disturbing proposal proffered via spiritual thought arises from indigenous traditions claiming humans can only eat nonhumans if the latter willingly give themselves to the former. While there is at least some thought given to the lives of animals exploited and killed for human survival, these ideas promote a hierarchy in which animals freely sacrifice themselves so humans can eat. If they are content to serve human purposes, there is little room for considering that we shouldn't eat animals. Kemmerer details the following:

Indigenous peoples who believe the brush rabbits and ruffed grouse *choose* to die to feed and clothe humans also believe that they will make this compassionate and generous choice only if people maintain proper, respectful behavior and attitudes toward those they hunt. Those who do not wish to die for humans will not do so [. . .] Similarly, the Inuit (Arctic) believe that the mother of the anymals (sic), Sedna ("She Down There"), dwells deep within the sea, from which vantage point she decides whether or not her children will become food for humans—she decides whether or not humans will eat. (33; 48)

This perspective effectively absolves humans of wrongdoing because other animals are making choices to become human food, assuming the human killing them is nice about it. Of course, hunting for food *is* different than maintaining or buying food that comes from an animal farm, and some tribal customs, such as that of the Anishinaabe, fully denounce human ownership of other animals. However, presence of "proper, respectful behaviors and attitudes" toward animals is regularly claimed by small-scale farmers who allege that their "happy" grass-fed cows become "happy" meat for the wealthy few who can afford the artisanal animal flesh (a system of animal agriculture that is not sustainable on a large scale and, as some have argued, possibly just as bad for the environment as factory farms[30]).

This quaint idea that animals willing sacrifice their lives to feed humans is not a mere remnant of indigenous belief systems. It is prevalent today through the common notion of "that's why animals are here, to serve humans." Ideologies such as this integrate people into a normalized meat-eating, animal exploiting culture. Again considering Nowatzki's critique of speciesist children's media, he analyzes a scene from *Sesame Street* in which a cow happily gets milked, exclaiming how proud she is to be a cow who can

---

30. For an accessible analysis of this issue, see James McWilliams's December 7, 2010 article "Why Free-Range Meat Isn't Much Better Than Factory Farmed" on *Theatlantic.com*.

produce such a healthy food for humans (82). Missing is the reality that cows produce milk for *their* offspring, not human children, who are soon taken away from them. Cows then mourn the loss of their calves and spend their lives hooked up to milking machines that cause irritations and infections. Once they are done making a profit for their "owners," they are killed.

The myth of nonhuman animal self-sacrifice, with a basis in religious/spiritual thought, has more recently been adopted by companies marketing meat products. The term "suicide food" refers to depictions of nonhuman animals willingly and excitedly preparing themselves or offering up their bodies, or those of their same species, for human consumption. The blog *Suicide Food* offers a storehouse of such images showcasing animals—often pigs, clearly the most maligned animal species in the Western world—announcing the "Pleasantville Pig Out" and "Uncle Piggy Smoker Grill," among others. In the latter image, a smiling pig lays with his legs crossed, "hands" behind his head, and a sly grin on his face as his roasts himself on a grill. The popular restaurant chain Subway has offered similar ads in which a pig entices prospective patrons to add bacon to their sandwiches.

Yes, nature is "red in tooth and claw," but I refuse the idea that it is populated by masochistic animals who like being tortured for human fulfillment, which is what our culture, propped up by religion, would have us think. I also reject the idea that every day in the wild is a bloody massacre (more on this in the next chapter). All animals don't die every day on battlefield Earth. Rather, as we can see via video footage and direct experience, animals play games with each other, they bathe in the sun, they preen, they have intercourse, they investigate; mothers tend to and teach their young. The list of pleasures that nonhumans enjoy could go on and on. And when/if they do die at another animal's teeth and claws, they at least spent their lives free from the myriad prisons humans have created for them.

I want to end by noting one spiritual pathway, much like indigenous traditions, that at least acknowledges the dignity of nonhumans, if only on a theoretical level: Wicca. Indeed, I am prepared to say that after an exhaustive review of world religions,

Wicca and native spiritualities provide the only religious perspectives that show any honest respect for nonhuman animals *as* nonhuman animals, but they do not promote veganism, which is why they too fall under the category of "better doesn't mean good enough." Wicca is a neo-pagan religion with ancient roots that reveres nature; the mystical aspects of Wicca arise through its practitioners' use of magic and veneration of gods and goddesses; it's "a personal, positive celebration of life" (Cunningham).

A positive element of Wicca is that it acknowledges humans are animals. We are a part of nature, not apart from it. Animals are not wicked for killing other animals, and they won't someday shake off their "violent lifestyles." Thus, Wiccan spirituality can help mend the many Western binaries that lead to hierarchy and oppression. However, aligning oneself with nature can lead to rationalizing the slaughter and consumption of other species. Wiccan practitioner Diane Sylvan states that her religion considers

> the cycle of the seasons to be a holy metaphor for the cycle of creation and destruction [. . .]. Some people use this metaphor to justify taking life for food, and many neopagans eat meat (and hunt); they claim that the relationship between predator and prey is natural and sacred, and consider themselves to be natural predators. (227)

How natural is it to sit in a tree with a gun (or bow and arrow) waiting for an unwitting buck to wander by and nourish himself in a field? How sacred is it to kill a duck and make orphans of her ducklings? How natural and sacred are these actions when humans have developed the means to do otherwise and survive quite healthfully? As with native religions, Wicca harkens back to a previous era in which killing other species may have been required for human survival. For many, this is simply not the case anymore, so the appeal to tradition underpinned by supernatural sanction fails to liberate animals as well. Sylvan does not agree with the hunting justification of her fellow witches, so she is also vegan, taking literally the Wiccan Rede: "And it harm none, do what you will." Ultimately, Wicca is not very different than any other religion whose creeds and doctrines will be interpreted differently depending on the practitioner, but it may be amongst the best of the worst.

Is there any hope for animals within religious and spiritual pathways? Perhaps there is, but only if one will settle for modified exploitation and slaughter. No, if one wants animal liberation. And some individuals, I sadly recognize, will simply never care about other animal species. This leads me to now explore what happens when we forgo religious doctrine, when we refuse the ideas of higher powers and holy books, of gods and goddesses, of crosses and talismans, when we acknowledge, without prevarication, that we are primates and our ethical codes do not arise out of fear of punishment in this or another life. Is there any hope for nonhuman animals in a world without the supernatural? I begin to answer that question in the next chapter.

Chapter 2

Animals Minus Myth

> The history of Western civilization shows us that most social and moral progress has been brought about by persons free from religion. In modern times the first to speak out for prison reform, for humane treatment of the mentally ill, for abolition of capital punishment, for women's right to vote, for death with dignity for the terminally ill, and for the right to choose contraception, sterilization and abortion have been freethinkers, just as they were the first to call for an end to slavery.
>
> —Freedom from Religion Foundation

In the previous chapter, I argued that religious arguments for animal liberation are brittle Procrustean beds or secular ideas ascribed to religious doctrine. To be clear, I am not asserting that religion created every ill that plagues our world, but I do argue it bolsters and sanctions many of them. Further, since religion was constructed by humans, as opposed to supernatural forces, then humans are the culprits of said oppressions.

Consider the epigraph from the Freedom from Religion Foundation (FFRF) with which I begin this chapter. It serves two purposes. First, it shows that many of Western history's social and ethical wrongs sprang from religious institutions. For example, the mentally ill were once seen as demon possessed and the storied history of religion's stranglehold on women's bodies continues

into the present day the world over. More to the statement's purpose, freethinkers (some with ties to radical, progressive religions
such as Quakerism[31]) have led the charge against the varied social
injustices that religion generated or condoned, even American
slavery. The abolitionist movement is often portrayed as led by
benevolent religious white folk. In truth, it does not take much
historical digging to learn that African Americans and freethinkers
were at the forefront of the movement as well, and the two are
not mutually exclusive. Black abolitionist Frederick Douglass was
critical of Christianity, which he deemed "the *slaveholding religion* of this land," although he notably differentiates that religion
from "Christianity proper," of which he was rather accepting.
Nevertheless, his famous narrative showed that Christianity did
nothing to diminish his "owner's" cruel treatment of him and
other enslaved people. In fact, Christianity justified and amplified
the slave owner's malice.

The FFRF epigraph also demonstrates that with religion per-
petuating so many unjust cultural norms, it makes sense for those
freed from religious thinking to be at the forefront of various social movements toward positive change. Civic-minded atheists of
the U.S. agitate against the human subjugation religion perpetuates in a country that claims separation between church and state.
Along with all of the concerns noted in the epigraph, atheists are
activists for LGBTQIA rights because prohibiting gay marriage is
clearly about politicians' religious beliefs and those of their con-
stituents.[32] As I defined political atheism in the Introduction, it
is an ethical stance against the heterosexism, sexism, ableism, and
racism that arise from religious traditions. However, as I also state
in the Introduction, the secular community has not yet sufficiently
addressed, or acknowledged the existence of, speciesism.

---

31. Quakerism is possibly the only strain of Christianity that includes
and welcomes atheists. In fact, some declare themselves Nontheist
Quakers or Quaker Atheists.

32. I am not asserting that atheists are never racist, sexist, homopho-
bic, or overall horrific individuals. Rather, I am specifically focusing
on those from the freethought community who are also social justice
activists.

In atheist philosopher Peter Singer's influential *Animal Liberation*, he defines speciesism as "a prejudice or attitude of bias in favor of the interests of members of one's own species and against those members of other species" (6). More recently, Joan Dunayer, also a freethinker, describes it as "a failure, in attitude or practice, to accord any nonhuman being equal consideration and respect" (5). An ethological retort might be that all species of animal are speciesist, solely concerned with those of their own kind, and more specifically, of their own kin. However, as I am a human being with moral agency writing a book for other humans with moral agency, and speciesism is, as far as we know, not comprehendible by other species, my concern is with speciesism as it manifests in Homo sapiens against other animals.

We know nonhumans eat other nonhumans both within and outside of their own species, and perhaps they even delight in the hunt. But we also know that in 2010, about 63 billion animals were slaughtered for food in the U.S. alone (10.2 billion land animals and 53 billion aquatic); worldwide, land animal deaths exceed 65 billion, and the number of sea animals killed globally for human consumption is so vast as to be unquantifiable ("Report"). We also know that in 2009, again just in the U.S., "1.13 million animals [were] used in experiments (*excluding* rats, mice, birds, reptiles, amphibians, and agricultural animals used in agricultural experiments), plus an estimated 100 million mice and rats" ("Animal Experiments," emphasis added).[33] Finally, we also know that animals are exploited and abused in untold numbers for sport, fashion, and entertainment. These outrageous statistics

---

33. The "food animals" data was amassed by the Farm Animal Rights Movement using numerous reports from the United States Department of Agriculture (USDA) and United Nations. People for the Ethical Treatment of Animals supplies the data on "research" animals from the USDA's Animal and Plant Health Inspection Service's "Annual Report Animal Usage by Fiscal Year" from July 2011. With numbers so vast, there is a tendency to question data from organizations working to improve nonhuman animals' lives. Thus, I felt it prudent to explain the source of these final statistics.

should be enough for any sensible reader to see that human speciesism is far more violent, prevalent, and expansive than the supposed speciesism that some would argue manifests in other animal species.[34] So, why is speciesism not yet important enough to add to the list of other "isms" against which the secular community contends?

I believe an answer lies in Michel Onfray's *Atheist Manifesto*, although he does not write it with nonhuman animals in mind (at least not that one can observe). Onfray states: "Secular thought is not de-Christianized thought, but immanent Christian thought. Couched in rational language, it nevertheless preserves the quintessence of the Judeo-Christian ethic" (217). His words echo those of other atheist thinkers. In "The Failure of Christianity," published in 1913, Emma Goldman made analogous note of those who "have rid themselves of the letter, but have retained the spirit; yet it is the spirit which is back of all the crimes and horrors committed by orthodox Christianity" (385). Goldman's contemporary Voltairine de Cleyre likewise observes that even "those who have utterly repudiated the Church, are nevertheless soaked in this stupefying narcotic to true morality. So pickled is the male creation with the vinegar of Authoritarianism, that even those who have gone further and repudiated the State still cling to god" ("Sex Slavery" 362). In other words, we may declare ourselves atheist or agnostic, but being raised in a culture saturated with the ideologies of those religions, even if we were raised in a secular environment, we cannot help but have internalized the cruel worldviews and mindsets embedded in religious doctrine. One of those worldviews is human exceptionalism, which is part of the problem of hierarchy addressed in the first chapter:

> Alas, like the religious, the majority of atheists don't embrace veganism. For many, the atheist view that there is no gods ends up elevating humanity to the position of god within the

---

34. A further problem with this argument is that since nonhumans can't realize they are speciesist, they cannot actually be speciesist.

hierarchy of being. Since there is no god, the argument goes, humans make the rules and can rightly position themselves at the pinnacle of the chain of being. Anthropocentrism either goes unexamined or is celebrated. The appeal to nature fallacy is embraced as a defense of the status quo. (Nowatzki "Religion")

In this passage, Al Nowatzki epitomizes the human tendency to maintain hierarchies even when the divine is missing, thereby relegating humans, as the dominant species, to the role of gods. Indeed, when considering the many ways Homo sapiens use other species, it is clear that humans determine when and if other species will be born, how they will live, how or if they will procreate, how much they will suffer, and when that suffering will end. If that is not a god-like position, then I cannot imagine what is from a secular standpoint.

To offer a brief case study of the areligious behaving religiously, consider how Onfray's assertion explains the oft trotted out commentary by religious advocates that some of the world's most notorious genocidal leaders were atheists. The argument is that when one forgoes God, s/he is without any moral or ethical code and mayhem will ensue. First, a strong case can and has been made that Adolf Hitler wasn't an atheist, nor was he a vegetarian, as is often claimed (Patterson 127), as if his possible vegetarianism somehow negates the ethics of that diet for anyone who adopts it. In *Mein Kampf*, Hitler shows belief in a higher power that he used to justify his egregious acts of violence: "And so I believe today that my conduct is in accordance with the will of the Almighty Creator. In standing guard against the Jew I am defending the handiwork of the Lord" (64). In a 1933 speech in Berlin, he states, "We were convinced that the people needs and requires this faith. We have therefore undertaken the fight against the atheistic movement, and that not merely with a few theoretical declarations: we have stamped it out" (378). Vox Day (real name Theodore Beale) argues that the notorious despot was not a Christian or an atheist, terming Hitler's religious views "pagan totalitarianism" (213). About a decade after his 1933 speech, Hitler lost faith in Christianity,[35] but he did not lose faith in religion, with plans to form a nationalistic church. As Michael Lackey effectively explains, Hitler made "use of the Bible's epistemological/ontological recursive loop" to construct "a political system that is based on a theological model of knowledge" (134). In other words, one need not have faith in God to use theological power constructions.

Other infamous dictators Josef Stalin and Pol Pot were raised in the religious traditions of Catholicism and Theravada Buddhism, respectively. In fact, Stalin studied for the priesthood and relied on the Greek Orthodox Church to underpin his brutal regime. Hence, even if one argues that Stalin and Pot were atheists, it is important to consider the role religion may have played in their worldviews. Religious ideologies inform the ways people think even for those who don't consciously accept them. Indeed, philosopher and physicist Victor Stenger asserts that "with its dogmatic policies and authoritarianism, communism more closely resembles a godless religion than secular atheism" (24) due to the many rules, policies, and procedures one must follow to be a "good communist" under authoritarian rule.

Richard Dawkins offers a fine retort to religious advocates who propose "atheist" genocides are far worse than religion-based brutalities such as the Crusades or the 9/11 attacks: "What matters not is whether Hitler or Stalin were atheists, but whether atheism systematically *influences* people to do bad things. There is not the smallest evidence that it does" (*God Delusion* 309). Hitler, Stalin, Pot, and other historical monsters were not slaughtering people because of sacred atheist doctrines (there aren't any), they were not necessarily free from the religious thinking that leads to violence, and some strategically used religion, via the Church, as a means to control people. In sum, one can be non-religious but still maintain religious attitudes and worldviews. History's worst genocides were constructed by men who understood the evil that

---

35. The Catholic Church did not lose faith in him. In fact, up to the fall of the Third Reich, the Nazis had the papacy's support.

could be done in the name of God and made acceptable to those who believe in a higher power. History proves the case.

In *Atheist Manifesto*, published in 2005, Onfray explores the reasons an atheology—a corpus of literature that both critiques and offers alternatives to religious thought—is needed to offset the damaging influence of religion on contemporary culture, with special focus on the monotheistic traditions. Coterminously, an atheology has surely blossomed over the last decade or so with the rise of both New Atheism and books promoting secular ethics. From this budding atheology, I focus on New Atheist writers in this chapter for a few particular reasons. First, the New Atheists are the most culturally influential secular theorists and the most controversial. Even many within the freethought community see the New Atheists as too radically anti-religion and are wary of their refusal to adopt a more sensitive approach to moderates within religious traditions (Stenger 14).

While I don't identify as a New Atheist ("atheist" is just fine), I am drawn to their perspectives because similar schisms are found within the animal liberation movement. Although there is a wide spectrum of animal activist styles, there is also a divide between those willing to work with animal industries to better animal treatment and those who find that strategy counterproductive. This latter group, often called "abolitionists," is similarly accused of being too radical and unyielding. I align myself with this faction, though I am cautious of using the term "abolitionist" for its connection to the American slavery abolition movement.[36] Finally, I center on the New Atheists, specifically Richard Dawkins, Sam Harris, and, briefly, Christopher Hitchens because they have considered nonhumans in their work, although their conclusions are ultimately unsatisfactory, even objectionable.

Peter Singer argues that a new form of politics, with ethics at its core, would and should be radical, meaning "it could change

---

36. In "The 'Dreaded Comparisons' and Speciesism: Leveling the Hierarchy of Suffering," in *Confronting Animal Exploitation: Grassroots Essays on Liberation and Veganism*, I analyze in greater detail the reasons to be cautious of using trans-species oppression analogies.

things from the roots" (*How Are We to Live?* 18). But even when attempting to develop a system of ethics divorced from religion, the ethicist's inherent speciesism often goes uninterrogated. Ralph Acampora maintains that "the foremost transhuman ethics remain all-too-humanist in that they fixate on human-like mentation in other organisms" (131–132). With humans doing the thinking, there is a natural tendency to determine the bar for personhood through assessment of human capabilities. Thus, although ethics can be divorced from religion, the presumption of human superiority surreptitiously and unquestioningly continues. In sum, human supremacy over nonhuman animals is deeply rooted in the human psyche, even amongst the non-religious. This also explains why I interrogate not just the theories and words of Dawkins, Harris, and Hitchens, but also their actions. I hope these are not seen as *ad hominem* attacks, but as a plea for freethinkers to more deeply consider the ways in which their professed beliefs, and disbeliefs, do not align with their practicable ethics.

This chapter aims to consider what an atheology may and should mean for other-than-human animals. I explore how animals are situated in New Atheism and also reflect on the work of individuals creating definitive connections between atheism and animal liberation. I am seeking deep connections in which vegan atheism and atheist veganism manifests in the critical ways needed to integrate animal liberation into the history of the freethought movement, which has been at the forefront of many important social changes. I want to see how animals fare when religious myth and the essence of religious thought are removed from our perceptions of them. In other words, I investigate animal treatment minus myth.

New Atheism, Old Anthropocentrism

It is worth noting that Victor Stenger begins his book *The New Atheism: Taking a Stand for Science and Reason* with "Ingersoll's Vow." Robert G. Ingersoll was a nineteenth century lawyer, politician, orator, and freethought advocate. Stenger comments that although Ingersoll was a spokesman on many social justice issues, he is most well known as "The Great Agnostic" for his speeches praising secular ethics (9). "Ingersoll's Vow" offers powerful commentary on the joys that arise when one is free from "ghosts and gods," "from the winged monsters of the night," when one is "free to investigate, to guess and dream and hope" (qtd. in Stenger 9). Stenger neglects to mention that Ingersoll also produced persuasive polemics against the abuse of nonhuman animals and the environment.

To be fair, there is not much reason for Stenger to include mention of nonhumans within his examination of New Atheism, which is, like religion, predominately anthropocentric. Stenger declares early in the book that "all evidence points to a purely material universe, including the bodies and brains of *humans*, without the need to introduce soul, spirit, or anything immaterial" (16, emphasis added). Clearly, humans are his focus. Just as religions give a nod or two in the nonhuman's direction while remaining almost wholly invested in the human animal, so do the New Atheists. The main difference is the religious look to gods and other supernatural forces to guide their decisions, while the most well-known spokespeople[37] of New Atheism—Richard Dawkins, Sam Harris, and Daniel Dennett—come from scientific and philosophical backgrounds. The late Christopher Hitchens, trained as a journalist, is an exception amongst this quartet the media has dubbed "The Four Horsemen" of New Atheism, an ironic reference to the biblical Four Horsemen of the Apocalypse whose arrival will announce the end of days. In this case, Dawkins, Harris, Dennett, and Hitchens are here to announce, or at least encourage, the end of religion and god(s).

In *The New Atheism*, Stenger explains the movement's scientific and rational bases, but he also argues that this foundation need not negate human appreciation of music, art, and other aesthetic pleasures that cannot be readily explained by formulae

---

37. "Spokes*men*" would be a more apt term, as the New Atheism movement, like religion, is dominated by men, which is not to discount the work of female atheist writers such as Annie Laurie Gaylor and Ayaan Hirsi Ali, both of whom I cite in this book.

and mathematical quantifications. Thus, "Ingersoll's Vow" is a suitable way to begin such a project, as it explores the abstract delights one experiences when looking at the world free from religious restraints. It is an expressive and inspiring bit of prose, but equally eloquent are his remarks against vivisection, which I quote at length for full effect:

> VIVISECTION is the Inquisition—the Hell—of Science, All the cruelty which the human—or rather the inhuman—heart is capable of inflicting, is in this one word. Below this there is no depth. This word lies like a coiled serpent at the bottom of the abyss [. . .] But what excuse can ingenuity form for a man who deliberately—with an un-accelerated pulse—with the calmness of John Calvin at the murder of Serviettes— seeks, with curious and cunning knives, in the living, quivering flesh of a dog, for all the throbbing nerves of pain? The wretches who commit these infamous crimes pretend that they are working for the good of man; that they are actuated by philanthropy; and that their pity for the sufferings of the human race drives out all pity for the animals they slowly torture to death. ("Vivisection")

Ingersoll's critique of the status quo arising from religious institutions also caused him to bemoan the environmental destruction resulting from humankind's desire to encroach ever more deeply into nonhumans' habitats: "The destruction of game and of singing birds is to be regretted greatly [. . .] The people of America have been too busy felling forests, plowing fields, and building houses, to cultivate to the highest degree, the aesthetic side of their nature" (30). Unfortunately, while many of Ingersoll's successors make similar associations, as I will demonstrate, they do not follow up with seemingly appropriate ethical actions such as going vegan. Richard Dawkins is an apt example.

Before becoming the rock star of New Atheism, Dawkins made his living as an ethologist, evolutionary biologist, and highly respected scholar in both of those disciplines. As such, he wrote a chapter for *The Great Ape Project* anthology in 1993, offering commentary I wish were as well known to atheists as is his later work *The God Delusion*:

> What's so special about humans? [. . .] The speciesist assumption that lurks here is very simple. Humans are humans and gorillas are animals. There is an unquestioned yawning gulf between them such that the life of a single human child is worth more than the lives of all the gorillas in the world. The "worth" of an animal's life is just its replacement cost to its owner—or, in the case of a rare species, to humanity. But tie the label *Homo sapiens* to even a tiny piece of insensible, embryonic tissue, and its life suddenly leaps to infinite, uncomputable value [. . .] But the melancholy fact is that, at present, society's moral attitudes rest almost entirely on the discontinuous, speciesist imperative. (81; 86)

The last two sentences of this passage clearly speak to the influence religion has had on making the human animal of "infinite, uncomputable value" (recall Pope John Paul II's commentary on embryo research in Chapter One). And again, this is a vestige of religious thought that freethinkers cling to even when recognizing they are animals and that various religions have been mistaken in their rankings of women, children, people of color, people with disabilities, and the LGBTQIA community. Could it be they've been wrong about animals too? Dawkins's essay is appropriately called "Gaps in the Mind," and surely atheists, agnostics, freethinkers, and secularists have let our fellow animals fall through those gaps. Even Dawkins has let them fall, for despite such elegant writing and reasoning, he is not even vegetarian.

This inconsistency has earned him a place of recognition on the Web site *Why Cultured Meat*, devoted to both promoting in-vitro meat production (created through animal cells without animal slaughter) and to identifying individuals whose commentary seems at odds with their omnivorous diets. As noted on the site, Dawkins is a "rational," "intelligent" man who is both aware and critical of speciesism, but he is also unwilling "to give up a piece of [his] high-level and convenient lifestyle" ("Is Richard Dawkins Vegan?").

Why this hypocrisy? In a 2007 interview, in response to a question from audience participant Peter Singer, Dawkins explains that he has not developed the "moral courage" to cease eating meat because it is so normalized in Western culture, and although he is troubled by his own dietary habits, he does not plan to change those habits until there is a mass movement demanding that people stop eating meat ("Richard Dawkins"). This response seems insincere. First, there *is* a worldwide movement encouraging vegetarianism and veganism of which Dawkins must be aware. Second, Dawkins finds no compunction in critiquing, sometimes in the most arrogant and unforgiving terms, culturally accepted religious ideologies without apology or hedging. He has not shown himself afraid of shaking things up, so is he really *that* afraid of what people might think if he orders pasta with marinara instead of salmon? I would say not. Rather, Dawkins is thinking and eating like a Christian, or a Muslim, or a Buddhist. And in a 2008 interview from the documentary series *The Genius of Charles Darwin*, Singer calls him out on that very point, albeit with stoic politeness.

In the extended interview on *YouTube* entitled "Peter Singer— The Genius of Darwin: The Uncut Interviews with Richard Dawkins," Dawkins declares Singer a "more moral" person than himself because Singer refrains from eating meat. While I will explore the latter's commentary in more depth in the next section, the very idea that Dawkins sees vegetarianism as a "more moral" lifestyle but continues to eat meat is indicative of cognitive dissonance and an example of why many who care about animals continue to eat them; fancy rhetoric aside, eating meat is a convenient, tasty custom. Surely there are others things one might do to make life more convenient and enjoyable, but one doesn't do those things because convenience and pleasure are not always apposite when determining proper action.

To illustrate, let's say a married man of considerable means is sitting in a McDonald's restaurant and wants a beverage. He could either steal one from the stranger sitting beside him or get up from the table and wait in a long line to make his own purchase. My guess is that man would find it immoral, or at least socially unacceptable, to steal someone's drink, even if doing so would be more convenient. Plus, he has the means and ability to pursue other options. Later that night, this man is propositioned by an attractive woman to engage in a night of passion. Assuming this man is faithful to his wife, he gives up the momentary pleasure of a sexual dalliance in favor of the more ethical choice not to break his marital vows. My point is that this theoretical man and many real humans regularly give up pleasure and convenience because they believe certain actions are wrong (and some without a higher power to punish them if they falter).

In the case of eating meat, Dawkins appears to acknowledge it is wrong and he has the resources easily allowing him to go vegetarian or vegan. Nonetheless, Dawkins—atheist extraordinaire, one of "The Four Horseman" of New Atheism, and an overall smart guy exceedingly capable of critical thinking—is unwilling to challenge speciesism's religious roots deeply enough to make a lifestyle change that many before him have made, most with far fewer cultural, social, and financial dispensations than he. Dawkins's rationalizations for eating meat are awkward at best. Aside from his specious explanations above, in his interview with Singer, he compares his diet to celebrating Christmas; it is an aspect of being human so ingrained in our culture that abstaining is too difficult. This is a false analogy. Many in the secular community acknowledge the value of and engage in cultural customs because disbelief in God does not negate the need for familial and social interactions, community, and tradition. Taking part in these rituals is far different from ingesting the reproductive excretions and flesh of slaughtered animals when less invasive food alternatives are ample. In response to Dawkins's commentary, Singer declares that "vestiges of religious beliefs" are the real reasons underlying his continued meat eating, the reasons Dawkins consigns himself, in quite a staid, blasé manner, to being a less moral person than Singer.

In that same interview, Singer states that "[Charles] Darwin knocked out a lot of the foundations for thinking humans are so special and we can do what we [want] to animals." Indeed, Darwin's evolutionary theory leads us to conclude there are no particular rights of humankind as detailed in a holy book. Humans do not get assigned to a special place after death while other animals decompose in the earth. Darwin also noted displays of other emotions within nonhuman animal species traditionally reserved for humans alone, such as jealousy, love, and mischievousness. Dawkins knows this, as do others in the New Atheist cohort and within the secular community as a whole. We know humans aren't as special as the religious seem to think we are, nor are we as vile. And I maintain that positive atheists[38] must do better than Dawkins when considering what we owe nonhumans and to what extent our beliefs about them are underpinned by the religions we claim to eschew.

Perhaps one might wonder why Dawkins's non-veganism, for lack of a better phrase, is any more important than another's. It isn't more important in terms of the ripple effect when any one person chooses to live more ethically. However, considering Dawkins's commentary on speciesism and his cultural influence, it is frustrating when someone of great authority should so obviously know better—indeed, when one does know better and admits he knows better—but does not act accordingly.

Similar inconsistencies are found within the work of Christopher Hitchens. As explored in the first chapter, Hitchens is critical of the hostile perception of pigs in the Abrahamic religions, especially Islam. He asserts in *God is Not Great*: "The pig is so close to us, and has been so handy to us in so many respects, that a strong case is now made by humanists that it[39] should not be factory-farmed, confined, separated from its young, and forced to live in its own ordure" (41). Admittedly, he puts concern for pigs on the

---

38. By "positive" I mean the activist atheist in the vein of Ingersoll who sees disbelief in the divine as liberation and seeks to identify and challenge social and ethical problems arising from spiritual traditions. Positive atheism has different connotations in philosophical vernacular.

39. Like Dawkins, Hitchens refers to animals as "its," not by gender, thereby maintaining the speciesist standard that aligns nonhumans with inanimate objects.

shoulders of humanists, not himself, but he was critical enough of the species' demonization to devote a whole chapter of his book to them. Yet he was not critical enough to stop eating them.

In fact, in a 2006 *Slate.com* article against what he terms the "international Muslim pogrom against the free press," he petulantly states in defiance of the Islamic view of pigs: "I am not asking for the right to slaughter a pig in a synagogue or mosque or to relieve myself on a 'holy' book. But I will not be told I can't eat pork." I imagine he wouldn't be told by Muslims or vegan activists that he can't eat the pigs whose very victimization he elsewhere decries. Once again, the disparity between ideas and actions are apparent and they maintain the hierarchy, speciesism, and anthropocentrism intrinsic to religion.

I hope readers will keep in mind the interesting dichotomy at play here. One on end, we have animal advocates futilely attempting to make religions animal-friendly. On the other, we have rationalist scientists and philosophers showing that atheism is clearly more animal-friendly than religion, but ignoring the ramifications of those findings. The causes of these rifts in both cases are speciesism and anthropocentrism. However, while religion proper (meaning not altered by secular thought) is innately speciesist and anthropocentric, atheism, devoid of divine beings making unalterable pronouncements in sacred texts, is more prone to progress, growth, and to finding real, not fantastical, motivations for fostering animal liberation.

Accordingly, as a final remarkable example of New Atheism's old anthropocentrism (and those who should know better), I move to Sam Harris, the philosopher and neuroscientist commonly seen to have started New Atheism with his 2004 bestseller *The End of Faith: Religion, Terror, and the Future of Reason*. However, I focus on his more recent book *The Moral Landscape: How Science Can Determine Human Values*. As noted, the New Atheists predominately arose from the scientific community, and in *The Moral Landscape*, Harris attempts to wrench morality, ethics, and human values away from religion and fold them into the sciences. This is a bold task that led to much praise and criticism from religious and freethought communities alike; Harris addresses those critiques in the 2010 edition's Afterword. Unlike Harris's usual critics, my concerns are quite different. If science and Sam Harris can tell us something about human values, what do they say about how we should approach the lives of other sentient species? Spoiler alert: not much. However, Harris's commentary on nonhumans is still worth analyzing, mainly for how his peculiar equivocations à la Richard Dawkins show the New Atheists preserving some of the worst elements of religious ideology while contradictorily offering some of the most solid reasoning for why animals matter.

Like Dawkins, Harris is noted on the *Why Cultured Meat* Web site as "one of the most rational philosophers and public intellectuals of our time" whose body of work appears animal-friendly, but who continues to eat meat and dairy products nonetheless ("Is Sam Harris Vegan?"). They likely focus on Harris's rationalism because his reason for consuming animals and their by-products comes across as surprisingly irrational. Before getting there, though, I want to emphasize those elements of *The Moral Landscape* that appear to point in a much different direction.

One of the most important facets of a secular worldview is it sees humans as just another animal species trying to survive in a not-so-intelligently-designed world, ushered into life by happenstance, not divine spark. In other words, human beings are animals as much as are dogs, lemurs, lizards, earwigs, and elephants. I think this perspective can benefit other-than-human animals immensely, as there is no heavenly being or book one can point to saying, "Here, see! God says it is okay for animals to serve human ends."[40] And as one who has some faith in the human animal, I don't think absence of God means absence of good, with life as a free-for-all in which pleasure and convenience outweigh careful consideration of ethical practices.

---

40. Coincidentally, the day on which I wrote this page I also reviewed a student essay explaining that meat eating is ethical because the Quran says it is. Case closed.

In contrast, with this life being the only life, there is more reason to enjoy it. Again, I turn to Ingersoll: "The Agnostic believes in developing the brain, in cultivating affections, the tastes, the conscience, the judgment, to the end that man (sic) may be happy in this world" (2). Ingersoll poses this view of humanity against the religious one: "Christianity has such a contemptible opinion of human nature that it does not believe a man can tell the truth unless frightened by a belief in God" (3). The New Atheists, the majority of whom come from scientific disciplines, reiterate Ingersoll's conception of life while also accepting that humans are animals. As such, Harris's book contains insightful passages that integrate nonhuman animals into the moral mix without qualifying those inclusions.

Harris argues that literal readings of scripture lead to an "intolerance of diversity" and acceptance of human *and* animal suffering (5). Indeed, he offers a long list of "bizarre and unproductive" deeds sanctioned by scripture. Female genital mutilation, rape, slavery, and elder abuse are among those behaviors, as one might expect, but he also includes "the torture of animals" on the list, placed between infanticide and scarification (20). He feels no need to defend his insertion of nonhumans amongst those who have and continued to suffer because religions command or are indifferent to it. His commentary also addresses the vilification of animals by religious animal advocates (see previous chapter) by declaring that "evil" would be an erroneous way to describe the actions of a grizzly bear who eats a human with whom he shares a cage (100). Survival or instinct are more genuine ways to describe such an occurrence, as opposed to the idea that the bear is acting in accordance with Adam and Eve's original sin and the subsequent sinful lives of all who succeed them.

While religious arguments for animal liberation falter when interrogated—that is, unless secular thoughts are aligned with them—Harris offers further examples of how atheism fosters more reasonable and compassionate notions of nonhumans. As Mark Rowlands states in his recent book, history's philosophers have come to the "near unanimous" conclusion that animals cannot

be moral, an anthropocentric assumption he then successfully
defends as "spurious" (14).[41] Similarly, in an argument against
geneticist Francis Collins's assertion that morality is the province
of humans alone, Harris details moral and altruistic behaviors
observed in mice, monkeys, and dogs, and he shrewdly notes that
"[w]hile no other species can match us for altruism, none can
match us for sadistic cruelty either" (170). To illustrate, while a
grizzly bear may wind up killing and eating a human with whom
he shares a cage, to date, there are no examples of other-than-human animals strategically, methodically, and expansively confining
and slaughtering another species, or those of their own species, for
food, clothing, sport, religious or ethnic differences, or simply for
the cruel, and sometimes sexual, pleasure of it. Of course, other
animals do not have the capacity (or intelligence) to take part in
these human pastimes, and while we may observe acts of "cruelty"
amongst other species (i.e. a cat toying with a mouse she plans to
kill but not eat), the point here is other species do not exhibit the
same penchant for cruelty that humans do.

Harris identifies the core of speciesism in a few key passages,
noting religion as the root of the problem. For example, upon exploring human beings' close genetic connection to other primates,
he comments: "Many of the world's major religions ignore these
awkward facts and simply assert that humans possess a unique
form of subjectivity that has no connection with the inner lives
of other animals," sarcastically wondering when humans split far
enough from our chimpanzee ancestors to garner souls (159). He
further notes that focus on the elusive soul has a damaging effect
on other species—and, I add, so do concepts such as karma. Harris
argues that "[c]oncern about souls is a very poor guide to ethical
behavior [. . .] Rather often, a belief in souls leaves people indifferent to the suffering of creatures thought not to possess them"
(171). And like Dawkins, he makes a case for how absurd it is that

---

41. While Rowland's book is quite intriguing, I remain cautious of
arguing that animals should be treated humanely only based on "they
are like us" reasoning.

some see the human embryo as imbued with more rights than animals such as apes, whales, and dolphins.

These are important observations and comments. Harris's thoughtful remarks about the myth of human supremacy and his belief that humans can be ethical creatures without god(s) to fear coincide with Ingersoll's conviction that freedom from religion is liberation. Atheism does not necessitate a species of animal (humans) bent on pursuing hedonistic pleasures with no thought to those we might harm in the process. For whatever reason, and for reasons we may never know, there are benefits to kindness and compassion even when there is no payoff, be it eternal life or kindness in return. Harris and the other "Horsemen" care about the world they live in. They decry the oppression of women, nature, people of color, the global poor, *and* nonhuman species. And like Ingersoll, they care about the environment too.

Stenger argues we will only flourish if issues of education, economics, *global warming, overpopulation,* and *energy resources* are acknowledged because if these problems were solved, people could cease looking to magical solutions to end life's suffering (234). Rather, life on Earth would be better. Singer agrees by stating that "[w]e cannot afford to wait for some coming glorious day when everyone will live in loving peace and harmony with each other" (*How Are We to Live?* 234), as is promised in the Bible and other religious texts and customs. In kind, Dawkins notes that wildlife and environmental conservation have attained a previously non-existent "moral status" historically reserved for religious holy days and other practices (*The God Delusion* 304).

Aside from Singer, not one of these atheist thinkers seriously includes nonhuman animals on their agendas, although animal issues are bound to environmental troubles. This correlation is of such importance that in 2006 the Food and Agriculture Organization of the United Nations, surely not a group with an animal rights agenda, reported the following:

The livestock sector emerges as one of the top two or three most significant contributors to the most serious environmental problems, at every scale from local to global. The

findings of this report ["Livestock's Long Shadow"] suggest
that it should be a major policy focus when dealing with
problems of land degradation, climate change and air pollution, water shortage and water pollution and loss of biodi-
versity. (Steinfeld, et al. xx)

Four years later, the United Nations' Environment Programme
determined that a "global shift toward a vegan diet is vital to
save the world from hunger, fuel poverty and the worst impacts
of climate change [. . .]. Agriculture, particularly meat and dairy
products, accounts for 70% of global freshwater consumption,
38% of the total land use and 19% of the world's greenhouse gas
emissions" (Carus). Surely these intellectuals, concerned with the
environment as they obviously are, must know of these statistics
and warnings. So why are nonhuman animal issues not of greater
importance to them? Again, I pose religious thinking and the
refusal to give up pleasurable habits as part of the answer, for the
responses they offer are far from adequate.

One of Harris's responses to questions of ethics and animals
mirrors Dawkins. He tells the story of a friend's young daughter
questioning why humans eat baby lambs. Her father basically
responds that they are killed for food because people like to eat
them (nothing like circular reasoning to answer a child's query).
The child determines: "It's not good. But I can't stop eating them
if they keeping (sic) killing them" (qtd. in Harris 71).[42] Harris
sums up this anecdote by averring that ethics and morality are an
outcome of "cultural norms to a great degree," which may be why
some are unwilling to forgo eating and otherwise using animals
and their byproducts (71). If that was Harris's best rationalization,
it would be as suspicious as Dawkins's. However, Harris does not
stop here.

For all of the animal-positive commentary Harris includes in
The Moral Landscape, much of which centers on just how un-

---

42. I cannot help but comment that someone should tell this child she
can stop eating them even though people keep killing them.

special human animals are, the book is still highly anthropocentric. For example, though he defends animals against Collins's commentary, he also states the following: "While [human] [. . .] mental states undoubtedly have analogs in the lives of other animals, we human beings experience them with a *special* poignancy [. . .] [W]e alone, among all earth's creatures, possess the ability to think and communicate with complex language" (114, emphasis added). According to Harris, it would seem Homo sapiens have divine favor after all, albeit in a lay sense. In contrast, science writer Tim Friend notes in *Animal Talk*:

> Humans are regarded by humans, of course, as the savants of communication. It may seem logical to conclude that the complexity of communication systems follows a hierarchy leading from humans to apes to mammals to birds and on down to insects. But it's not so simple. The most complex system of communication next to that of humans is found in the dance steps of the honeybee. (8)

Friend's book details the myriad other avenues through which nonhuman species communicate in complex ways (their forms of language) that Harris feels is reserved for us "special" humans. Further, Harris does not explain what makes human experiences any more poignant than those of other animal species. How could one even determine poignancy? I have no reason to think a prairie dog's playful activities in a field are any less meaningful than whatever the human equivalent of that play is in my own life. (Indeed, such equivalencies may be impossible to determine.) Harris is simply making a speciesist assumption not sufficiently backed up with reason. This is because, as with Stenger and other New Atheists, nonhumans are not on his ethical radar. The sciences were created for humans to help them better understand their world, and it cannot be explored from anything other than a human perspective.

Aside from that which I've already investigated, Harris's most decisive commentary on nonhuman animals occurs in his book's endnotes. How telling that an anthropocentric author relegates animal issues to the margins of his substantial text. It is only in

these margins of moral theory that he offers any real discussion of
the lived realities under which animals suffer immense deprivation,
exploitation, and agony. And his consideration of them is speciesist and hollow, manifesting the hierarchical thinking of religious
ideology.

In the fiftieth endnote of his second chapter "Good and Evil,"
Harris uses factory farms as an example of moral hierarchy and
philosopher Robert Nozick's concept of "utility monsters" as
a critique of utilitarian philosophy. In his classic work *Anarchy,
State, and Utopia*, Nozick explains utility monsters as those who
would obtain greater gains from the "sacrifice" of other beings
than those beings would lose (41). Although Nozick's concept is
hypothetical, Harris prudently notes that paying others to kill and
butcher nonhuman animals makes human beings just such utility
monsters. He then hedges a little, stating that while animal slaughter is certainly bad for the animals slaughtered, the farming system
might be right, but then again, it might be wrong. He explains:
"For many people, eating meat is simply an unhealthy source of
fleeting pleasure. It is very difficult to believe, therefore, that all
the suffering and death we impose on our fellow creatures is ethically defensible" (226–227). So, how does Harris justify meat eating? Because there may be superbeings somewhere in the universe
who could someday need to harvest humans as a food source, to
which Harris, it seems, would accept his lot as suicide food. Harris
takes a highly implausible future condition and uses it to justify
present day animal consumption as "ethically defensible."

Harris is not the only one to make such a case. In a video series
entitled "Atheism, Animal Rights, and Ethical Veganism," produced by the Atheist Community of Austin, a caller named Miles
remarks that "atheism is not equivocal to veganism [. . .] [but]
the two make pretty good bedfellows." The show's hosts Tracie
Harris and Matt Dillahunty respectfully bring up the usual reasons
one uses to justify eating animal products: nonhumans eat other
nonhumans, the "us/them species mentality" is natural, you can
buy "humane" animal products, and evolution.

Dillahunty adds his own response by claiming other animals can
eat him if the situation arises. Sitting comfortably in his land-based

studio, Dillahunty declares that a shark has the "right" to eat him. Let's look at some numbers here for perspective. Worldwide, there are approximately 60 shark attacks each year and five to fifteen shark-related fatalities (Handwerk). In stark contrast, about 100 million sharks are caught for human use per year, and 273,973 sharks are killed by humans per day ("How Many Sharks"). Finally, out of approximately "400 species of shark, only 11 have been known to attack [humans]" (Moore 95). In this case, the numbers truly do speak for themselves, and what could have been an opportunity for critical discussion turns into a Harris-style thought experiment that is very unlikely to happen. Dillahunty also states that all humans speak from a "spoiled, privileged position." Indeed, that is true, and as "spoiled, privileged" humans, we have a choice in what we consume while other animal species do not. In the end, Dillahunty comes across as more honest than Harris when contemplating his unlikely scenario (one that is still more likely than Harris's) which he admits is a "lame copout" to the caller's comment. Harris makes no such concessions.

Again drawing on Nozick, Harris ponders if it would be ethically acceptable for the human species to be "sacrificed for the unimaginably vast happiness of some superbeings"; his conclusion: yes, so moral hierarchy is not problematic and human beings do not necessarily have to stand at the pinnacle of the moral landscape even though they currently do (227). I must clarify that Harris does not overtly express any need to justify his omnivorous diet, and he does state how unlikely it is that humans will ever become a food source for superbeings (227). Thus, what began as an occasion to address the reality of animal exploitation and integrate those concerns into the moral landscape lapses into an arrogant and bizarre assertion that since Harris seems willing to sacrifice himself as food to beings who don't exist, the argument against using animals as food is irrelevant. I wish I could offer further analysis, but again, there is so little to work with because nonhumans are mere sidebars in Harris's world.

And should happiness be the sole criteria, as Harris claims, by which we justify sacrificing one sentient group for another? For that matter, are tradition and cultural norms the criteria by which we base our ethics? Yes, for some, but this should not be the case for those whose goals are to circumvent the dangerous cultural capital of religious traditions. Yet both Dawkins and Harris employ the appeal to tradition, a logical slip, as justification for meat eating. Further, Harris's fantasy superbeings aside, along with many omnivores' proclamation of how much they love bacon, I am prepared to state without equivocation that there is nothing nonhuman animals give to humans that results in, to use Harris's terms, "unimaginably vast happiness." There is nothing on this planet that offers humans "unimaginably vast happiness," and as an atheist Buddhist practitioner, Harris knows this, but he indulges in fancy, as do his religious nemeses, to justify the morally questionable.

The handling of nonhumans in *The Moral Landscape* also leads me to question what Harris thinks qualifies as animal torture. Thus, I here quote the full passage paraphrased above, one in which the author provides a list of "bizarre and unproductive behaviors" sanctioned by religion:

> [F]emale genital excision, blood feuds, infanticide, the torture of animals, scarification, foot binding, cannibalism, ceremonial rape, human sacrifice, dangerous male initiations, restricting the diets of pregnant and lactating mothers, slavery, potlatch, the killing of the elderly, sati, irrational dietary and agricultural taboos attended by chronic hunger and malnourishment, the use of heavy metals to treat illness, etc. (20)

I propose that of this list, it is only "the torture of animals" that is ambiguously proffered, the only area where interpretations can differ. There is no acceptable way to scar or starve a human person, no middle ground in terms of rape or a woman's immolation on her husband's funeral pyre. So what, exactly, is "the torture of animals" as Harris sees it? He seems to be against it, or it wouldn't have made his list, right?

In response, I offer some examples of animal treatment as a complement to Harris's catalog: *infanticide*—in the chicken industry, male chicks are not profitable, so after birth they are immediately ground alive or suffocated atop one another in large bins; *scarification*—livestock are branded with hot irons to identify to which humans they belong; *rape*—dairy cows are forcibly impregnated their whole lives with human arms inserted into their rectums so as to position the uterus to receive bull semen; *the killing of the elderly*—in all animal industries, from food to entertainment, animals are killed when their bodies are deemed unprofitable; *chronic hunger and malnourishment*—chickens are purposely starved for one to two weeks in an unnatural attempt to increase egg production, also known as forced molting. This list of the ways animals are exploited for food could go on and on in disturbing detail, and all examples come from the farming system of which Harris has no major criticisms.

These practices are clear acts of pitiless domination perpetuated by supremacist ideologies humans have created, but I am sure Harris does not see them as "the torture of animals." Perhaps "cultural tradition" would be a more apt description for him; it works for Dawkins. Harris never actually explains what animal torture is, though he would likely sneer at the inhumanity of bull mutilation as a way of thanking God amongst Zulu. I assume that fits his definition of animal torture, not the kind in which he indulges at meal time. Indeed, 99 percent of the animals humans consume are products of the industry whose regular practices include those listed in the preceding paragraph (Foer 12), which is not to applaud so-called "humane" farming practices that still leave a preventable body count.

In sum, Harris—at the pinnacle of the cultural landscape as a white, able-bodied, wealthy, highly educated male—can engage in whimsy when posed with genuine questions about animal suffering.[43] This is the luxury that comes with sitting atop the hierarchical design. Within this moral hierarchy, Harris argues, again in an endnote (the eighth of his first chapter "Moral Truth"), that

---

43. I am certainly not the first to make this observation. In *Godless America*, Sikivu Hutchinson ably critiques the racially segregated nature of New Atheism, arguing they need to more regularly integrate issues of economic and racial injustice into their dialogues (144–146).

all animal lives are not equivalent; thus, experiments on monkeys are more unethical than experiments on mice (215). And in an offhand fashion akin to Dawkins's, he also asserts that all human lives are not equivalent, even acknowledging there may be some human beings whose deaths would have a greater impact on the world than his own. However, and this is of the utmost importance, as human beings, we should "collectively act *as though* all human lives [are] equally valuable" (215). Other species get no such dispensations in the moral landscape Harris has painted. How pleasurable and convenient for humans.

Harris's responses to the animal question rest too easily on speciesist cultural norms, capricious thought experiments, and "vestiges of religious beliefs," to use Singer's accusation against Dawkins. Further, never once does Harris consider that animal experimentation and consumption are not necessary for human survival. They are surely not necessary in the industrialized world in which Harris writes his bestsellers. If his conclusion is that neither human nor nonhuman animal lives are equivalent, I wonder by whose standards this equivalency is judged. He tries to address these questions with his consequentialist based idea that certain beings are able to experience more happiness, and since the goal of existence is to maximize happiness, those beings should get more consideration. He does not, however, question the premise of his own argument. One reviewer of *The Moral Landscape* critiques the text for just this reason, observing that "Harris takes consequentialism as an obvious assumption that we can all start with. Harris also assumes that we can all agree that the 'best outcome' part of the consequentialist equation equals 'the well-being of conscious creatures'" (Lehto19). In Bill Lehto's review, which is generally positive, he concludes that despite the subtitle of Harris's book, science is not capable of determining human values; rather, "it can—at best—help us achieve our pre-determined values" (19). Like many human beings, Harris does not appear to highly value nonhuman animals. In his moral landscape, just as in mainstream secular and religious communities, animals remain in the margins of thought, consideration, and value.

New Atheism is sustained by scientists and philosophers who veer in the direction of a post-speciesist world but pull back the promise of liberation by ultimately maintaining speciesist norms on very shaky and inadvertently religious premises. This makes the New Atheists part of a rather old tradition. Singer reports that during the late eighteenth and early nineteenth centuries, nonhumans began to receive some consideration from a few of the West's most prominent philosophers. However, with exceptions such as Lewis Gompertz and Henry Salt, "these writers, even the best of them, stop short of the point at which their arguments would lead them to face the choice between breaking the deeply ingrained habit of eating the flesh of other animals or admitting that they do not live up to the conclusions of their own moral arguments" (*Animal Liberation* 207). Dawkins, Harris, and Hitchens, it appears, are in highly esteemed company in terms of both Western philosophers and religious animal advocates, for denigration of nonhuman animal worlds also arise amongst the New Atheists.

As noted in the preceding chapter, while nature is traditionally seen as "red in tooth and claw," there is a tendency to overstate that case to the extent that confining animals for human use can be made to seem preferable to leaving them to their natural states of existence. To read this passage from Dawkins's *River Out of Eden*, one might think we humans have a moral imperative to exact our concepts of the good life upon other species:

> The total amount of suffering per year in the natural world is beyond all decent contemplation. During the minute that it takes me to compose this sentence, thousands of animals are being eaten alive, many others are running for their lives, whimpering with fear, others are slowly being devoured from within by rasping parasites, thousands of all kinds are dying of starvation, thirst, and disease. It must be so. [. . .].
> The universe that we observe has precisely the properties we should expect if there is, at bottom, no design, no purpose, no evil, no good, nothing but pitiless indifference. (131–132)

Surely, a similar case can be made about human civilization. In the United States alone, *not* counting individuals under age twelve, a sexual assault occurs every two minutes ("How Often"). According to the Federal Bureau of Investigation's 2010 Crime Clock, a violent crime takes place every 25.3 seconds, someone is murdered every 35.6 minutes, someone is forcibly raped every 6.2 minutes, a robbery occurs every 1.4 minutes, and an aggravated assault every 40.5 seconds. Again, this is *just* in the U.S. (one of approximately 200 countries) and does not include property crimes. Perhaps such statistics only serve to prop up Dawkins's view of the universe, but considering his other comments on morality and ethics, he certainly thinks there is more than "pitiless indifference" in the human realm. Thus, such assessments only serve to enforce the human/animal binary and justify speciesism.

Author J.M. Coetzee makes a comparable observation in his introduction to animal behaviorist Jonathan Balcombe's *Second Nature: The Inner Lives of Animals*:

> Balcombe is particularly forthright in his criticism of the *idée reçue* [. . .] that nature must always be red in tooth and claw, a site of relentless struggle, of kill or be killed. Far from being absorbed in a grim battle to survive, he contends, animals actually enjoy life minute by minute, day by day. [. . .]. He has harsh words for television producers who, to satisfy the human appetite for blood, favor scenes of cruelty in nature documentaries, as well as for such intellectual luminaries as Richard Dawkins and Daniel Dennett, behind whose delight in emphasizing the misery and destruction to be found in nature, he suggests, lies an undeclared motive: to excuse mankind for its cruel treatment of other species.

Coetzee's commentary is familiar to animal advocates who face similar responses when interacting with a general public who finds it easy to excuse human use of other species seen to live in the brutal, uncaring world Dawkins and Dennett paint. In *Pleasurable Kingdom*, Balcombe compares Dawkins's view of nature to the feelings humans get when reading about tragedy after tragedy in the daily news (see FBI crime statistics above). In response, he expressively notes that

> this creeping paranoia is quite out of proportion with reality. For every tragic child abduction hundreds of millions of kids get to school safely every day. And so it goes for cheetahs and gazelles. Nature is not nearly so grim as she (sic) is made out to be. A gazelle, like you and I, will die only once, and that death is usually a fairly fleeting event compared to the life that goes before. A violent end on the African savannah typically lasts minutes, at most. Tens, hundreds or thousands of days precede it, few of which are punctuated by any serious threat. The same goes for gulls, sea lions, leopards, sea turtles and guenon monkeys. Especially once an individual gets past the precarious infancy, he or she has good prospects of a long and mostly peaceful life. For every moment of fear, suffering and/or death, there are multitudes of opportunities to experience life's calmer moments and its pleasures. (35–36)

Considering Balcombe's commentary, it should be more challenging to insist that humans have an innate right to disrupt these nonhuman lives. Other species, like humans, have moments of terror and torment just as they have times of peace and joy. To ignore the latter reality and emphasize the former is akin to the vilification of animal natures that takes place within progressive revelation, thereby providing another example of New Atheism's old anthropocentrism. But the criticism does not stop here.

Law professor and animal liberation advocate Gary Francione proposes a valid critical assessment of New Atheism and its theorists. In his article "New Atheism, Moral Realism, and Animal Rights: Some Preliminary Reflections," Francione questions the either/or binary that New Atheism appears to propose: one either accepts "scientific rationality" or they are banished to a world of "supernatural" beliefs and/or moral relativism or subjectivism. I too oppose such either/or thinking, and I agree with his assertion that "science is a social activity that *cannot* be divorced from political and moral considerations." As Francione states, there is "something beyond rationality" when it comes to determining moral beliefs and human values.

He further claims that scientific rationality ignores any type of evidence that cannot be measured. He is not alone in this supposition. Will Tuttle argues the following: "This materialist mythos (scientific reductionism) ignores spirituality and the mysterious adventure of consciousness, and tends to reduce both animals and humans to mere survival machines propelled by genetic and chemical forces" (155). Yet in clarifying the New Atheist perspective, Stenger notes that many erroneously believe atheists see science as the only knowledge base. In contrast, atheists can enjoy things reason cannot fully explain such as "the beauty of art, music, and poetry [. . .] along with the joys of love, friendship, parenthood, and other human relationships" (Stenger 22). In both cases, Francione and Tuttle, whether intentionally or not, are presenting false depictions of atheists because atheists, even those of the "New" variety, are not limited to appreciating only those things science can explain. Still, Francione and Tuttle's circumspection is not without premise.

As noted, Francione cautions against believing that "science as practiced is somehow separate from political and social institutions." This is an important statement, especially as it regards the scientific community which continues to exploit and kill untold numbers of nonhumans in research labs and experimentation rooms. And as Sikivu Hutchinson powerfully declares in *Godless Americana: Race and Religious Rebels*: "In the mainstream imagination, science and God are united in mystery. Both are contested terrain whose authority is defined, governed and controlled by powerful elites. Both promise transcendence, a taste of the immortal, a swipe at redemption" (40). As products of the human brain, science and religion can be allied to the benefit or detriment of nonhuman species. To illustrate, David Clough argues that genomic findings about humans and other species can lead to "theological recognition of what living creatures have in common" (29), thereby implying a leveling of hierarchical judgments.

It is highly unlikely that the scientific community will suddenly cease using other species as a means to an end upon discovering that humans share a certain percentage of our genes with other life forms, even non-animal organisms.

Nothing humans produce is separable from the political and social elements of our world. My concern is with Francione's inability, or refusal, to see that his avenue of choice for ending animal exploitation—the law—is an institution as much as are science and religion, yet he intractably argues that animals will be liberated when they are no longer viewed as property. They will, in effect, have legal rights.

As I argue in *Confronting Animal Exploitation*, "Francione's assumption that rights of any kind could ever be unmoored from the financial interests of dominant groups within a capitalistic [. . .] and speciesist culture is both naïve and circumscribed" (Socha, "'Just Tell the Truth'" 53). In sum, the law would be an effective way to liberate nonhumans if it were not corrupted beyond redemption in our current plutocratic legal and political system. In that same collection, Travis Elise supports Francione's method for abolishing the property status of animals. However, Elise also finds it deficient, for there are many instances in which non-property animals are harmed: "Hunting is a classic example [. . .]. The harm done to wild animals by never-ending human expansions such as deforestation, mining, oil drilling, and urban sprawl is another example of this" (31).

With these criticisms comes acknowledgement of why Francione is suspicious of New Atheism and scientific rationality in general. As he skillfully states, those who care about animals "are in error if they think that there is some notion of 'objective' rationality, or some combination of rationality and scientific facts, which, though rejecting moral premises, can secure the moral conclusion that we ought to stop exploiting animals." I agree wholeheartedly that science will never come to that moral conclusion, but I do not think the law will either, nor will religion, nor the moral realism on which Francione's abolitionist philosophy relies, defined crudely here as the idea that there are moral facts ("New Atheism, Moral

Realism, and Animal Rights"). I reject this notion for the same
reason as Peter Wilson, who argues that "[c]laiming that there
exists a natural order on which a morality can be based and actions
can be objectively judged just substitutes one make believe god
with another." Moral realism and moral facts are just as influenced
by society and politics as is scientific rationality. Ethics are also
a part of society as well, and people will come to different ethical conclusions based on their society, politics, and culture. It is
within this larger social context that individuals arrive at the ethical
conclusion to stop exploiting animals via exposure to educational
resources about animal abuse, as opposed to institutional decrees
or proclamations of ultimate truth.[44]

On his *Animal Rights: The Abolitionist Approach* Web site, as
a note after "The Six Principles of the Abolitionist Approach to
Animal Rights," Francione assures readers that all religious and
non-religious perspectives are adaptable to his approach to animal
rights; both the religious and the atheists should become vegan
educators and animal advocates. Similarly, in "New Atheism,
Moral Realism, and Animal Rights," he states: "I often say that
ending animal exploitation requires 'a revolution of the heart.'
What I mean by that is that we must reject *all* ideologies of domination and power, whether religious or secular." By secular, we
can imagine by the tenor of his article that he refers to scientific
institutions. However, reminiscent of the theological eco-feminist
perspective, he does not acknowledge that religion is built upon
"ideologies of domination and power." Even the Rev. Andrew
Linzey admits "it is impossible not to conclude that religion has
been complicit in animal cruelty and abuse" ("Is Religion Bad for
Animals?"). Just as Francione neglects to pinpoint the legal system
(and its connection to corporate interests) as a foundation upon
which animal cruelty flourishes, he misses the opportunity to expose religion's damning effects on nonhuman animals.

----

44. This idea, which approaches the topic of veganism as a religion,
will be addressed in greater detail in the next chapter.

Francione's supposed rejection of "all ideologies" that sub-jugate others is also suspect in other ways. As Elise points out, although Francione claims to be a pacifist, he sanctions the state, via legislation for nonhumans, as the enforcer of any laws that might miraculously materialize to usher in a more animal-friendly nation (38). Max Weber explains of the "modern state" in "Politics as Vocation": "Ultimately, one can define the modern state sociologically only in terms of the specific means peculiar to it, as to every political association, namely, the use of physical force" (78).[45] Comparative philosopher Jin Park likewise asserts that to enforce the law, "the exercise of force is required, which limits an individual's freedom. As much as law protects people from violence, law is also violence—legitimized violence." Aside from acts of clear civilian self-defense, the state is the only body authorized to use violence against others. This is even true in the case of animal industries. For example, hunters are not supposed to kill animals willy-nilly. Rather, they must purchase the right to kill via permits issued by the government and within guidelines determined by governmental bureaucracies. Thus, although a presumed pacifist, Francione is relying on the violence of the state within his abolitionist approach.

This brief diversion from Francione's critique of New Atheism is meant to demonstrate the ways in which "ideologies of domina-tion and power" are quite insidious. If not critically examined in ways that may cause us to question our own identities and ideolo-gies, they are tacitly normalized, as is hierarchy, which results in further injustices against human animals, nonhuman animals, and the environment. Francione does not see the intrinsically violent nature of the state and religion. In kind, the New Atheists avoid or ignore their sometimes unsuspecting and sometimes conscious acceptance of the "quintessence of the Judeo-Christian ethic" (Onfray 217). The remaining task of this chapter, therefore, is to

---

45. Elise similarly uses Weber's "Politics as Vocation" within his argu-ment against Francione.

dig more deeply into the nature of oppression and domination as they arise from religion and affect the lives on other-than-human animals. With this, a vegan atheology may commence.

Animals Minus Myth

In the Bible, God gives humankind dominion over the planet and all of its resources: "God blessed them [Adam and Eve] and said to them, 'Be fruitful and increase in number; fill the earth and subdue it. Rule over the fish in the sea and the birds in the sky and over every living creature that moves on the ground'" (Gen. 1:28). Humans have taken this authorization and run with it, especially that whole being fruitful part; we are now at over seven billion human beings. Even the many who consider themselves free from religion live by this mythical passage, this "immanent Christian thought," to again reference Onfray, by assuming that everything is at the service of the human animal, both other animals and the Earth's resources. A vegan atheology, in contrast, demands that freethinkers question their unspoken supremacy and dominion over the planet, starting with their treatment of other animal species. Just as the Freedom from Religion Foundation declares freethinkers to be the vanguard of social and moral advancement in other areas, more individuals from the secular community must consider the religious remnants causing them to embrace the stratified thinking that renders other sentient/conscious beings disposable bodies.

Animal advocate Will Tuttle notes that although religion and science often seem to be at hopeless odds, they "are in actuality strikingly similar in their underlying assumptions. This mentality is required to sustain the practice of enslaving and eating large animals, and to support an economic system based on exclusion and exploitation" (154). Matthew Scully makes an observation about religion that easily applies to secularism of all kinds. He asserts that religions do not actually require the abuses humans inflict upon our fellow species; rather, "they're merely overlooked, or tolerated, or dismissed as unworthy of serious attention" (351). The dismissal of animal concerns is clearly exemplified in the work of the New Atheists, as demonstrated. Vestiges of hierarchy and assumptions of human superiority remain deeply embedded in the secular community. And I would argue to the staunchest atheist who defends human use of other animals that he is thinking like a Christian . . . or a Neoplatonist.

Through the Great Chain of Being, Greek philosophers Plato and Aristotle proposed a pyramid scheme with God at the top (or above the chain as creator) as the greatest being, followed by angels, demons, men, animals, plants, and minerals. This is a simplification, as there are other levels to the chain (i.e. angels, animals, and plants are sub-categorized and the stars and moon are placed above humankind). Men of royal lineage are placed above the everyday Joe. Although Plato and Aristotle were obviously not Christians, their ideas greatly influenced Christian thought. In a classic study of the Great Chain, Arthur Lovejoy asserts the following: "It is true that the God of Aristotle had almost nothing in common with the God of the Sermon on the Mount—though, by one of the strangest and most momentous paradoxes in Western history, the philosophical theology of Christianity identified them, and defined the chief end of man as the imitation of both" (5). Man, therefore, is firmly established in Western culture as an almost divine being made in God's image, whereby "the human [is treated] as a naturally superior species rather than a cognitive and morphological norm [that] conceals how the idea of a 'divine chain of being' isolates humans from caring relations with other-than-human worlds" (Jenkins and Stănescu 75). This is the myth, both religious and secular, leading to the massive animal exploitation we see today. It is even older than Christianity.

A key aspect to understanding Aristotle's view of being and subsequent Western hierarchy is the concept of rational thought; those seen to possess it rank more highly on the Great Chain. Christian theology, as formerly explored, customarily placed women below men, as they were seen as less rational, as were those suppressed because of skin color, mental capabilities, and species. This stratified thinking led to a historical paradigm in which all humans are to serve God, women are to serve men, people of color are to serve whites, and animals—thought incapable of any reason—are to serve all humans.

For decades, eco-feminists and those espousing a feminist care tradition have noted how the ability to reason has been *the* criteria for determining one's cultural status. Cathryn Bailey argues that when "Reason sets the parameters of the discourse [. . .] only Reason can be heard" (350). Thus, a woman's tearful response to a sorrowful event, a dog's yelp in response to a cruel human's kick, and a slave's rebellion against his captor are deemed unreasonable. Marti Kheel proposes that rationality itself is a deception by which a culture's powerbrokers wield their own feelings and morality as natural and normal (53), so anything that goes against those strictures are deemed irrational and unworthy of serious concern.

In critical response to reason's reign, questions of consciousness and sentience are now seen as more valid grounds upon which to base ethical arrangements. Below I offer an image of and alternatives to the Great Chain of Being as it still manifests in contemporary Western civilization, even amongst freethinkers. Figure 1 offers a simplified example of the traditional, Judeo-Christian ranking system. Figure 2 demonstrates a secularized chain with supernatural beings removed but with hierarchy still intact. Finally, Figure 3 offers a spectrum of being that addresses speciesism by including nonhuman animals amongst atheists' concerns within the industrialized Western world.

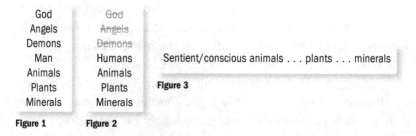

Figure 1	Figure 2	
God	G̶o̶d̶	
Angels	A̶n̶g̶e̶l̶s̶	
Demons	D̶e̶m̶o̶n̶s̶	
Man	Humans	Sentient/conscious animals . . . plants . . . minerals
Animals	Animals	**Figure 3**
Plants	Plants	
Minerals	Minerals	

Before one accuses me of playing fast and loose with my verticals and horizontals, I will explain why I group all sentient/conscious beings together through explication of what sentience and consciousness are and why they lead to such a broad categorization (and why I don't include plants therein). As Joyce D'Silva states, sentience has been the topic of much debate amongst philosophers for centuries, but "the consensus seems to be that sentient creatures are those who have feelings—both physical and emotional—and whose feelings matter to them" (xxiii). One of the biggest boosts to this concept of animal sentience came in July 2012 when a group of internationally respected neuroscientists, presided over by famed physicist Stephen Hawking, developed "The Cambridge Declaration on Consciousness" at the Francis Crick Memorial Conference. The declaration was geared toward a public audience, and part of it states that

> [c]onvergent evidence indicates that non-human animals have the neuroanatomical, neurochemical, and neurophysiological substrates of conscious states along with the capacity to exhibit intentional behaviors. Consequently, the weight of evidence indicates that *humans are not unique* in possessing the neurological substrates that generate consciousness. Nonhuman animals, including all mammals and birds, and many other creatures, including octopuses, also possess these neurological substrates. (Low, emphasis added)

Admittedly, this proclamation seems self-evident to anyone who has spent time amongst certain nonhuman species. As Mark Bekoff asks of the declaration, "Did we really need this statement of the obvious?" He also notes a few drawbacks to the document. For example, fish are not included in the declaration, and all but one of its signers based their conclusions on lab research, as opposed to studying animals in the wild. Bekoff goes on to state that there are still some within the scientific community who do not see animal consciousness as reason enough to conclude animals matter. Evelyn B. Pluhar gives concise reasoning for why some continue to ignore the reality of nonhuman sentience and consciousness. In this case, she applies her critique to philosophers, observing how cleverly they can lead themselves off course because they have "such powerful incentives to deny nonhuman suffering as a devotion to vivisection, factory farming, or theodicy, and a common vision of human superiority" (39). Indeed, Pluhar's commentary applies to most humans who choose to ignore the painful reality of animal suffering, not just scientists and philosophers.

Along with the reasoning proposed above via Onfray, I also propose that animal liberation is not given greater thought within the secular community because humans, religious and areligious, like the taste of nonhuman animal flesh and reproductive excretions such as milk and eggs. They don't want to give up things they enjoy, even if that enjoyment causes others immeasurable pain. There are other reasons as well. For example, Dallas Rising offers a more sympathetic theory for why people, especially those who claim to love animals, are not willing to speak up for or cease using them: fear of social rejection and alienation (15), which is imbued in Richard Dawkins's reasons for not being vegetarian. Rising's is a valid assessment, but I also think that pleasure is a seemingly simple factor that should not be dismissively overlooked. In *Anarchy, State, and Utopia*, Robert Nozick states this case well: "Suppose (as I believe the evidence supports) that eating animals is not necessary for health and is not less expensive than alternate equally healthy diets available to people in the United States. The gain, then, from eating animals is pleasures of the palate, gustatory delights, varied tastes" (36). Nozick's commentary is important not just for what it says of pleasure, but for what it says of choice.

My vegan animal advocacy is premised on the supposition that the people I reach out to—via activism, education, and writing— are those who can viably and easily make changes to their diets, purchasing choices, and entertainment venues. There are prudent reasons I am not in the arctic climes of Canada, where vegetation is scarce, admonishing Inuit for not being vegan. I am concerned with what each individual can do here and now within the place I write this entreaty, in the United States and, more generally, the Western world and other industrialized countries.

In "Secular Ethics and Animal Rights," Peter Wilson makes a similar argument. First, he confirms what is now commonly accepted: animals feel pain and can suffer. Thus, both humans and cows should live free from the suffering that comes from being another's food source. Wilson equivocates slightly by stating that the "extent to which the cow has this right may arguably be less than that for humans because there are (minor) differences between the two species." Therefore, in a situation of necessity, it may be more ethical to kill a cow for food than a human. Wilson concludes his point by asking, "But is it in modern society a necessity? If cows did not exist would humans die? Certainly not." Despite this seemingly inarguable reality of our modern world, most people still maintain their right to eat other animals as both a natural right and a necessity for human survival. Neither of these ideas is true, but they are maintained as such in quite dogmatic ways reminiscent of religious ideologies. These ideologies negatively affect both human and nonhuman animals.

Despite social progress, people (the non-heteronormative, women, children, the poor, and people of color) are still subjugated not just because of religious doctrine, but religious thinking as well, which can be divorced from one's affiliation with a particular spiritual practice (see my commentary on genocidal dictators in the previous section). Atheist activists would never find it acceptable to throw acid in a woman's face because of religious ideology. Yet the majority of atheist activists do not acknowledge the horrors nonhumans undergo by the billions for human pleasure, nor have they sufficiently acknowledged that the "quintessence of the Judeo-Christian" ethic is at the heart of this dissonance. They have bought and swallowed the myth, perpetuated by all religions, that nonhumans are disposable bodies, their capacity for pain and emotion isn't as relevant as humans', and they are stepping stones to human pleasure. For all of these reasons, I call foul on the freethought community while still believing it offers the most fertile ground for fostering a more compassionate view of nonhumans.

Humans have historically drawn moral baselines to determine appropriate actions and protocols. Thankfully, these baselines aren't static. A prime example is scientific research and experimentation. As a society, Americans have decided that although certain types of experimentations on human beings—i.e. vivisection and forced drug addiction—could be highly beneficial for scientific progress, such practices lead to an ethical abyss from which we may not return. All humans, we decided, are sentient, conscious creatures, and as much as we can learn from poking, prodding, and drugging their bodies, it is not worth the moral cost. We have drawn a moral baseline that, barring consenting volunteers taking part in specific types of studies, it is not acceptable to conduct scientific research on human beings. This was not always the case.

For centuries, experimenting upon people with disabilities and people of color was acceptable in the scientific community. In the late eighteenth century, a physician named Benjamin Moseley had this to say about native people of the West Indies:

> Negroes [. . .] are devoid of sensibility to a surprising degree. They are not subject to nervous diseases. They sleep sound in every disease; nor does any disturbance ever keep them awake. They bear [surgical] operations much better than white people: and what would be the cause of insupportable pain in a white man, a Negro would almost disregard. I have amputated the limbs of many Negroes, who have held the upper part of the limbs themselves. (475)

To a modern reader, this is racist nonsense, but it exemplifies what was once the status quo of scientific thought. And lest one think this a relic of a bygone bigoted era, remember the Tuskegee experiment in which the United States government, under the guise of providing free healthcare, surreptitiously infected African American men with syphilis to see what happens when it goes untreated. This went on from 1932 to 1972. Today, we are (hopefully) horrified by this mindset and perceive that the moral baseline of the medical and scientific community has thankfully shifted. The Great Chain of Being can be altered. As a culture, we have a history of reflecting on our actions and revamping our ethical standards as needed. It is time to give nonhumans that same consideration, and with atheists challenging millennia-old assumptions arising from religious dogma, other species must be on that agenda as well.

Before moving on to what others have said about secularism and animals, I want to return to Figure 3, in which I placed plants on the spectrum next to, not allied with, sentient/conscious animals. Obviously, I find it ethically acceptable to eat plants. As explored in the Introduction, one of the most popular "I gotcha" questions proposed by those hostile to veganism is centered on the idea that plants are alive and feel pain. Thus, they assume that because plants are living beings who may or do feel pain, then eating animals, along with all of the other horrors we subject them to, is acceptable. I don't think there is much logic to the argument, but I do acknowledge plants as worthy of respect, which is why I want to address that dreaded "I gotchya" rather than slough it off as some vegan activists are wont to do. In sum, while I find plant sentience to be a red herring against the argument for veganism, I still think it deserves some consideration.

In "The Ethical Matrix as a Decision-making Tool, with Specific Reference to Animal Sentience," Ben Mepham reviews the work of Laurence Johnson, an environmental ethicist who argues that plants have interests in both existing and "flourishing"; Mepham also notes that plants are still "non-sentient" (140) in the ways described above by D'Silva and the authors of "The Cambridge Declaration on Consciousness." Arguments from the vegan arsenal against plant sentience are that plants don't have a central nervous system, brains, or the fight or flight response that most pain-feeling beings have. As Christine Korsgaard states in a lecture about what it means to be an animal, pain and terror are actually gifts allowing one to flee predators (2). It seems a cruel trick of evolution to develop a group of about 300,000 living species who are subject to the same emotional and physical pain that, for instance, a primate undergoes on the vivisector's table, without any ability to flee their environments or empirically respond that they don't want to be so treated.

This is not to deny the less overt ways plants respond to attacks and other stimuli, which do indeed show an impulse to flourish. However, the chemical defenses of broccoli cut from a field or on one's kitchen counter are clearly distinct from the blatant defenses of the chicken's terrified reaction to being dunked into a vat of boiling water or of the fox hung by his legs, skinned alive, futilely writhing away from his murderer's knife. What we have here is a difference of kind, not degree. When determining the ethics of my diet, I do consider plants, and at this point, to quote Peter Singer and Jim Mason, I believe "the evidence for consciousness [. . .] in plants [is] vanishingly slight" (133).[46] Similarly, in "Secular Ethics and Animal Rights," Peter Wilson explains a seven-point process developed by The Institute of Medical Ethics to determine a being's ability to feel pain. Of the many animal genera, all were found to experience some level of pain and suffering, albeit at different levels and with insects failing to meet almost all criteria.[47] As for plants, they were not even considered because "lacking any known mechanism for consciousness, they may reasonably be considered incapable of suffering" (Wilson). If one wants a more popular resource debunking plant sentience/consciousness, see the fifth episode of the popular television series *MythBusters* from the 2006 season.

I address plant consciousness because, as stated, I think this common argument is most often a diversion from the ethical quandaries surrounding human use of other-than-human animals. Further, there is an implicit misrepresentation of veganism within the concept of plant sentience that allows omnivore apologists to dismiss veganism as too radical or aberrant. In 1944, Donald Watson defined veganism as follows:

> The word "veganism" denotes a philosophy and way of living which seeks to exclude—as far as is possible and practical—all forms of exploitation of, and cruelty to, animals for food, clothing or any other purpose; and by extension, promotes the development and use of animal-free alternatives for the benefit of humans, animals and the environment. In dietary terms it denotes the practice of dispensing with all products derived wholly or partly from animals. (qtd. in "Veganism")

There are a few important ideas to take from this definition. First, veganism is not about ceasing to be cogs in the cycle of life and

---

46. I should note that they claim the same of bivalves/mollusks as well, beings not included in the vegan diet.

47. And like bivalves/mollusks, consuming insects is not considered vegan either.

death (re "possible and practical"). As vegans, living organisms die so that we continue living, and unless we decide we don't want to live anymore, we will cause death—we just want to cause less of it and want it to be less violent. Second, veganism is not just about food choices, but about what people wear, the products they buy (tested or not tested on nonhumans), and their choices of sport and entertainment. Third, veganism is also about the environment, which includes the plants and minerals on my proposed spectrum of being (Fig. 3).

For those who show concern for plant sentience, either sincerely or for giggles, choosing a vegan diet results in less plant deaths. To briefly illustrate, thirteen pounds of grain are needed to produce one pound of cow meat. Thus, a non-vegan not only eats plants but also consumes other animals who have been fed vast amounts of plants before slaughter. Vegans go right to the initial food source, thus causing less plant loss in their lifetimes while also using less natural resources such as the water and energy needed to support animal agriculture.[48] As implicated in Watson's initial definition of veganism, while animals are of primary concern, the environment in which we all live (minerals included) benefits when humans choose a plant-based diet.

While the plant question remains on the periphery of animal ethics since no one at this time is claiming plants are animals, there are individuals making definitive connections between animal liberation and secular thought. Before exploring some contemporary resources I find encouraging, I want to briefly recapitulate what Peter Singer has said about religion and animals in *Animal Liberation*.[49] In sum, Singer argues that religion has been used as

---

48. This is a point of contention within the anti-vegan agenda. For a notable counterargument to the idea that more living beings are killed to support vegetarian and vegan diets than omnivorous ones, see: "Number of Animals Killed to Produce One Million Calories in Eight Food Sources." *AnimalVisuals.* AnimalVisuals: Visual Resources for Animals, 12 Oct. 2009. Web. 8 Apr. 2014.

49. Singer has since softened his critique of Christianity after dialogues with Charles Carmosy (see Mark Oppenheimer's "Scholars Explore Christian Perspectives on Animal Rights," cited in Chapter 1).

a tool by which "to mask the naked self-interest of human dealings with other animals" (186). As his book is seen as a founding text of the animal liberation movement, it is of great import that he includes a whole chapter on the role of Western thought and religion in relegating animals to their low cultural status. Singer argues that Western attitudes toward animals are based in Judaism, ancient Greek philosophy, and the aggressive Roman Empire. All three united in Christianity, which would go on to become one of the most influential religions in human history (188–89).

Just as Lovejoy connects ancient Greek and Christian conceptions of existence, Singer notes that two ancient Greek philosophers, Pythagoras and Aristotle, held differing views on animals; only one would have lasting impact on Christian thought. While Pythagoras was a vegetarian who promoted kindness toward nonhumans, Aristotle, as would those after him, proposed that animals exist to serve humans, just as he argued some humans are born natural slaves. Against the backdrop of human and nonhuman slaughter in the Roman Coliseum, Christianity arose with the unique idea, "inherited from the Jewish tradition," that humans, "alone of all beings living on earth, were destined for life after bodily death. With this came the distinctly Christian idea of the sanctity of all human life" (Singer 191). As an illustration of this paradigm shift, Singer reports that as the Roman Empire converted to Christianity, human-to-human combat as entertainment ceased. However, animal combat continued, eventually ending for economic, not moral, reasons (Singer 192). Of course, this human indulgence continues into the present day. While human-on-human fighting is a popular sport, today's fighters consent to be in the ring and are often well-compensated for their years of training. On the contrary, bullfighting, cockfighting, and dog fighting remain forms of entertainment in which nonhumans are forced to engage, with a painful death as the most common recompense.

In between the rise of Christianity and modern times, progressive answers to the animal question have arisen. But for all of the insight to be found within that history, animals are exploited and killed in greater numbers today than ever before, especially in industrialized societies that have mechanized animal exploitation and slaughter. Renowned freethinkers throughout Western history have observed the ways in which animal oppression is an outcome of religious dogma. Robert G. Ingersoll is one of them. Eighteenth-century revolutionary writer Mary Wollstonecraft held "strong opinions against conventional religion" while championing "women's rights, children's rights, and animal rights," amongst other entrenched Western customs (Gaylor, "Mary Wollstonecraft" 17). In fact, her classic treatise *A Vindication of the Rights of Women* (1792) would inspire Thomas Taylor's *A Vindication of the Rights of Brutes* (1792) in which he satirically proposes the absurd idea of an animal liberation movement to poke fun at Wollstonecraft's work, ending with the even more unheard of concept of environmental liberation. Surely, Taylor was on the wrong side of history.

Many of the Romantic poets of nineteenth-century England were vegetarian because it "undermined the normative hierarchy between humans and other sentient beings: the eater and the eaten [. . .]. To eat a diet of vegetables was a form of solidarity, an eschewal of class distinctions, as well as species ones" (Morton 196). In "The Necessity of Atheism," Romantic poet and vegetarian Percy Bysshe Shelley (husband of Mary Wollstonecraft's daughter Mary Shelley, who penned the novel of the vegetarian Frankenstein's "monster") wrote the following: "If ignorance of nature gave birth to gods, knowledge of nature is made for their destruction." Here, Shelley unwittingly encapsulates the core of the New Atheist standpoint. My hope is that knowledge of speciesism in religious traditions can help dispel the ignorance that leads to so much destruction of other-than-human animal species.

The title of this section is "Animals Minus Myth" for it proposes a view of nonhumans undistorted by religion. This is a difficult proposition because humans are the dominant species in terms of our control over other species, and anything we might say of other species is, albeit at varying levels, a product of the culture in which we are born. The challenge, therefore, is to remain ever critical of the ways in which oppressive thinking disguised as normative ideology guides our ethical judgments.

In Rob Johnson's "Are Atheism and Veganism Related?" he identifies the tautological mentality that animals are just animals so we can use them as we see fit as the "final myth" he let go of as veganism, atheism, anti-sexism, and anti-racism began to coalesce in his life. Johnson implores atheists to promote veganism and for vegans to "take up a rationalist position" within their advocacy. By doing so, vegan activists can pack their advocacy "with real punch that has real world relevance and a focus on causes rather than symptoms" (Johnson). While I cannot speak for Johnson, I interpret his commentary to mean the many symptoms of a speciesist culture—animal agriculture, animals in entertainment, animals in research, general indifference toward animal suffering—spring from a core cause. That cause is the religious ideology I have proposed thus far. If we accept the studies and stories indicating high levels of atheism, agnosticism, and humanism in the animal liberation movement, then encouraging vegans and atheists to see those connections can benefit both movements and, most importantly, other animal species.

On the American Humanist Web site, Jason Torpy makes an argument similar to Johnson's for why vegan priorities are also humanist priorities (in fact, that is the article's title). Likely foreseeing the typical antagonistic responses to pro-vegan sentiments, Torpy admits that although humans evolved as a species able to eat meat, we have moved past that point and have found alternative ways to be healthy without animal exploitation. Here, Torpy touches on another cultural myth humans are hesitant to renounce: we need to eat animals to be healthy. In contrast, the official position of the American Dietetic Association, as detailed in Winston J. Craig and Ann Reed Mangels's 2009 report, is that vegetarian and vegan diets are suitable, and perhaps even healthier than omnivorous diets, for humans from infancy onward, from average individuals to athletes.

Torpy continues by stating that "[h]umanist values [. . .] put a premium on health, animals, and the environment. Humanists should be able to suffer some inconvenience to reduce their carbon footprint and their cruelty footprint [. . .] Humanism should be about being the best humans we can be, not asserting our human dominance by breeding, exploiting, torturing, and slaughtering animals." Responses to Torpy's essay on the Web site vary. Of course, there is the ubiquitous retort that eating plants is akin to a carnivorous diet. Another respondent states humans should focus on reforming the ways animals are raised and slaughtered for food, while also accusing Torpy of relying too heavily on emotional appeals as opposed to rational thought.

In response to those who cite the "circle of life" argument for animal agriculture, a respondent named Dani wisely acknowledges that hunting for survival is far detached from the systems through which animals become food in the industrialized world. In other words, humans have attained such a destructive position of dominance that they have warped the "circle of life" argument beyond moral or ethical viability. Finally, a respondent named Colleen supports Torpy's essay in a critical fashion not unlike the arguments I've been making in this chapter thus far: "Being 'good' without 'god' surely means leaving behind this notion of man as the pinnacle of creation, able to consume ravenously other thinking, feeling beings." As demonstrated through analysis of Dawkins, Harris, and others, many who have given up God have not yet given up this notion of human ascendancy. This can change, and one hope for changing human perceptions of their own supremacy is making the word "speciesism" more commonly known.

For instance, Michael Shermer, secular writer and Executive Director of the Skeptics Society, recently published an article in *Scientific American* titled "Confessions of a Speciesist" after seeing Mark Devries's 2013 documentary *Speciesism: The Movie*. Shermer states that humans' "superior intelligence, language and self-awareness" have traditionally been used to excuse our domination of other species. However, he acknowledges a collapse in that logic when hearing Peter Singer and Devries argue that some species have superior intelligence and awareness over humans "such as infants, people in comas, and the severely mentally handicapped." Although Shermer makes no declarations of going vegan after seeing the film, his conclusion is telling:

Mammals are sentient beings that want to live and are afraid
to die. Evolution vouchsafed us all with an instinct to survive, reproduce and flourish. Our genealogical connected-
ness, demonstrated through evolutionary biology, provides a
scientific foundation from which to expand the moral sphere
to include not just all humans—as rights revolutions of the
past two centuries have done—but all nonhuman sentient
beings as well. (88)

This is quite a revelation coming from the founder of *Skeptic*
magazine. However, there remains the problem of Shermer's blasé
attitude toward admitting he is speciesist. He would surely never
admit to any other kind of "ism" in such a casual manner, nor
would he admit to taking pleasure in human suffering through
eating their meat, wearing their skin, or laughing at jokes made
at their expense. Nevertheless, he confesses to all of those things
in regard to other species. Perhaps he does this because the term
"speciesism" is so new to him and he hasn't fully interrogated
what it means to "expand the moral sphere" beyond humans.
Ultimately, while Shermer's article both exposes and reinforces
speciesism, such a response from one so prominent in the secular
community is promising.

Singer's conversation with Richard Dawkins in the uncut interviews from *The Genius of Charles Darwin* also questions the myth
that humans are the apex of life on Earth, but not without some
qualifiers. For instance, both Singer and Dawkins agree humans
are not nearly as special as religion would have us believe, but they
also appear to agree that human ability to see life in a "biographi-
cal sense" and plan for the future make our lives more relevant.
Dawkins says "there is no need to draw lines [. . .] [because] there
is a continuum of capacity to feel pain [. . .]. Our moral responsibility to oysters is quantitatively less than our moral responsibility to pigs, quantitatively less than our moral responsibility to
humans." Similarly, Singer concludes that if there is a concrete
benefit to helping humanity, animal testing is justified; consistent
with his utilitarian philosophy, he says the same of human beings
with severe brain damage. The difference is the human will need

familial consent while nonhumans get no such allowances. Here, we see both an interrogation of human exceptionalism along with incidental reinforcement of it.

Dawkins also poses a question to Singer that many a believer has asked about non-believers. To paraphrase: Without belief in God, why should one care about others and from where does one acquire morality? First, Singer amusingly responds by questioning the example God is setting for ethical behavior when considering all of the suffering in the world. He further comments that "living ethically is not just thinking about yourself, but putting yourself in the position of other beings who are affected by your actions." There are many without religious belief who want to make the world a better place before they die. Singer continues by noting that such altruism is found in nearly every religion and "tradition of ethical thinking." In other words, doing the least amount of harm is a conclusion many humans will come to whether it is through a religious or atheistic philosophical stance. And from my point-of-view, humans created religion; thus, any altruism found therein comes from humans, not divine beings. I must add, however, that as religions come with texts and leaders meant to serve as guides for human behavior, religion will always stop short of including nonhuman animals on the ethical agenda in a way that fosters true animal liberation.

There is no known religious doctrine or spiritual tradition that is not also speciesist, anthropocentric, and hierarchical, as demonstrated in the prior chapter. In contrast, there is no atheist doctrine at all, so there is no limit to the human ability to broaden our circle of compassion within a secular framework. Angela P. Harris states that "as we continually 'widen the circle of the we,' we learn to recognize that the social arrangements taken for granted today as normal, natural, and necessary are always historically and socially constructed" (25). Removing religion as a dominating social force is a necessary hurdle in defeating those oppressive and violent human behaviors that, much like hierarchy, are seen as "normal, natural, and necessary."

While books such as Harris's *The Moral Landscape* attempt to understand moral action from a secular, scientific perspective,

other philosophers prefer the term "ethics" to "morality." Wilson
explicates the terms here: "Whereas morality deals with the inherent worth of actions themselves and the motivations behind them,
ethics deals with the worth of the probable effects brought about
by actions." What some may seem as a case of semantics within
Wilson's parsing out of terms is really an important commentary
on the differences between moral action and ethical action. Moral
action, as Wilson defines it, maintains the egoism intrinsic to
religious conceptions of good living. Ethics, on the other hand,
looks at the effects of our actions on others, and Wilson includes
"non-consenting individuals" as those affected by human choices.

Singer identifies another way in which nonhuman animals
are disserved by religion, noting how the "religious viewpoint
reinforces the boundary" between humans and animals (qtd. in
Dawkins "Peter Singer"). This traditional Western binary makes
it appear natural for humans to use nonhuman animals because
it makes humans extraordinary amongst all animal species. For
some believers, it even removes humans from the realm of animals.
Wilson expounds upon the importance of challenging this binary:

> Once the link between humans and animals (and plants)
> is recognized and the absolute supremacy of humans shat-
> tered there can no longer exist a sharp line separating "us"
> from "them." This prevents any *a priori* justification for
> excluding animals from all ethical consideration [. . .]. The
> recognition of these [ethical] rights is drastically different
> from the western view which is dominantly theistic. Had a
> god created each species separately or directed evolution to
> form humans, a line would definitely exist between humans
> and animals that could be used to restrict rights to humans.
> Humans would have a soul or a divine spark missing from
> the "lower" animals.

Atheism removes the soul and the spark, but for the majority of
secularists, it does not remove the dispensations that belief in the
soul and spark has given humans throughout our relatively short
history on Earth. Resultantly, we have a culture built upon the
backs of nonhuman animals, from food, to clothing, to education,

to science, to entertainment, to arguably any industry or institution one might imagine. Indeed, even our language maintains the speciesist paradigm. While using the terms "human" and "non-human" or "other-than-human" animals is a step up from the traditional human/animal dichotomy, it still maintains a divide between humans and all other persons (Dunayer xi).

Humans are certainly unique, but so are other animal species. We all differ in ways as evident as the bodies we inhabit and as inconspicuous as our mental capacities. Somewhere along the evolutionary way, human uniqueness was recast as preeminence. As both Harris and Wilson affirm, the sole criterion of the soul was primary in ushering in the myth of human ascendency. Belief in the human soul regularly necessitates the further belief that non-humans do not have souls, and this idea is "so ingrained in people's consciousness that they announce it as if it were simple fact. As if they honestly don't realize that souls are not an identifiable part of human anatomy" (Sullivan). In *Speciesism*, Joan Dunayer tells the story of a kosher slaughterer who justifies his business of killing cows by declaring that only humans have souls (15). As she further notes, the claim that only human animals possess souls cannot be disproven, and even though such a belief lacks any basis in "evidence or logic" and generally "makes no sense," the conviction that humans have some immortal attribute persists much to the detriment of other-than-human animals (15–16). Religion, consequently, is not only an egotistical tradition; it is supercilious as well. As early twentieth century atheist Voltairine de Cleyre asserted: "The question of souls is old—we demand our bodies, now. We are tired of promises, God is deaf, and his church is our worst enemy" ("Sex Slavery" 363). For those willing to expand the circle of compassion to include other species, we demand that animals have mastery over their own bodies as well. All of us soul-less creatures can only benefit from giving up the ghost.

Once again, *atheism*—no god(s), no souls, no divine sparks, no rebirths, no reincarnations, nobody gets out of here alive, even and especially after your physical body has perished—lays those myths to waste. What, then, do animals look like minus myth? For humans, being without myth allows us to appreciate the one life we have. To paraphrase the work of Ingersoll, it allows us to approach the world's mysteries with curiosity and awe, freed from fear of vengeful gods, tormenting monsters, and constant reminders of how truly awful yet contradictorily splendid we are. There is a saying amongst animal advocates that "animal liberation is human liberation." Indeed, nonhuman animal liberation is not about opening all of the cage doors in one fell swoop, a near impossibility; rather, it first comes with liberating the human mind from speciesism. As the dominant species, before liberation of other species occurs, humans must come to believe that animals deserve ethical concern on par with humans. Although there is anecdotal evidence of nonhumans liberating themselves,[50] other species do not have the capacity for organizing resistance movements as do humans. Thus, humans must see other species differently to render animal liberation viable.

For animals who are not human, taking away religious myths allows human animals to see other beings with whom we share this world as having inherent worth apart from what they can offer us. We can then leave nonhumans alone. They too only have one life and feel emotions, and they experience physical and psychological suffering. They matter without qualifiers that differentiate between the evils of factory farming and the supposed kindness of "humane" farms. They matter despite what sacred books would have us believe. They *all* matter, even the fish Jesus ate and the pigs Buddha may or may not have consumed.

As a species that claims a history of moral and ethical progress, we must be willing to consider that other animals are like us in more ways than they differ. Despite growing exploitation of nonhumans—by 2050, meat production is expected to double (Halweil)—they are now being considered more closely than ever in academia and the mainstream media from non-religious perspectives. Kari Weil notes that while Peter Singer's attempt to align speciesism with racism and sexism in *Animal Liberation* has been

50. See Jason Hribal's *Fear of the Animal Planet: The Hidden History of Animal Resistance.*

somewhat unsuccessful overall, a change is taking place in higher education with an sudden increase in books and conferences that consider what's been called the "animal turn" (1). There is also an "animal turn" in popular culture as well, with the violence of animal farms and research labs coming under more frequent scrutiny.[51] While such contemplations are not necessarily employed by those promoting veganism or comprehensive alternatives to animal usage, there is hope in that animals are more commonly acknowledged as beings with agency, even with languages that we may one day understand:

> On the one hand are those who look to our nonhuman others with envy or admiration precisely because they remain outside language and thus suggest the possibility of unmediated experience. On the other are those who would prove that animals do indeed speak and can tell us, however imperfectly, of their lives, if not of their traumas. (Weil 5)

Until that time when other species can speak in a way the masses will hear, the media is rife with photographs and videos of their lives, suffering included. And as I and others see it, their trauma is spoken every day quite clearly; animal language is not inadequate, as Weil suggests. As an experiment, *listen to*, do not watch, a slaughterhouse video and try to argue that nonhumans do not speak of their trauma. Humans know that other species feel, and that should be reason enough to avoid causing needless suffering.

Life without God and religion need not be one of nihilism and agony; just the opposite is true, as many who live without myth feel an ethical imperative to expose and circumvent injustice in the many ways it manifests. This book is proof that such people exist because I and some of those cited herein are trying to make the world better without the promise of earthly or celestial reward. Indeed, I find it an ethical imperative to do so even when feeling

---

51. In response, corporations and the government are reacting with draconian laws that label animal activism as "terrorism." Research the Animal Enterprise Terrorism Act (AETA) for more details.

like I am banging my head against the proverbial wall when met with human refusal to really look at nonhuman animal suffering. Within the continued project of putting myths into their proper place amongst other fantasies of the vast human imagination, we head into the final chapter in which I offer concluding thoughts on how to rhetorically and contextually proceed with a concept of vegan atheism, atheist veganism, and a vegan atheology.

Chapter 3

No More Room
at the Inn

Hungry child,
I didn't make this world for you.

—Langston Hughes, "God to Hungry Child"

I emancipated myself from the concept of God and
religion because I educated and empowered myself
to move away from oppressive and dehumanizing
narratives.

—annalise fonza

Just as Joseph and a magically pregnant Mary were told on that
starry night in Bethlehem, there is no more room at the inn.
There is no more room at Hotel Procrustes. And I title my chapter as such because by this point in the text, the reader may have
asked, perhaps multiple times: Isn't an atheist argument for animal
liberation another Procrustean bed? Hasn't the author just cherry-
picked animal-*un*friendly passages and practices from religious traditions to prove them incapable of addressing animal liberation? I
obviously do not think this is the case, but I believe the questions
merit some response by way of my introduction to this chapter.

In a text exploring anthropology and religious conversion, Lewis Rambo asserts "that each discipline [studying the topic] must be self-critical and willing to modify assumptions, goals, and methods in the face of a phenomenon that cannot be forced into a Procrustean bed" (*Understanding* 217). In the first chapter, I showed the ways in which religious animal advocates are not critical enough of religious practices and texts, thereby forcing nonhuman animal issues into the Procrustean bed that is religious mythology. These authors approach texts and traditions with preconceived ideas and force them into the bed, however uncomfortable the fit might be (like Cinderella's sister jamming her foot into a tiny shoe to win Prince Charming's affection). At worst, they are supporting traditions that condemn nonhumans to their lowly cultural position.

In the second chapter, I surveyed the work of those who have foregone the religious Procrustean bed, leading some to more conscientious views of other species, but not enough of a changed view to more ardently challenge speciesism in their work and through behavioral changes such as diet. Although awakened from the bed and checked out of Hotel Procrustes, they maintain a form of religious Stockholm syndrome that allows hierarchy, anthropocentrism, and speciesism to continue unchallenged through the very worldviews they criticize.

In this final chapter, after explaining how atheism escapes the Procrustean bed, I analyze and critique the use of religious rhetoric in animal advocacy and the propensity to pose veganism and animal rights as a religion, while also proposing nonhumans as heirs apparent within the advancement of social progress. Just as do those whose words begin this chapter, individuals from historically oppressed groups have noted the ways in which religion has been a primary tool of subjugation, and their wisdom can benefit a vegan atheology. For instance, as Michael Lackey declares in *African American Atheists and Political Liberation*: "[F]or African-American atheists, atheism is a cause for rejoicing, since it effectively divests the dominant political powers of their most powerful weapon against culturally designated inferiors" (3). While I am always wary of making trans-species analogies too closely, my hope is that by now, religion's role in assuming non-human inferiority is unmistakable, just as religion has done with women, people of color, and those with nonconformist sexual identities and disabilities. Thus, I trust atheism, when critically applied, also deprives humans of their supposed right to dominate other species. As such, I am compelled to look at other social justice causes while maintaining the singularity of the animal liberation movement.

The questions I ask above about making a Procrustean bed out of atheism align with the somewhat frequent assertion that atheism is a religion. Secular thinkers of all sorts have likely heard this observation before from those wary of a world without god(s), and they presume that since some atheists hold gatherings and form organizations, we are trying to create a new religion. In contrast, being atheist or agnostic does not mean one no longer enjoys the community and social bonding that can arise from religion. Victor Stenger states: "Certainly, one of the appeals of churchgoing is the social life that comes with it, for young and old [. . .]. I can't see why this cannot continue in a nonsupernatural environment. I am gratified to see atheist and humanist groups that include considerable socializing forming in increasing numbers around America" (234). We can still have community, but it will not be bound to the sacred, to symbols and order, nor to divine beings, which are part of Émile Durkheim, Clifford Geertz, and Daniel Dennett's definitions of religion, as respectively related in this book's initial pages.

Although almost all of the major recognized religions do include a mystical element, to be fair, religion is not solely about the paranormal. In *The Anthropology of Religious Conversion*, Andrew Buckser and Stephen B. Glazier explain the perspective that religion is not just about the paranormal, seeing it also as a concept of existence that appears unique and valid to the spiritual individual (xi). The same can surely be said of non-believers. We have theories of the world that seem legitimate to us. This does not make atheism a religion proper because, even from an anthropological perspective, the supernatural does somewhere manifest within world religions, but it does not, by definition, do so in

atheism. Indeed, after appraising recent definitions of religion developed by William Alston and Monroe and Elizabeth Beardsley,
philosopher Michael Martin concludes that over and again "atheism fails to meet the conditions of being a religion." Still, atheism
is an unmistakable perspective *on* religion, and for some atheists,
the destructive power of belief in nonexistent gods is in dire need
of subversion.

Atheism is not a Procrustean bed because there are no divinely
inspired or pre-determined frames into which an atheist must fit
her ethics. On the other hand, the world's most common religions
offer books, traditions, and gods to which one can seemingly fit
any perspective, be it for good or ill. Religion's real world power
ironically comes from its imaginary foundations that can be
molded into anything one wants. In effect, religion is "content-
less, because it has justified and can justify anything and everything, from polygamy to monogamy, from subjugating women
to liberating women, from genocide to pacifism, and from rabid
capitalism to monastic poverty" (Lackey 7). Anne Nicol Gaylor
articulates this idea quite well: "It is possible to speculate endlessly
about the nonexistent" (qtd. in Gaylor "Introduction" 13); and
when those in power are doing the speculating, they will likely
favor themselves as the governing authorities. Lackey goes on to
note that "the God concept is simultaneously nothing and everything; it is an idea that ultimately sanctions an 'anything goes'
philosophy" (142). Many a believer will say the opposite, arguing
that forgoing God leads to "anything goes" hedonism. Recent
polls and studies demonstrate this popular premise.

A 2011 Pew Research poll reports 33 percent of those asked
would be unlikely to vote for a presidential candidate who is ho-
mosexual, but that number nearly doubled for those unlikely to
vote for an atheist candidate (R. Bailey). While numbers such as
this actually show improvement regarding popular views of the
godless when compared to previous decades, a 2011 Gallup poll
found that only 49 percent of respondents would vote for an atheist president, even if he or she was highly qualified for the position (R. Bailey). A 2010 study from scholars at the Universities of
British Columbia and Oregon detail the following:

Recent polls indicate that atheists are among the least liked
people in areas with religious majorities (i.e., in most of the
world). [. . .] [A] broad sample of American adults revealed
that distrust characterized anti-atheist prejudice, but not
anti-gay prejudice (Study 1). In subsequent studies, distrust
of atheists generalized even to participants from more liberal,
secular populations. A description of a criminally untrust-
worthy individual was seen as comparably representative
of atheists and rapists, but not representative of Christians,
Muslims, Jewish people, feminists, or homosexuals (Studies
2–4). (Gervais, Sharif, and Norenzayan 2)

All of this research reveals how the majority of people judge non-
believers. However, there is no data supporting these perceptions.
Once again, the religious believe in non-existent "truths." As
Benjamin Beit-Hallahmi reports after studying decades of research
on the subject, the "claim that atheists are somehow likely to be
immoral or dishonest has long been disproven by systematic studies" from the 1950s onward; and he concludes by stating: "In
short, [atheists] are good to have as neighbors." In a brief article
on secular ethics, Kevin Drum notes that "there's never been the
slightest evidence that religious believers behave any better on
average than the nonreligious."

Still, the perception of the godless perpetrated by religious
domination persists, even though there is cause for some to believe God can be an impediment to moral action:

Religious indoctrination can easily draw human beings away
from difficult moral goals of social justice, gender and racial
equality, peace, and environmental sustainment. There is a
real danger that religious service can promote acquiescence
in the status quo, either seeing it as part of God's created
world or hoping for redemption in an afterlife. Belief in God
is a moral encumbrance. (Overall)

Indeed, as an atheist, I engaged in a year-long Bible study with
Jehovah's Witnesses who implied that my social activism is point-
less, and I should be preparing for the end of days (right around

the corner, evidently) by giving myself to the Lord and helping persuade others to do the same. This is not meant as a blanket statement against all believers, many of whom advocate for social justice because their religion demands it (i.e. Quakers and some strains of Catholicism). Rather, Christine Overall's commentary provides hope for determining a system of ethics developed by something beyond the unseeable, a system that will alter as humans evolve, a system that will not have to be matched against a mysterious, celestial authority who has written a paradoxical book for us to live by. This is why an atheist argument for animal liberation is not a Procrustean bed. There is no sacred atheist dogma against which to confirm or contradict our morals and ethics, while the religious must always return to their founding principles or engage in intellectual contortions to make their spiritual paths non-oppressive.

Other freethinkers have made analogous observations. Stenger argues that "science and atheism must never be dogmatic" (164). In *How Are We to Live?*, Peter Singer acknowledges a fear people have that if God goes, good goes with him (187), but he also asserts that principled living is not about rule following; rather, it involves a life of reflection to determine how we can act most ethically in particular situations (ix). In terms of morals and ethics, however, there is freedom in giving up God, and it doesn't take much work to determine right from wrong without looking to an overseer for assistance. Religion, in a sense, is just a long entrenched habit one need not follow to live an ethical life. On the failure of Christianity, Emma Goldman states that the "average mind is easily content with inherited things, or with the dicta of parents and teachers, because it is much easier to imitate than to create" (384). Individuals should be inspired by this sentiment, for what lies before us is a surfeit of ways to look at the world and the various injustices contained therein unburdened by supernatural and religious dogma (which often cause injustice to begin with). In fact, life can be better without those things: "You will not be bored, or lack fulfillment in your life [without God]. [. . .] [Y]ou will know that you have not lived and died for nothing, because you will have become part of the great tradition of those who have responded to the amount of pain and suffering in the universe by trying to make the world a better place" (Singer *How Are We to Live?*, 235). This is the promise of an atheology, a system of ethics based on an ever-evolving world that expands consideration of who gets counted in the moral community.

Individuals, of course, may always search for that absolute truth and those unconditional promises religion provides. Religion is an endpoint for determining right action, an idea which is, in itself, problematic, for the very proposal that some (i.e. the priest, rabbi, shaman, imam) have greater access to mystical truths is essentially hierarchical and maintains a culture of advantage for a select few. On the other hand, atheists do not "think that the believer has privileged epistemological access to a God-created Truth" (Lackey 13). But without knowledge of "God-created Truth," one might wonder where to look as we figure out the complexities of existence. In her essay "Crime and Punishment," social revolutionary Voltairine de Cleyre offers an ideal answer by stressing that we arrive at ethical arrangements "not by revelation from any superior power, not through the reading of any inspired book, not by special illumination of our inner consciousness; but by study of the results of social experiment in the past as presented in the works of historians, psychologists, criminologists, sociologists, and legalists" (378). In other words, we look to history, which includes religion, and to social experiments documented for us by those de Cleyre mentions. Most importantly, we can also look to our experiences as we give ourselves authority over our lives, as members of other species should have over theirs.

Only then can we see that "[i]deas do not have 'truth,' but 'value,' that is, an effectiveness that is measured by their capacity to enhance life" (Caputo). This concept is the antithesis of dogma, and what was true at one point in history need not be true anymore, nor does it need to be true at all places at the same point in history. For example, naysayers will call upon the "humans have always eaten meat" argument to reproach vegans. Yet while human slavery has always been a part of our species' cultures as well, it is unlikely one would use that to justify contemporary human slavery. The concept of truth as an illusion of sorts also strengthens my earlier argument that vegan activists must be ever cognizant of their audience. For instance, it is absurd to denigrate the Mansi people of Russia for continuing to eat animal flesh when there are little to no other food sources in their Siberian climate. We do not have to like it, but such practices must be contextualized lest we too become dogmatic, culturally ignorant, and closed off from realities and privileges other than our own.

Social justice theorists have long discussed the concept of a social contract, which maintains that human beings are willing to give up certain dispensations to those elected to positions of authority so that our rights are protected in return. With a few exceptions, most individuals in the Western world have "signed" this contract, whether they are aware of it or not. And I admit there is value to it (though not necessarily truth, to echo John Caputo). However, all would do well to envision the social contract as "a human-constructed idea that should be subjected to a never-ending process of interrogation, deconstruction, and a subsequent reconstruction" (Lackey 145). Like other ideas created by humans, the social contract has not been friendly to animals, mainly because they lack the rational capacity to knowingly enter into a contract (Bernstein 50; Rowlands "Contractarianism and Animal Rights," 235). Mark Bernstein argues that the most contractualists have awarded nonhumans is "'indirect' moral status, effectively implying that the only moral engagements we can have with them are instrumental" (50). Only by continued inquiry into the social contract and other social norms will we be able to identify and subvert oppressions long disguised as truthful and natural, including the moral status of nonhuman beings.[52]

Unlike religion, atheism is not essentially static (same gods, same words, same books, same ideas, albeit occasionally dressed in modern liberatory rhetoric). Religion is old. It comes from a past when knowledge and life itself were different, and many religions

---

52. Bernstein's essay "Contractualism and Animals" and Mark Rowland's "Contractarianism and Animal Rights" go into greater philosophical detail as to how other species can be included in contractualist theories.

remain mired in times of yore. As Taslima Nasrin affirms in regard to the tensions between a secular and Islamic East: "While some people want to go forward, others are trying to go back. It is a conflict between the future and the past, between innovation and tradition, between those who value freedom and those who do not" (616). Religion requires fealty to a higher power, an imaginary being who can cause strife as easily as s/he can give comfort. And as we've seen, sometimes God's way of comforting one is to cause strife to another. That is not freedom (and it doesn't sound too praiseworthy either).

The notion of evolving ethical norms applies to veganism as well, for "being vegan" is not a set condition one reaches. As formerly stated, the idea of living without causing any harm to other organisms is unfeasible. Ethical veganism will never find a fixed point for reasons well stated by Critical Animal Studies scholar James Stănescu: "What we are interested in is conceiving of veganism as a practice of the self, as a method that does not come from having the truth revealed, but is itself a practice of truth and of learning truth. Becoming-vegan is not an end, but a process, an always ongoing process" (36). For instance, I recently stopped eating chocolate products not certified as "fair trade" due to issues of child slavery on Africa's Ivory Coast. When I first went vegan, the truth about chocolate wasn't magically revealed to me as I settled into a new ethical code. Just as Lackey asserts about the social contract, ethics must constantly undergo examination and transformation. Vegans, atheists, and atheist vegans have not had the truth about life miraculously disclosed to them; such an assertion would merely replace the vegan or atheist for the priest as one with privileged information, thus mirroring dubious religious dynamics. Put plainly, vegan atheists/atheist vegans are trying to navigate a sometimes violent world filled with unnecessary inequality. Fortunately, we don't have the contradictory word of God nagging us to the conclusion that human beings are at the apex of life on Earth.

In the remainder of this chapter, I ponder where we go from here. I first analyze and caution against the religious rhetoric that has made its way into animal liberation (and even secular) vernacular with thought to improved ways for animal advocates to talk about nonhumans, activism, and veganism. Surely we can do better than recycle the oppressor's verbiage. Next, I borrow select ideas and passages from traditionally marginalized and subjugated human beings who have identified religion as intricately bound to their domination. With that, I explicate the correlations between human and nonhuman exploitation and consider ways in which other-than-human species can be counted within the progress of an all-encompassing justice advocacy movement that begins with letting go of God.

Conversion, Paradise, and Losing Our Humanity
Religious Rhetoric and Animal Advocacy

There is a tendency amongst those who undergo major life changes to frame their transformations using religious terminology, to speak of revelations, seeing the light, and awakening to a new reality. I too have used "conversion" to explain how I became atheist and vegan because it seemed apt in a world dominated by religion to use terms with which others are most familiar. Once becoming vegan, I have, as do others, also promised a vegan paradise if all would cease exploiting other species.

At a Critical Animal Studies conference in 2013, a group of panelists explained how to use ideas from Christianity and Islam to advocate for nonhumans. When I asked one speaker which came first for her, Christianity or liberation, she openly explained her purpose was animal advocacy, and she did not seem interested in Christianity as anything other than a vegan conversion device. Considering my view of religion as a tremendously repressive cultural institution, this has led me to re-evaluate the use of religious rhetoric as a method of animal advocacy and to consider the shortcomings of using the oppressor's language to subvert oppression.[53] To accomplish this, I started with two seemingly

---

53. As I often do in my writing, I cannot help but quote womanist poet and activist Audre Lorde here: "For the master's tools will never dismantle the master's house."

easy questions that I speak to below: Is becoming vegan akin to a religious conversion? Is the vegan animal advocacy movement a religion? The answers are not as simple as I thought. Rather, my findings give credence to Al Nowatzki's contention that "[t]he words 'convert' and 'conversion' come up a lot when vegans talk about choosing to be vegan. In many ways, this makes sense. In others, it's problematic" ("Conversion Narrative").

First, I must caution that conversion is a culturally-specific phenomenon that most readers of this book will understand from a Western perspective bound to the "legacy of Christian hegemony. [. . .] The Pauline [St. Paul] model of conversion combines notions of an unexpected flash of revelation, a radical reversal of previous beliefs and allegiances, and an underlying assumption that converts are passive respondents to outside forces" (Rambo "Anthropology," 213). This definition does not exactly epitomize a typical route to veganism or atheism, especially the idea of being passive recipients of truths that can only be revealed by "outside forces." Becoming vegan is often an *active* process of discovering truths long withheld from one by animal exploitation industries, whether through reading a book or watching a video about the realities of nonhuman suffering.

The idea of a "flash" of knowledge leading to a "radical reversal of previous beliefs" does have some bearing on becoming vegan and atheist, at least for me and others I've met in the animal liberation and freethought communities. As explained in this book's Introduction, I became vegan while viewing a documentary called *Behind the Mask: The Story of the People Who Risk Everything to Save Animals*. When I recently explained this during a presentation at a college, a student asked me to repeat the name of the movie because she was struggling with going vegan and hoped she would have the same reaction as I did, one I compared to flipping on a light switch. I cautioned her that what worked for me might not work for her. The same has been said of religious conversion: "Conversion is usually an individual process, involving change of world view and affiliation by a single person" (Buckser and Glazier xi). Conversion is rarely, if ever, described as a communal experience in Western traditions.

Religious anthropologists have also used terminology similar to James Stănescu's, as cited in the previous section, with the notion that conversion is not a straightforward once-and-done event. Lewis Rambo asserts: "Given the complexities, messiness, and diversity of individual human experience, complete conversion is a goal to work toward, not a 'finished' product" ("Anthropology" 214; *Understanding* 1). Diane Austin-Broos similarly states that "[c]onversion is a form of passage, a 'turning from and to' that is neither syncretism nor absolute breach" (1). Conversion does not involve a complete break with one's past behavior at which point all of life's experiences and intricacies merge into a new mode of existence. Getting back to Rambo's "messiness," the converted must navigate the same world with new perceptions, including "ideas about race, religion, and politics that preclude or discourage religious passage" (Austin-Broos 7). The same can be said about becoming vegan or atheist, for doing so does not mean the world, including beloved family and friends, goes vegan or atheist with you. One's newfound veganism and/or atheism must be integrated into other elements of life that can either encourage or discourage a person's new outlook. In response, one may become fervent in trying to sway those within his or her immediate circle to get on that same path. This explains why religious ideas and expressions frequently make their way into the vegan community.

James McWilliams, a history professor who covers animal rights issues in the popular media, posted a number of vegan conversion narratives on his Web site in 2012. He explains his purpose: "I envision these accounts as diverse reminders that—no matter how cogently we present an intellectual rationalization for going vegan—everyone approaches conversion through specific emotional angles and personal histories." While true, the use of the term "conversion" always includes the specter of religion that not all vegans will include in their individual histories. Thus, it can be off-putting to secularists and lead to the familiar assertion that veganism is a cult.

On the site, Gena Hamshaw writes of "revelations" and being "illuminated" after touching live animals. Another contributor, Emma Wilson, notes the dangers of zealotry in relation to her sister-in-law who became "obsessed with conversion" after going vegan, making her appear "caustic, self-righteous and unbecoming" as she reveled in her vegan bubble; meanwhile, those closest to Wilson's sister-in-law either abandoned her or remained unconverted. Popular vegan writer Melanie Joy compares veganism to matrimony: "Veganism and marriage are so interconnected because veganism is not simply a diet, but a way of life." Does this also mean choosing to remain *un*married is like veganism? Is every way of life akin to veganism? Possibly, which makes Joy's comment somewhat empty and also problematic in that she compares veganism to a heteronormative cultural institution in which individuals seek the sanction of church and state to legitimize their union.

The idea of the spirit is also popular in vegan conversion narratives. On McWilliams' site, Joy writes of veganism as a spiritual path, and Melissa Tedrow explains how she became vegan after connecting "with the spirit of the being who once inhabited" a nonhuman animal carcass. The problem with terms such as "spirit" and "spirituality" is not that they have no meaning, but that they have so many different meanings (which, one could argue, leads to meaninglessness). For many, being spiritual means they believe there is something larger than they are, something they do not understand. *Who doesn't?* Even the most learned atheist evolutionary biologist will admit she cannot comprehend and explain all of life's mysteries. But although the term borders on the hollow, it still includes association of the spirit as a cosmic, paranormal element with substance, albeit one we cannot quite put our fingers on. And this road of spirituality inevitably leads to New Age religions with nothing new or promising to offer in terms of animal liberation.

To borrow language from the field of addiction recovery, there is a notion of being on a "pink cloud" when a new conviction sets in. As bluntly explained on *Urban Dictionary*, the pink cloud is "12 step recovery jargon referring to someone new who talks about how great life is now that they're sober. Usually meaning that the person is out of touch with reality." This may sound harsh, but I find it *apropos* here (and below when I talk about the vegan paradise mythos). The newly religious and newly vegan may embark on quests to make others see the world as they do. They come prepared with "a new rhetoric or language system" and a burning desire to tell their story (Rambo *Understanding*, 137), and they are often disappointed when others do not follow suit. But despite these similarities, spiritual proselytizing and vegan activism are not precise counterparts. Religious missionaries, while they may have an earnest desire to help others, are giving of their time and resources to please a superior being (Rambo *Understanding*, 74–75). For some Christians, these actions raise their image in God's eyes and ensures reciprocity in an afterlife.[54] Animal advocates, most of whom are secular, have no such celestial goals. Rather, the burning desire to tell stories and take to the streets with pamphlets, banners, and chants comes from consideration of the billions of sentient beings slaughtered for human consumption, along with the myriad other ways humans utilize other species. We are, in effect, attempting to dismantle the idea of superiority, while religious missionaries sustain it by nature of their religiosity.

Ultimately, no matter the similarities between religious and vegan conversion, the element of the divine is not part and parcel to the latter, but it is endemic to the former. Conversion "marks the time when the hand of the *divine* is most plainly visible; conversion narratives overflow with expression of *supernatural* agency, in which the individual feels guided, or coerced, or enraptured by a *divine* presence" (Buckser and Glazier xii, emphasis added). Psychologists have noted that religious conversion is almost always bound to a concept of the celestial (Rambo "Anthropology," 217). In stark contrast, there is nothing divine or supernatural in exposing the gruesome horrors of animal exploitation, and I have yet to meet an animal activist, even a religious one, who explained her advocacy as a stairway to heaven or a way to fulfill God's will (which doesn't mean such activists don't exist).

---

54. This is not true of all Christians, of course. Some engage in missionary work simply because God says to, and still others argue there is nothing one can do to raise one's image in the eyes of God—one is forever a sinner, even if forgiven.

Despite these clear distinctions between conversions to veganism and religion, scholars, mainly sociologists, have declared animal rights and other social movements to be secular religions, as others claim about atheism. There is certainly valid, well-researched reasoning for doing so. To begin broadly, scholars have demonstrated the ways in which religious tendencies subversively manifest in contemporary culture even amongst the non-religious. In Edward Bailey's *Implicit Religion in Contemporary Society*, he defines implicit religion as something that requires commitment, an integrated focus within one's life, and a consistent influence, as opposed to a passing fancy (8–9). He does caution against thereby viewing everything through a religious lens: "To suggest that anything may be implicitly-religious, by no means suggests that everything is (implicitly or otherwise) religious" (9). This caveat is important because based on Bailey's initial definition, one can say having a child or a companion nonhuman animal constitutes a religion, for if done well, it requires commitment, integrated focus, and consistency, just as do jobs and other types of intimate relationships.

Sociologist Milton Yinger also developed a noteworthy definition of religion in his classic 1970 study on the science of religious belief:

> Religion, then, can be defined as a system of beliefs and practices by means of which a group or people struggles with [the] ultimate problems of human life. It expresses their refusal to capitulate to death, to give up in the face of frustration, to allow hostility to tear apart their human associations. The quality of being religious, seen from the individual point of view, implies two things: first, a belief that evil, pain, bewilderment, and injustice are fundamental facts of existence; and second, a set of practices and related sanctified beliefs that express a conviction that man can ultimately be saved from those facts. (7)

From this characterization, Yinger concludes that the Ku Klux Klan, communism, humanism, and nationalism can be perceived as secular religions (193). These examples plainly demonstrate that religion in no way necessitates taking the moral high ground (i.e. the KKK). And clearly, animal advocates do accept that pain and injustice against other species are facts of existence and that with the right set of strategies we may be able to save animals from those cruel realities. (Yinger's human-centric focus lessens when applied to animal advocates, but it does still pertain.) Definitions such as Bailey and Yinger's explain why other sociologists have continued to make the "animal activism/veganism = religion" argument.

For example, Harold Herzog equates animal activism with religion for the following five reasons: first, activists undergo a radical shift in basic beliefs; second, their lives change because of this shift; third, they want to convince others to accept their beliefs; fourth, they view activities that do not align with their beliefs as sinful; and finally, they think they are right (117). Other scholars have focused on "the elements of conversion, community, creed (system of belief), code (prescriptions for behavior), and cult (symbols and rituals) as they are found in the animal rights movement" (Jamison, Wenk, and Parker 307), while also highlighting the ascetic-like quality of veganism (Jamison, Wenk, and Parker 317).

These comparisons are justifiable, but not without some problems. To wit, Herzog cites an activist named Lucy who chooses to frame her activism in this way: "Jesus didn't beat people over the head with [his message]. He just tried to live an example and show them that his was a better way to live. I guess that's the way I feel about it. So here I am—Jesus walking on the Earth with my message" (114). Lucy is an extreme example of one who would compare herself to a divine being, and I charge Herzog with being a bit heavy handed by including a quote such as that in his work when it is not representative of how most activists view themselves. As to the work of Wesley Jamison, Casper Wenk, and James Parker, I explicitly disagree that vegan animal activists are de facto ascetics (or near ascetics). Just as in the general population, the animal liberation movement is comprised of a variety of individuals, many of whom do not feel they are denying themselves pleasure by refusing to consume animal products. In fact, vegan activists often partake with bountiful potluck dinners, bake sales, and other events celebrated with food not taken from other animal species.

Nonetheless, there are some benefits to these sociological studies, for they emphasize the ways in which human beings can feed their psychological or biological need for religion without engaging in historically destructive cultural practices. As Yinger states, many reject religion but "will get emotional support from various symbols, acts, and ceremonies (worship), and will join with others in groups that seek to sustain and realize these shared beliefs" (9). Jamison, Wenk, and Parker also note the seemingly innate human desire to maintain religious beliefs, further explaining how social movements offer "alternative communities that provide a degree of meaning through which [activists] can interpret their world" (320). While I am loath to look at my compassion for other species as dreck left over from my religious upbringing, I find it acceptable, even promising, that there are ways to find meaning in life without engagement with oppressive institutions. Yet I am troubled by the implication that activism is simply another way for human beings to find meaning, for that once again takes the spotlight off the exploitation and suffering of other species. Ultimately, as with conversion, while there are similarities between activism/veganism and traditional religious practices, the former should not be posed as parallel to the latter.

One might wonder what the harm is to make that association. By now, I hope readers have come to accept, or at least seriously consider, that the harm is religion itself. In his blog article "Religion and Vegan Advocacy," Nowatzki deftly explains the danger of using religious vernacular in animal activism:

[R]eligious texts and traditions generally don't support the idea that animals are due equal consideration, and so they would likely not be the true cause of the embrace of veganism among the faithful. [. . .] It seems strange, then, to hold veganism up as a religion, or to incorporate the language of religion within veganism, when religion has historically been a major perpetrator of the greater/lesser divide. [. . .] Since the majority of religious leaders are not vegan, it's too easy for adherents to dismiss arguments for veganism. If veganism was really what their religion demanded of them, the defense would go, their holy leaders would already be vegan. Secondly, veganism stands on its own just fine. It doesn't need to be incorporated into a religion and it doesn't require buttressing by the language of religion.

With no culturally influential religions on record advocating for animal liberation for the primary sake of animal liberation, as opposed to human ascendency, there is no compelling reason to promote veganism or the animal liberation movement as a religion even if there are similarities from certain disciplinary perspectives. In fact, it would be dangerous if such a religion did exist, as it might simply raise nonhuman suffering above human, thereby maintaining what Nowatzki terms "the greater/lesser divide."

Further, religions always include a supernatural component, but vegan activism is about the lived realities of animal exploitation, torture, and slaughter. If anything, people need to stop looking to the heavens—or wherever their god(s) reside(s)—and start looking at the research labs, the slaughterhouses, the entertainment venues, in their closets, and on their plates when thinking about living moral lives. The God concept has, at best, offered a foundation for weak arguments against extreme animal abuse, and humankind has offered weak arguments for the existence of God, gods, and goddesses. In contrast, being vegan "requires no more faith than is required when we see a dog yelping in pain and say, 'That dog is in pain'" (Nowatzki "Veganism"). Consequently, the "veganism as religion" idea ranges between wishful and foolish thinking.

Another problem with raising veganism to religious status comes down to simple classification. In "The Church of Veganism," Mariann Sullivan asserts that the main question isn't whether or not veganism is a religion, "but what 'religion' really is. And, unsurprisingly, that is a pretty tough question in our very diverse society, and one the courts have struggled with." With humans still trying to define religion after millennia, perhaps we should leave the term alone and express veganism as a system of worldly ethics attempting to do the least amount of harm. Sullivan further states: "I would say that for most vegans, certainly for me, veganism—regardless of its roots—is *exactly* the sort of belief system that religion plays in (at least some) people's lives." I see the benefits of this position, for it may garner vegans greater consideration in terms of food choices (akin to kosher or halal) and other cultural norms such as animal dissection choice in schools. However, there is also risk in "substitut[ing] one faith-based way of thinking with another faith-based way of thinking" (Nowatzki "Conversion") because faith-based ways of thinking have traditionally sanctioned hierarchy and intolerance.

With all of this said, although veganism is not a religion and there is danger in positioning it as such, it is still an ethical choice worthy of respect in the same ways as religious food practices. In fact, at the time of this writing, in the capacity of faculty adviser of my college's Animal Rights Club, I took part in a presentation with the campus' Muslim Student Association. We were attempting to get the Food Services Committee to take halal and vegan food options more seriously. It was quite difficult trying to explain that while veganism isn't a religion as is Islam, our ethical codes are just as significant as religious food prohibitions.[55] But without sacred texts and traditions to refer to, the vegan part of the presentation was not an easy sell, although some effort has been made on the committee's part to demarcate vegan food options.

Despite my firm assertion that veganism is not a religion, I do think one's moral choices should be respected within our culture's

---

55. Although my goal was to show vegan dietary concerns to be as significant as religious ones, an argument can surely be made that they are *more* significant because they aim to cause less suffering from an "animals matter" perspective in contrast to a "pigs are vile creatures and I don't want a knife that cut impermissible dead pig flesh to then cut permissible dead chicken flesh" perspective.

institutions. To illustrate, there are animal liberation activists serving prison sentences who must fight for access to vegan meals, but because their requests are not affiliated with a recognized religious belief, they are often ignored. For these political prisoners and their advocates, it may be tempting to pose veganism as a religion to pull upon legal precedent that will allow access to animal-free foods. I understand that perspective, but I ultimately think it is misguided in terms of long-range planning.

In fact, secularists have much older precedent than the US court system to pull from when attempting to have their ethical choices count in a religious society. As Kevin Drum points out in a *Mother Jones* article, Aristotle initially championed a secular code of ethics (one eventually absorbed by the church), and there are "plenty of modern, secular states in Europe and elsewhere, which appear to effortlessly practice an ethics every bit as praiseworthy as that of more religious states." Of course, we do not live in such a secular state. Therefore, more pressure is needed to enforce the concept that one's moral choices should be respected regardless of whether or not they align with the religious status quo. Otherwise, for secular ethics and veganism to matter, they will be forced to meet the nebulous criteria of being a formal belief system. I think the goal in legal cases should be to pose veganism as significant as, but not the same as, religious perspectives. In theory, using the "veganism as religion" model could make the fight for ethical food choices easier, but as veganism does not meet the criteria of being a religion, I don't think the courts would ever recognize it as such. As an alternative, we can continue to build upon a system of secular principles and demand that it receives the same respect and recognition as religious ones.

Atheist scholars have offered other alternatives to the religious rhetoric that finds its way into explanation of ethical mores and stories of personal change. For example, annalise fonza says of her move toward godlessness: "I find myself repeating, over and over again, that my transition from being a minister or preacher to atheism was not that dramatic or complicated. In fact, it happened with very little 'hullabaloo'" (188). Similarly, I have heard activists explain their veganism as a clear-cut ethical stance against violence and oppression. And although I credit a documentary as causing my veganism, in truth, I started becoming vegan about a decade or so before when I first began reading about animal issues. Once one removes the mysticism and "hullabaloo" surrounding change, going vegan may become more palatable to a broader audience because it will seem less complex and mysterious. Becoming vegan or atheist need not include a bolt of lightning nor a "this is a religion" stamp of approval.

Donald Watson, who coined the term "vegan," argues that to be effective, "the [animal rights] movement must consist of people who are self-critical, truth loving, scientific, careful in judgment and eager to yield to evidence even if it tends to weaken their case." In kind, people often come to veganism and atheism after a process of critically analyzing violent cultural norms, which leads to the next alternative.

In opposition to the traditional conversion narrative, Michael Lackey proposes the idea of the touchstone narrative as a proper way to explain one's transition to atheism, and this is applicable to becoming vegan as well. First, he defines the religious conversion narrative as a three-stage process: the individual thinks life is worthless, he then comes in contact with God either directly or through a religious group, and finally, with newfound meaning, the convert begins to evangelize (15). He next offers a four-stage touchstone process of becoming atheist, of which I am most intrigued by the final step in which one "interrogates the sociocultural consequences of religious belief" (Lackey 16). The touchstone narrative is much more relatable to ethical veganism than narratives of conversion. Admittedly, vegans are sometimes seen as zealous missionaries when engaged in outreach, but they are much more directly interrogating the sociocultural consequences of human dominance over other species, as opposed to evangelizing.

Evangelism and animal advocacy also differ in a key way involving the cliché of the "personal choice." While there are atheists who actively oppose religion, others don't pay it much mind as long as the religious keep it to themselves, away from our doorsteps (and, ideally, out of our schools and divorced from our nation's laws). This is clearly not the reality of religion in our culture, but for the sake of argument, let's say religion is a personal choice that shouldn't be forced upon those unbelievers deemed in need of salvation. People can worship their god(s) at home or in designated buildings and cease using God's will as a political platform. That would certainly be better than the reality of religion, but it is *not* comparable to vegan activism. In fact, even if religion was just a silent personal choice and atheists still aggressively opposed it, that would not be the same thing as vegans advocating to "innocent bystanders" that they should stop participating in animal abuse.

Nevertheless, meat eating is posed in the same way, with vegan activists often hearing this response during outreach: "I respect your veganism, but it is my personal choice to eat meat and dairy, and you do not have any business telling me not to." However, others' choices to engage in animal exploitation *are* my concern for a couple of crucial reasons. First, many would agree that opposing rape, torture, and murder is justifiable, and it is our business as human beings to stop such abuse, if possible; vegan activists extend that element of the social contract to other-than-human animals. Second, as a US citizen, my tax dollars support farm subsidies, animal research, meat- and dairy-based school lunch programs, and myriad other forms of animal exploitation. For those two reasons alone, I find it ethically imperative to advocate for nonhumans. Thus, religious proselytizing is far removed from animal activism, further making the "veganism as religion" paradigm invalid while also emphasizing the harm of using religious rhetoric to foster animal liberation.

Indeed, in Donald Watson's 1948 essay "Should the Vegetarian Movement Be Reformed?" he argues that "[v]egetarian literature should be secular. There must be thousands of vegetarians, both theists and atheists, who regard most religious doctrine as mythical and unintelligible and who do not, therefore, wish to be associated with it." And he warns against the "disharmony" that will likely ensue if religion, mainly Christianity, is used as a strategy in animal activism, advising that vegetarian literature "should not include articles concerning irrelevant cults and superstitions." His reasoning, as cited here in detail, shores up one of my motivations for writing this book:

> The association of the vegetarian movement with religious bodies should be one of enquiry, if not of open challenge. Probably the chief reason why otherwise decent people behave so callously to creatures as highly sentient as themselves is because the Church teaches that such creatures were sent by a provident creator for man's use. It is the duty of the movement to recognise and oppose this sinister aspect of religion which can readily be proved absurd and which bars the way to vegetarian reform. The foundations of the slaughter house are safe so long as this falsehood survives.

Religion is such a vital force in promoting anthropocentrism and speciesism that to use it to combat those ideologies is a proverbial exercise in futility, akin to running in a circle. In contrast, religion must continually be critiqued for its function in the roles humans have assigned to other animals. It is also ill-advised to pose the animal liberation movement and veganism as religions when they don't meet the criteria in core ways, as argued above. Watson wisely cautions that those creating vegetarian literature "should use more care in sorting out facts that can be demonstrated, from personal beliefs and wishes." Thus, we come to the myth of the vegan paradise.

As discussed in the first chapter, many religions speak of paradise, whether in terms of a literal place where the faithful will reside near their creator (maybe with virgins, maybe not) or a state of existence comparable to bliss. In *Good News for All Creatures*, Stephen R. Kaufman and Nathan Braun remind readers of the Bible's promise: "According to Isaiah [. . .], at the end of time, all the world's creatures will once again be vegetarian and enjoy peace [. . .]. Thus, each meal symbolically anticipates Creation's reconciliation—a restoration to the harmonious peaceful world God originally intended" (49). No matter what myth one is pulling from, paradise is a good place to be, an Edenic locale filled with harmony, peace, balance, and joy. Back on planet Earth, there are some within the animal rights community offering parallel visions of a material paradise, if only everyone would become vegan:

> The word "vegan," newer and more challenging than "vegetarian" because it includes every sentient being in its circle of concern and addresses all forms of unnecessary cruelty from an essentially ethical perspective, with a motivation of compassion rather than health or purity, points to an ancient idea that has been articulated for many centuries, especially in the world's spiritual traditions. It indicates a mentality of expansive inclusiveness and is able to embrace science and virtually all religions because it is a manifestation of the yearning for universal peace, justice, wisdom, and freedom. (Tuttle 27–28)

This passage from Will Tuttle's *The World Peace Diet* packs quite a pledge, as does the book's title (much like Kaufman and Braun's): veganism will lead to both concrete and abstract blessings for all! This is a promise worthy of the Bible. Similar arguments are made in the video "A Life Connected: VEGAN," created by Nonviolence United. They persuasively provide solid data to support the idea that veganism can change the planet to benefit people, the environment, and animals. The video asserts that if we stop growing plants and grains to feed nonhumans, that land could be used to feed the world's hungry; it identifies the rampant environmental destruction resulting from diets based in meat and dairy; and finally, "A Life Connected" asks viewers to consider the other species with whom they've felt a bond and to carry that compassion over to those beings humans have deemed food. I have shown this video quite a few times in activist contexts, but whenever I do, I am troubled by the promise of paradise inherent in the content, although the content itself is trustworthy.

The general public sees "going vegan" as replacing animal-based commodities with non-animal ones, which is surely part of the process. But the promise of a vegan paradise is inaccurate when based upon the premise of mere commodity exchanges: the bad ones for the good ones, Walmart for Whole Foods, cow's milk cheese for non-dairy "cheeze," leather for pleather. Such exchanges may benefit those in wealthy, industrialized countries who do not consider human beings in their definitions of "animal liberation," but they will not end suffering the world over. Veganism requires less black and white thinking, as I see it, and more expansive critique of the realities of our modern age.

There is still, and may always be, the issue of human *natures* to contend with when considering the promise of a vegan utopia. For example, on the subject of feeding the world's poor with grains and on land traditionally used to make "food" animals fat for slaughter, Brian Dominick reveals the following hindrance:

> If North Americans stopped eating meat next year, it is unlikely that a single hungry person would be fed newly-freed grains grown on U.S. soil. This is because the problem of world hunger [. . .] is not at all what it seems. These problems have their root not in the availability of resources, but in the allocation of resources. Elites require scarcity [. . .]. First of all, the market value of goods drops decisively as supply increases. If grains now fed to livestock were to become suddenly available, the change would drop the price of grains through the floor, undermining the profit margins [. . .]. Second, it is the case that the national and global distribution of food is a political tool. Governments and international economic organizations carefully manipulate food and water supplies to control entire populations. (9)

Dominick's commentary is not meant to dissuade one from being or becoming vegan, but it is a point worth acknowledging when animal advocates make promises about social change and world peace resulting from nonhuman animal liberation. And lest one think Dominick's concern is extreme and pessimistic, a quick Internet search of the terms "food politics" or "food power" demonstrate the ways in which food is used as a means of political control across the globe. Model case studies of agricultural manipulation and selective distribution being used to oppress can be seen in the 1980 and 1990 famines in Ethiopia and Sudan.

Even if the United States suddenly had storehouses of grains to share with the world, there is no assurance the food would reach its intended recipients, and, sadly, there is no assurance the US government would share those resources if it was an unwise political maneuver. And so goes the promise of paradise. I believe the world becomes slightly better with each person who goes vegan, but I do not envision world peace based upon that hypothesis.

Watson likewise critiques false notions about vegetarian living that find their way into animal advocacy literature. The theories he details, often "quoted as facts" in vegetarian literature, go like this: "all life is one," "vegetarian diets create peaceful dispositions," "cruel people must suffer for their cruelties," "man has fallen from a perfect state," and "the universe is moral." Aside from the idea that all life is connected, there is no reason to believe any of these notions. I know from direct experience that there are vegetarians and vegans who are complete assholes. I also know many unapologetic meat eaters who are quite pleasant to be around. And while it is nice to think cruel people will someday face their comeuppances—that is one element of religion I like—many such individuals, vegan and otherwise, will skate through life being generally dreadful people and never have to answer for their misdeeds.

Inherent in the idea of humankind's fall from a perfect state is the promise that eliminating animal products from one's life will make him perfect, an impossibility relegated to the faultless mythological beings of which religions speak. If perfection means one lives without causing the death of another, no one will ever reach that state until he or she dies, even the most hardcore raw fruitarian (one who eats only fruit because it falls from the branch as opposed to being pulled from the ground). Finally, as argued in the previous chapter by Peter Wilson, claiming there is a material order in the universe through which we can pinpoint morality merely exchanges one unproven idea (God) for another (a cosmic moral code).

In the animal rights/liberation movement, there is a penchant for making elaborate claims about veganism without critically assessing the realities of the world in which we live. Dominick is a notable exception to the tendency, but he writes from a radical perspective which is potentially off-putting to average listeners, even vegans, by nature of his being an anarchist. Even imaging a future in which nonhuman animals are left alone, I still envisage human beings at each others' throats even though they are consuming a plant-based diet and have ceased exploiting other species. This is why Tuttle's commentary from *The World Peace Diet* is so troubling, with its subtle guarantee that veganism is in tune with spiritual and scientific traditions and human nature.

Eliminating hierarchy in its many manifestations, religion and the sciences included, is a more holistic way of framing world peace: "Until human beings cease to live in societies that are structured around hierarchies as well as economic classes, we shall never be free of domination, however much we try to dispel it with rituals, incantations, ecotheologies, and the adoption of seemingly 'natural' lifeways" (Bookchin 39). I pose Murray Bookchin's commentary against Tuttle's because it is, in essence, saying the opposite of Tuttle, who implies that all ideologies align with veganism and that all human beings actually wish to live in a world of "universal peace, justice, wisdom, and freedom" (Tuttle 28). There are some who do not care a jot about peace and justice, and feeding them a vegan diet won't change a damned thing.

I ardently focus on the myth of the vegan paradise because it touches on a misrepresentation of vegans in popular culture. To illustrate, in Michael Pollan's wildly successful book *The Omnivore's Dilemma*, he dismissively writes of a "Vegan Utopia" populated by naïve, self-righteous people completely out of touch with our animal-killing, meat-eating natures. After discussing how he killed and ate a pig, Pollan continues: "I have to say there is a part of me that envies the moral clarity of the vegetarian, the blamelessness of the tofu eater. Yet part of me pities him, too. Dreams of innocence are just that; they usually depend on a denial of reality that can be its own form of hubris" (362).

Such a passage makes me wonder if Pollan has ever had any profound conversations with ethical vegans. If so, he may have learned what James Stănescu here states: "I have no doubt that if we try hard we would be able to find some vegans out there that take their veganism as a marker of innocence and a guarantee of blamelessness" (34), but the reality is much different. More often than not, ethical vegans "feel guilty by the actions we engaged in

before we were vegans, we feel guilty by the inability of veganism
to stop all cruelty toward animals, we feel guilty that we haven't
convinced more people to be vegans, and on and on" (Stănescu
35). We also feel guilty because we know our habits and lifestyles
cause damage to the environment and other animals, both human
and nonhuman. Consequently, vegan activists rarely live on pink
clouds of purity. But rather than ride the wave of blamelessness
or wallow in self-loathing, Stănescu ultimately suggests a middle
ground on which we acknowledge our lack of innocence without
becoming incapacitated by "guilt or rituals of purity" (47). With
that in mind, I suggest ethical vegans stop using religious rhetoric
that pledges a utopia we cannot deliver. Regardless of their entertainment value, the world does not need any more myths built
upon false promises.

The final example of supposedly liberatory rhetoric needing
disengagement from religious ideology is best demonstrated by
eighteenth century Prussian philosopher Immanuel Kant: "[A]s
far as animals are concerned, we have no direct duties. Animals
are not self-conscious and are there merely as a means to an end.
That end is man [. . .]. Our duties toward animals, then, are indirect duties toward mankind" (564). It is of little consequence
that Kant was not writing from a deliberately religious viewpoint,
for this popular idea that cruelty to animals may lead to cruelty to
humans is grounded in the same speciesism and anthropocentrism
prevalent in religion. In *Defending Animal Rights*, Tom Regan
affirms this reading of Kant, noting it as an influential mixture of
Aristotelian and Aquinian/Thomist views (12).

Modern philosopher Christine Korsgaard offers an essential
critique of those who remain in the Kantian camp. She explains
Kant's belief that only rational creatures (those not ruled by impulse, attachment, and craving) can make moral claims upon each
other (5). This effectively ejects all other-than-human animals
(and some humans) from the moral community. Ration, to use
traditional terminology, is what separates man from the animals.
However, Korsgaard wisely rebuts that many of the concerns we
most wish to protect are natural ones, such as "the desire to avoid

pain," and they "spring from our animal nature, not from our rational nature" (5). Many are willing to accept Korsgaard's premise, but stop short of using that premise as reason not to cause other species avoidable pain.

Still, the idea of "indirect duties" is often used in animal rights argot. Even in Robert G. Ingersoll's injunction against vivisection, as quoted in the first chapter, he writes that a "physician who would cut a living rabbit in pieces [. . .] would not hesitate to try experiments with men and women for the gratification of his curiosity." In Greg Epstein's more recent *Good Without God: What a Billion Nonreligious People Do Believe*, he questions if humanism, "with its semantic focus on humans," allows for mistreatment of other species, questioning if it is anthropocentric and speciesist to use the term humanist (34). In the end, he supports the ethical treatment of animals (which doesn't appear to indicate veganism), "lest we lose our own humanity" (Epstein 35).

Ingersoll's assertion isn't necessarily true. Yes, anyone who watches horror movies or television crime dramas knows that serial killers often start out hurting small animals before moving to larger human prey. But as difficult as it is to fathom, I would guess some, if not most, vivisectors will never ply their trade on humans even if given the opportunity, and they likely go home at the end of the workday to be adequate-to-good fathers, mothers, citizens, sons, daughters, friends, as well as being loving companions to their domesticated canines and felines. In less coarse terms, Epstein is saying the same thing as Kant and Ingersoll, that we should not be cruel to animals because it may result in the more significant cruelty toward humans. Although Ingersoll and Epstein's sentiments are certainly more sensitive than Kant's, both of them reinforce the Kantian view of "the natural order as existing to serve human interests" (Regan *Defending*, 13). Although these ideas arise from freethinkers, I see them as religious rhetoric in disguise and counterproductive to fostering a revolution in human perception of other species.

In place of these ideas, activists should pose other species as having intrinsic value by nature of their sentience. It does not matter how similar or different they are to Homo sapiens; it doesn't matter if cruelty to animals leads to cruelty to humans. Other-than-human animals have worth because their lives matter to them and we know it because we have seen animal suffering as well as animal joy. This is not to say comparisons between humans and other species are always ill-advised. Rather, the "indirect duties" argument for animal welfare is a tactic with a suspect foundation: Kant's declaration that since animals are not rational, they do not matter.

Religion fails other-than-human species at every turn. Indeed, it fails humans quite often as well, which speaks to why, "given the way the God concept functions to justify political and socio-cultural systems of oppression, responsible humans should not believe" (Lackey 19). This leads to the next section, an investigation into how those from social justice movements have identified religion as a primary cause of their oppression and to explore what this might mean for the animal liberation movement.

Animal Liberation, Atheism, and the Project of Parity

One of the goals of this book is to challenge secularists to think about the ways in which their views of other-than-human animals spring from and reinforce domineering religious social norms. While this book's theme may seem novel, I argue it continues a tradition of social justice activism that recognizes the role of religion in securing the subjugation of ostensibly less worthy individuals. While the animal liberation movement differs from other movements in that its participants are not members of the group for which they fight—which is species other than our own—the challenge to hierarchy is fundamentally the same. Therefore, I end with consideration of how those from other causes have used secular thought in their critiques of tyranny. The animal liberation movement is still relatively young, and even some from other radical movements do not see the value in its pursuit. However, when looking at commentary arising from the black liberation and women's movements, the parallels with this text are evident.

This is why I end with a focus on how animal liberation can be integrated into a secular history of social progress.

With religion as reinforcement, physical and corporeal criteria (skin color, the ability to walk on two legs, amount/texture of hair/fur) has been and still is used to determine who receives ethical consideration. And, of course, as noted by many past scholars, the animalization of people of color was as much a tool in their domination as was religious ideology; thus, history itself has made the comparison between nonhumans and oppressed human beings.

In Frantz Fanon's classic text *The Wretched of the Earth*, he asserts that the colonized revolted against their imperialist overlords partly because they "treated them like animals and considered them brutes" (89–90). This could only occur, obviously, if the colonized themselves viewed nonhumans as lesser beings. The colonizers responded to this upheaval by using politeness and humanizing behavior to keep the oppressed under control while still silently viewing them as animals, in the negative sense of the word (Fanon 89). Similarly, in the animal rights/liberation movement, there are efforts to make animal exploitation less egregious (i.e. use bigger cages to imprison other species) while keeping the assumption of human superiority intact.

Building upon Fanon's work, Michael Lackey observes the ways in which the imperialist animalization of native people included the presumption that they did not have the ability to understand "western values," arguing that "animalizing discourse relates to [and allows for] violence" (25). Therefore, it was permissible to subjugate those incapable of experiencing God: "Those who have epistemological access to true Religion, true Morality, or true Truth are full-fledged Humans, while those who lack such Knowledge are subhuman or nonhuman. In short, the theory of objective knowledge has been used to determine humanness" (Lackey 4), which then determines how other living beings are to be (mis)treated.

Even non-atheists from the African American community are cognizant of the power of religion, with its "anything goes" facility, to subjugate those judged socially inferior. For example, renowned early twentieth century social scientist and activist W.E.B. DuBois affirms: "The American Church of Christ is Jim Crowed from top to bottom. No other institution in American is built so thoroughly or more absolutely on the color line" (169). DuBois notes the Church was historically against all progressive social change, that is until popular opinion leaned in the other direction, after which the Church hypocritically "did not hesitate both to claim a preponderant share of the glory of victory and again to emphasize its supernatural claims" (170). The church has hypocritically used race as both an instrument of tyranny and a way to gain more adherents, resulting in more financial and cultural capital.

Radical activist Emma Goldman, a contemporary of DuBois, makes a similar, albeit more general, observation that "Christianity is most admirably adapted to the training of slaves, to the per-petuation of a slave society" (384). The exercise of religion as a method of social control was not lost on other radical activists in US history. For example, in the 1960s and '70s, the Black Panther Party challenged white hegemony through its secular approach to social change. A recent interview with law professor and former Party member Kathleen Cleaver confirms that "one of the things that the people in the Black Panther Party were very clear on [was] [. . .] that our group had no religion; that whatever your religion was [. . .] you keep it in the closet; that this was a secular revolutionary social-political movement." The Panthers knew that religion in the US was overseen by the oppressor and religion could be divisive in a movement requiring unity.

Admittedly, DuBois also saw much potential in the church (as, of course, Dr. Martin Luther King, Jr. would a few decades later), believing it could be a galvanizing source of power through which ministers could arouse the strength and moral fortitude needed to lift African Americans out of social, political, and economic despair. And in retrospect, Cleaver and other former Party mem-bers would rethink their views on religion—or more specifically, spirituality. Cleaver now believes the Panthers "misunderstood the profoundly spiritual nature of the energy that [they] needed to accomplish what [they] set out to do," while still critiquing those religious proponents within the African American community who are "selfish, self-aggrandizing puppets of the power structure."

In contrast to this moderate acceptance of religion and spirituality, in his study of black writers and activists such as J. Saunders Redding, Richard Wright, Nella Larson, and Langston Hughes, Lackey asserts that African American atheists "would argue that the God concept is the problem and thus cannot be part of the solution," and they are more content to "evolve a liberation antitheology or a liberation atheism" than to find a way to use an oppressive tool to paradoxically end oppression (38). This proposition is currently evident in the growing trend of African Americans coming out as atheist. Jamila Bey is one of those individuals. Although Bey notes "you commit social suicide as a black person when you say you're an atheist," she feels compelled to do so because the African American community "need[s] proactive solutions [to racial issues], and praying and churches is not the answer" (qtd. in Oduah and Bohn); in fact, "black churches can sometimes be part of the problem" (Oduah and Bohn) because they come from Euro-American conceptions of God initially forced upon Africans during the slave trade starting in the fifteenth century.

This issue is more complex than it may first appear, for it goes beyond a simple argument that whites used Christianity as justification for enslaving Africans (which is true) and slaves often adopted belief in the very religion used to enslave them (which is also true). However, there were slaves who maintained their native traditions even after being forced into a new land, while others syncretized those traditions with Christianity. Further, as Darnise C. Martin notes in *Beyond Christianity*, early black churches, while places of Christian worship, were also sites for planning escape and revolt, for seeking support and community, and for championing liberation (38). But acknowledging the uniqueness of black Christianity does not in any way speak to the question asked in different ways throughout this book: Why does one need a higher power, especially one of dubious merit if one really reads the Bible, to endorse liberation? Humans can gather to speak of escape, revolt, and freedom, as well as find community support, without the promise or threat of an almighty autocrat. Christianity fundamentally supports a "chosen people" mentality, and although ideas about who can be chosen have progressed throughout history, Christianity is always already hierarchical and demanding of subservience. Considering the history of Christianity and people of color, black atheists would likely agree with comedian Chris Rock's quip: "A black Christian is like a black person with no memory" (qtd. in Staff).

In Abrahamic religious traditions, to be considered a person, in the moral sense, one must be part of a group chosen by God or an individual with access to God-determined truths. For centuries, certain factions of human beings were seen as unable to be chosen, including those with dark skin. This has changed in contemporary culture. For the divine-seeking human, this means one can convert to the "right" religion and become a chosen person with the ability to experience God both on Earth and, if one's cards are correctly played, in an afterlife.

American culture is certainly not in a post-racial state, as some might claim, but even the Mormons are attempting to lift their long-standing prohibition against people of color having full participation in their Church (officially lifted in 1978). In 2013, they published "Race and the Priesthood," avowing that the "structure and organization of the Church encourage racial integration" and patting themselves on the back for having had at least two black Mormon priests in 1852. (Women, of course, are still prohibited from the priesthood.) Such progress, and I use the term very loosely and somewhat sarcastically, is evidence that glacial shifts in unjust behaviors are possible in organized religion. However, these slowly developing changes will only benefit humans—assuming one thinks being allowed to convert to Mormonism is a benefit—because only humans can be chosen by God. This means very little for the other creatures with whom we share the planet.

All of the arguments thus far exposing religion as an instrument for the oppression of humans apply to other species as well. However, nonhuman animals (even primates) can never be seen as human beings for the irrefutable fact that they are not biologically human. As such, they will always lack epistemological admission to the cosmic truths religions promise, and with no religion offering alternatives to this paradigm, religion is, in perpetuity, worse for nonhumans than it is for humans. The use of animalizing terminology against Homo sapiens of different races can be subverted, as history shows, but by its very nature it cannot be subverted in terms of its effects on other species, for it is from those species, filtered through anthropocentric mindsets, that the negative rhetoric arises. If there were no other species to look down upon for lack of their non-humanness, animalizing ideology and discourse could not have been used as tools of subjugation. The oppressor would not have had the "animals are inferior" rhetoric to use and the oppressed would not have been offended by it. Just as Lackey declares that "killing God would be the first step toward the construction of a truly tolerant and egalitarian democracy" for humans (2), it is also a step within abolishing the human/animal binary relegating other species as means to human ends.

The promise of "killing god" has not been lost within feminism either, the issues of which are not wholly disconnected from race. annalise fonza, a womanist, atheist advocate, and Humanist Celebrant, wisely affirms that "[w]hen most people think of dialogues that take place at the intersection of gender, religion, and human rights, they are not thinking of atheism" (185). Her objective is to include black atheist women in such dialogues because "civil rights for females/women are threatened worldwide by governance that is informed by patriarchal masculinity that conveys the need to control the fate of the female body" (186). Perhaps because of cultural saturation, critics of sexism and misogyny in religion rarely consider atheism as an alternative. In contrast, many endeavor to reform the religion itself, akin to the intellectual gymnastics detailed in the first chapter in relation to religious arguments favoring nonhuman animals. For instance, using Mormonism as an example once again, there is an organization called Ordain Women seeking a place for women in the Mormon priesthood, as opposed to challenging the religion as essentially gender-biased and of little worth for true parity.

fonza lists the names of black female theologians from the 1980s onward who began questioning male leaders, from religious scholars to black liberationists, for refusing to acknowledge the patriarchy intrinsic to both the Bible as a whole and the "Jesus narrative" specifically (190). fonza has a different goal than theologians such as Dolores Williams, Katie Canon, and Emilie Townes, for she seeks complete disengagement from religion as the only viable path to freedom from oppression. fonza puts special emphasis on women, with even more emphasis on women of color, because religion in its many manifestations has been especially harsh on them. (And women were/are often derogatorily equated with nonhumans in religious thought, along with "children and, in the parlance of the day, 'idiots'" [Gaylor "Introduction," 4].) Just as the atheist movement as a whole is seen as dominated by white males, a similar dynamic is at play within African American atheism. In 2007, the Pew Research Forum reported that "African-American men are significantly more likely than women to be unaffiliated with any religion (16% vs. 9%)" (qtd. in fonza 193). In sum, those most negatively affected by religion are incongruously less likely to forgo it.

Part of the reason women of color, indeed of all ethnicities, may be less likely to come out as atheist is due to the very patriarchy that inundates major world religions and other cultural institutions. There is extra pressure on women of color because, as Chika Oduah and Lauren E. Bohn report, in 2009 the Pew Forum on Religion & Public Life found African Americans to be one of the most religious US populations. It seems less "ladylike," more scandalous, and even an affront to one's ethnic heritage for women to be godless, just as it is more shameful for women to be sexually promiscuous than it is for men, an idea also propagated by many religions.

In her introduction to the anthology *Women without Superstition*, Annie Laurie Gaylor asks: "What do 'faithless' women have faith in? Themselves, their rights, the potential of humankind, and the natural world" (14). While this seems quite promising for women, it is not so for anyone who wishes to keep women marginalized and suppressed. Both fonza and Gaylor observe that once people of color and women give up God, they may be more willing to confront the debasing things religion has to say about them. For instance: "[T]here is a suspicion of unworthiness and uncleanness seductively infused into the books of Moses against the whole female sex, in *animal* as well as human life" (Stanton 126, emphasis added). In this passage, suffragist Elizabeth Cady Stanton makes clear connections amongst religion, women, and nonhuman animals, especially those female species whose reproductive capacities are used as commodities (i.e. eggs and milk).[56]

Observations such as Stanton's have subsequently been made by ecofeminists within the animal liberation movement, resulting in the questions: Why don't more feminists support animal rights? Don't they see the patriarchal structures condemning them as commodities are the same that condemn nonhuman animals?[57] However, some of the feminist vegans asking those questions are religious themselves. Hence, my question to them would be: Don't you see the patriarchal structures condemning women and nonhuman animals as commodities are informed and reinforced by religious institutions? As Gaylor affirms: "The status of women and the history of the women's rights movement cannot be understood except in the context of women's fight to be free from religion" ("Introduction" 3). In response to feminists who do not identify religion as a source of their oppression (and who, in fact, may rely on God for succor), fonza applauds other feminists who are willing to fight "anti-atheist prejudice" in its many forms (185) and argues their "willingness to identify as atheist is the very thing that has set them free, for it is in the naming or proclaiming of their realities that they have emancipated themselves, their

---

56. Not wanting to misrepresent Stanton here, although she was a champion of woman's rights, she was also "a mean-spirited, Saxon chauvinist" who denigrated other races deemed inferior to whites (Painter).

57. These questions are continually asked in the feminist animal rights movement, but they are commonly seen to have been best articulated in Carol J. Adams's *The Sexual Politics of Meat: A Feminist-Vegetarian Critical Theory* (1990).

families, and their children from oppressive frameworks" (195). I argue that proclaiming the realities of nonhuman animal lives from a non-religious perspective can aid in setting them free from human prisons. Here we see intersections of gender, religion, human rights, atheism, and now *species* that deserve further discussion amongst those concerned with positive social change.

For some feminists, religion's anti-woman deportment is quite uncomplicated, especially regarding the monotheistic traditions. Philosopher Christine Overall acknowledges the argument from evil as the most direct reason women should be atheists. The argument asserts that if there is an all-knowing, all-powerful God (in the Abrahamic sense) who loves those he creates, then evil should not exist in the human realm, for the two ideas are logically incompatible (Howard-Snyder xii). (To which some would respond with the cliché: "God works in mysterious ways.") Past and current harms done to women in the name of religion are reason enough for some feminists to lose any faith they once had in a benevolent higher power: "The existence of oppression and injustice to women and children and members of many other groups, both human and *nonhuman*, on this planet is evidence not just of the harmfulness of monotheistic religions, but also that there is no God in the traditional monotheistic sense" (Overall, emphasis added). Examples supporting Overall's contention abound.

In Ayaan Hirsi Ali's *Infidel*, the author, now living under a fatwā, details the treatment of women by men based on the latter's readings of the Quran. In the following passage, she provides examples of Muslim women's abuse from a film she was making with Theo Van Gogh, *Submission*, before he was assassinated for his anti-Islamic stance:

> There is the woman who is flogged for committing adultery; another who is given in marriage to a man she loathes; another who is beaten by her husband on a regular basis; another who is shunned by her father when he learned that his brother raped her. Each abuse is justified by the perpetrators in the name of God, citing the Quran verses now written on

the bodies of the women. These women stand for hundreds of thousands of Muslim women around the world. (xxi)

Certainly, Ali does not speak for every Islamic woman. There are feminists in Islam who object to analyses of their faith as essentially misogynistic and argue "that wearing stereotypically Muslim clothing [is] most often a matter of choice" (McElroy 31). Much of this feminist commentary arises from debates about whether or not wearing a veil (*hijab*) is oppressive.

In Leila Ahmed's "The Veil Debate Again," she documents her own shifting perspectives on the controversial head covering, having once been anti-veil but then coming to understand that many Muslim women do not see wearing the *hijab* as an obligation arising from the Quran, but rather as a preference representing their heritage (306). And for some, it is a conscious political statement against Western hegemony. Ahmed also muses on an insightful skit performed by members of the Young Muslim Women's Association. In this performance, one young woman frets about which outfit to wear and fiddles with her hair and make-up in despair, making her late for school; meanwhile, another young woman puts on her traditional Muslim garb and has time to spare for praying, eating, and making it to school on time (315). As many global feminists would rightly argue, Western women should worry about the social implications of their own allegedly independent choices of self-representation before they critique Islamic women for theirs. However, questions of the veil are minor when compared to the practices Ali mentions in her memoir, which no women, as far as I know, support in the name of Allah (which is not to say there aren't any). Some interpretations of the Quran are intrinsically oppressive, and as Taslima Nasrin concludes in "On Islamic Fundamentalism," until that inherency is challenged more rigorously, Muslim women "will have to suffer not only discrimination but also ignominy and violence, and human rights will remain just a dream for many" (620).

With atheist writers such as Christopher Hitchens and Sam Harris being accused of Islamophobia, I am compelled to reiterate that the Bible is no better in its depiction of women than the Quran, as demonstrated in the tongue-in-cheek *Skeptic's Annotated Bible* page "Misogyny and Insults to Women," which adds colorful commentary to misogynistic biblical passages, of which there are many. What I offer here is just a sampling. In Genesis: "Lot refuses to give up his angels to the perverted mob, offering his two 'virgin daughters' instead. He tells the bunch of angel rapers to 'do unto them [his daughters] as is good in your eyes.' This is the same man that is called 'just' and 'righteous' in 2 Pet. 2:7–8. 19:8." In 1 Samuel 21:4: "The priest tells David that he and his men can eat the 'hallowed' bread if" they have not laid with women, which would render them befouled.

And lest one thinks only the Old Testament is bad for women, Jesus Christ continued in like fashion. In Matthew: "Jesus says that divorce is permissible when the *wife* is guilty of fornication. But what if the husband is unfaithful? Jesus doesn't seem to care about that. 5:32, 19:9." In John (4:7–18), Jesus comes across a Samaritan woman who had been divorced multiple times; in that era, divorce was always considered the woman's fault, and they were resultantly made social pariahs. As *The Skeptic's Annotated Bible* states, "This was a great opportunity for Jesus to explain why the Mosaic marriage laws were unjust and correct them—if he thought they were wrong, that is, which apparently he didn't." The list of woman-hating rhetoric could continue, and all give credence to Overall's comment that "monotheistic religions harm women." Yet although there is humor in *The Skeptic's Annotated Bible*, we mustn't forget the real women who have been and continue to be abused, ignored, and killed in the name of all that is holy.[58]

---

58. As is the case with nonhuman animals, Buddhism has been historically more progressive in its view and treatment of women, but it is still dominated by men. Alan Sponberg calls this "*institutional androcentrism*: the view that women may indeed pursue a full-time religious career, but only within a carefully regulated institutional structure that preserves and reinforces the conventionally accepted social standards of male authority and female subordination" (13). Further, as in Christianity, in Buddhism there is also a traditional fear that women will "undermine male celibacy" (Sponberg 20).

Ideas about nature and what is natural also underpin religion's deprecating treatment of women and other species. As explored in the first chapter, one of the most insidious aspects of hierarchy and other tyrannical norms is that they are posed as natural and beyond modification. As Lillie Devereux Blake has cautioned: "It has been a favorite objection against woman's emancipation to say that it was a 'reform against nature,' that women have always been subordinate, and therefore always will be" (247). A "reform against nature" is also seen as blasphemy against God. See the religious war against the gay rights movement for a current example of fighting the "unnatural" in God's name.

Voltairine de Cleyre also addresses the argument from nature, beginning with the observation: "I can see no reason, absolutely none, why women have clung to the doom of the gods. I cannot understand why they have not rebelled" ("The Case of Women" 365). She continues her argument for women's emancipation with a significant analogy to human treatment of other species:

> As a horse is designed to draw wheels because it (sic) is a horse, so have women been allotted certain tasks, mostly menial, because they are women. The majority of men actually hold to that analogy, and without in the least believing themselves tyrannical or meddlesome, conceived themselves to be justified in making a tremendous row if the horse attempted to get over the traces [on a harness]. (366)

De Cleyre's observation[59] is at the crux of the argument from nature. Even today, we see violent human responses if women dare step out of line from the "natural" role assigned to them by God. An especially heinous example is the story of Malafa Yousafzai, a Pakistani girl who, at age twelve, was shot by the Taliban for championing women's educational rights.[60] And in a bizarre

---

59. Although primarily an activist for laborers' rights, de Cleyre was also sensitive to nonhuman animal issues, so there is reason to think she was criticizing animal use here as well as women's cultural roles.

60. She survived and continues to be a dynamic, unapologetic activist for women in Islam.

twist, nonhumans, as de Cleyre mentions, are often abused because they won't participate in the most *unnatural* positions
humans put them in because they believe it somehow natural
for other species to follow human edicts. To illustrate, elephants
in circuses are beaten with bull hooks when they won't balance
their tremendous weight on a ball. Bears are similarly abused if
they don't ride tricycles correctly. Pigs and other farmed animals
are treated viciously by slaughterhouse workers if they react with
fear and attempt retreat as they head toward their demise. Horses
are whipped if they do not run fast enough during races. There
are also more common ways human beings meddle with animal
behaviors seen as unnatural: declawing cats, cutting dogs' vocal
cords, shedding prevention treatments, and using shock collars as
training devices.

Questions of nature, and the dangers of doing the "unnatural," similarly arise amongst those hostile to veganism. A common
declaration by defensive omnivores, who often erroneously think
themselves to be carnivores, is it is natural for humans, as animals,
to eat other animals. Law professor and animal advocate Sherry
Colb explains this familiar argument from nature quite well:

> Given what we observe about them, it is plainly natural for
> lions, tigers, and bears to kill and swallow the flesh of other
> animals. If we cannot condemn anyone for doing what
> comes naturally, then it would be inappropriate for us to ac-
> cuse lions of immorality for consuming other animals. Thus,
> according to the reductio argument from lion behavior,
> because we and lions are both animals, it ought to follow
> that we cannot condemn the human consumption of animal
> products either.

This argument is not without logic, but I have never heard it
sufficiently followed by acknowledgement of other nonhuman
behaviors that many cultures deem immoral, such as rape, infanticide, and xenophobia (Colb). (These are all actions religions have
and still do sanction.) Further, such arguments neglect to consider
the differences between killing for survival and raising other spe-

cies for the purpose of exploiting, slaughtering, and eating them when other food options abound. There are also biological differences between those animals who can eat other animals and those for whom it is a necessity, but that is far afield from my purposes here. Rather, my endeavor is to expose the argument from nature as a distraction from the human ability to think critically about and advance systems of ethics and morality. Appeals to nature and tradition are often entangled with the divine appeal, and these errors in reasoning have been normalized to justify racism, sexism, speciesism, and other social ills for millennia.

My main focus within this feminist argument for atheism and its relation to nonhuman animal oppression has been on patriarchal monotheistic religions. Thus, I must also recognize older religious traditions with female and androgynous deities. In Buddhism, for example, Kuan Yin is a bodhisattva with both male and female traits representing balance and harmony. Shaktism is a branch of Hinduism whose devotees worship Devi as the Divine Mother who has no male overseer. There are also those who practice goddess worship of deities such as Venus, Ishtar, and Gaia, or who venerate Nature as a female conception. The worship of other-than-human animals, known as zoolatry, has also existed throughout history.[61] There are Japanese and Finnish traditions of bear gods and goddesses. Cows are sacred, although not necessarily worshipped, in Hinduism and Zoroastrianism. Ancient Egyptians famously idolized cats and developed cat cults with feline deities. However, these past and current positive valuations of women and other-than-human animals from religious and spiritual perspectives have done very little to promote liberation in lived reality. Indeed, as far back as the fourth millennium B.C.E., nearly all civilizations, although formed independently, would develop "new forms of inequality between men and women" and "deepen patriarchy" (Stearns 10). Just because there have been women in power does not mean women have power; just because some

---

61. Zoolatry can also include animal sacrifice.

species of animal have been revered does not mean nonhumans are treated with reverence.[62]

In "Feminism and Atheism," Overall addresses the issue of female and hermaphroditic gods by avowing that "the convenience and greater moral acceptability of a nonsexist divinity" still does nothing to prove the existence of a higher power. Moreover, she argues that the cult of the Goddess reinforces essentialism by "proposing a feminine God, an androgynous God, or a Goddess [who] retains an overgeneralized gender dualism, with all of its dubious implications for human interactions." Imagining a divine being who captures the essence of each gender ignores the wide range of ways one can express gender identity and, in the end, reinforces concepts of what it means to be male or female, ignoring those identities falling somewhere in between or outside of the normative dualism. But perhaps most importantly, Overall observes that "feminist objections to feminist reinterpretations of God are concerned with the role of hierarchy and power within any religious system." The presence of a God, god(s), or goddess(es), whether anthropomorphic or zoomorphic, cannot be extricated from hierarchy and differential power relations, those very things that lead to so much suffering in the world.

Feminist author Wendy McElroy, although an atheist, would argue with some of the contentions within feminist arguments for atheism. Even though she sees issues like abortion as creating tension between religion and feminism, she does not see the viewpoints as having a "natural schism" (28). McElroy even goes so far as to argue "the marginalization of religion by the dominant form of feminism over the past decades has been negative for the movement [. . .]. [I]t distorts feminist history, especially the rise of feminism within the United States" (29). Many of the early slavery abolitionists and suffragists in US history, even Elizabeth Cady Stanton cited above, were believers in the divine, albeit critical of man's untoward use of religion to justify oppression.

---

62. Similarly, from a racial standpoint, just because the United States has a black president does not mean we live in a post-racial country.

However, to use McElroy's words against her own argument, she notes how female abolitionists, even religious ones, objected to "slavery on the grounds that every man (sic) was a self-owner, every human being had a moral jurisdiction over his or her own body" (McElroy 29). What is intrinsically religious about that perspective, especially considering pro-slavery elements of the Bible? Adding the divine to that statement negates the notions of self-ownership and "moral jurisdiction" over one's body, for with God as creator, we owe him something, be it fealty, our souls, or the myriad other things he demands within the Bible.

Any arguments against oppression and violence offered by religious advocates—whether they be for humans, nonhumans, or even the environment—can be made without mention of divine beings. Any arguments made by slavery abolitionists, suffragists, and civil rights leaders that include appeals to God's will can be just as powerful and meaningful if the divine is omitted from the rhetoric. Just because positive social change has occurred due to the hearts and minds of religious activists does not mean there is a divine force at play or that the same spirit of progress cannot exist without religious belief. One of the most powerful and famous speeches in history is inarguably Martin Luther King Jr.'s "I Have a Dream." God is only referenced four times therein, and although Reverend King was a devout Christian man, the power of his words does not lie in his four references to God, but on potent metaphors of the "promissory note" and the "insufficient funds in the great vaults of opportunity of this nation" and his passion to end injustice because he saw his people treated abominably long after slavery's presumable end.

Compassionate people the world over would agree with this statement: "Child sex slavery is unethical." But what if the statement read: "Child sex slavery is unethical because God is against it." Non-believers would not agree with the second portion of that statement and believers would be tasked with looking for proof in their texts and traditions that their gods abhor child abuse and slavery. Christians would be in an especially difficult position, as the Bible shows instances of God condoning slavery and the abuse of children. My point here is that the divine is not necessary—and often counterproductive—when seeking the end of oppression and hierarchy because the divine is part of the problem to begin with. Why not remove the middlemen (God and religion) and oppose unjust acts because they are so evidently harmful? We know child sex slavery is wrong because of observations of the world leading to the conclusion that every being should be a self-owner and choose what happens to their bodies. Ethics can be as simple as that with no need for God muddying the waters.

Returning to the animal question, and more importantly, the animal *condition*, there is even less need for claims of God's will. Religion was created and is recreated by human beings, so other species are not on the religious agenda, barring those few animal-friendly passages, none of which speak of animals having ownership of their own bodies or inclusion in the moral community. As explored throughout this book, injunctions against using animals for certain purposes do exist in some religious traditions, but virtually always with a focus on how humans can ultimately benefit. Thus, by way of concluding, I speak directly to any readers who do not accept the premise of *Animal Liberation and Atheism: Dismantling the Procrustean Bed*. I start by addressing my presumed audiences, but I hope these final words contain meaning for anyone who happens upon this book.

Parting Messages and Conclusions

To the religious reader, with focus on animal advocates: It is time to give up your place atop Earth's hierarchy. Cease imagining your religion lends itself to true parity for animals. Your god is not vegan, and if animals were of great concern to him/her/it, they would have garnered much more attention in your holy books, rituals, and traditions. Religion is innately anthropocentric, hierarchical, and speciesist, none of which bode well for nonhumans. You are not special to some anthropocentrized divine being, neither are other species, but that is not cause to treat either yourself or others with disdain. This is good news because it means you and others of your species are not superior to other-than-human animals. We are all creatures living on a planet with very little idea of how we got here. Yes, we have different traits and abilities, all of which should be respected, even admired. One of your capabilities is moral agency. This means you can make choices that do not cause needless suffering. Everyone does not have that choice, including our ancestors (possibly) and some humans living today. That is of no import to the choices you can make in terms of food, clothing, entertainment, and other modes of consumption. Please take serious note of the destruction caused by religion, especially regarding animals, who are harmed more than any other oppressed human group. Stop looking to the stars for answers and focus on actualities. See the suffering of animals, but also their beauty, and think about what you can do to end that suffering besides making pleas to a God who, even if he did exist as other humans have constructed him, does not care a whit about nonhumans.

To the freethinking reader, with focus on social justice activists: If you are anything like me, when you gave up God you awakened to all of the injustices created by religion and permitted by passages from supposedly hallowed texts. You are frustrated by bans on gay marriage—or perhaps the very tradition of marriage—because it clearly arises from religion's stronghold on the state. You have acknowledged the role religion has played and continues to play in the subjugation of and violence against certain groups of people, especially women, people of color, and the non-heteronormative. You likely believe human beings created deities and religion, so injustices that manifest in the name of god(s) really exist because of *human* actions, inaction, needs, and desires. However, you also know that although religion is a myth, it has a very real power to exponentially ramp up human proclivities toward sexism, racism, heterosexism, xenophobia, child abuse, rape, murder, and mutilation. Conceding all of these points, do you not also see the affect religion has had on your view of other species? Why has religion been wrong about nearly everything else except how humans are to treat animals? Please consider the answer I propose in the second chapter, which is that you may have given up God, but you have not foregone the domineering, hierarchical essence of religion. Just as you believe the appeal to divine will is a logical fallacy, think about the fallacies commonly used to justify continued animal exploitation. Human beings have always used animals for a variety of practical purposes; this is the appeal to tradition, arguing that since something is a common or longstanding practice, it must be correct. Some respected nutritionists say human beings should eat meat and animal byproducts for optimal health; this is a version of the argument from authority, suggesting that the opinions of a few notable individuals equal de facto consensus. You have already questioned the very existence of God, so now question the (mostly financial) reasons meat- and dairy-heavy diets are promoted, especially in the US. You are capable of rejecting cultural norms as ancient as religion itself. Please use that capability to now question your unspoken assumption that other sentient species are yours to eat, hunt, rape, wear, confine, crush, slaughter, poke, prod, dissect, vivisect, electrocute, addict, and maim. Hopefully, you will then integrate nonhumans into a more holistic vision of social progress and justice.

It is not easy to deviate from the norm, especially when said deviation includes calling out long-held beliefs, some of which determine an individual or group's identity. Further, it is difficult to muddle these traditions when they have served humans well in some ways and continue to serve us well within specific contexts. Our species may not have survived without access to meat. Some Homo sapiens still eat meat for basic survival; unless they move to a different geographical location, they could starve to death without hunting for food. We may not have found cures for diseases such as polio if not for animal research; however, animal testing and research have also failed humans, sometimes leading to death. Thankfully, we have arrived at a time in history where many can live healthily on a plant-based diet, and there are alternatives to animal testing such as computer modeling and human cell and tissue tests. And from an ethical perspective, we have reached a point where it is not seen as totally incongruous to consider that the means (animal suffering) do not justify the ends (prolonged human life).

Religion, when not wreaking havoc, brings solace and peace to some in times of stress or simply in everyday life. Religions of the world have offered great splendor through their literature, art, and architecture.[63] On the other hand, our ability to create masterful works of art surely exist without God and religion. Diego Rivera's murals, Zora Neal Hurston's novels, and Oscar Niemeyer's buildings are proof of that. But I must reiterate that as it is humans who created religion, we have the ability to find within ourselves all of the positive things we believe come from outside forces. And again from an ethical perspective, we have reached a point where it is not seen as totally incongruous to consider that the means (religion) do not justify the ends (holy wars, genocide, infanticide, sexual abuse, misogyny, sexism, racism, ableism, speciesism, *ad infinitum*).

Nonhuman animal species are the mostly unacknowledged victims of human supremacy, as bolstered by religion. The extent to which humans continue not to see other species is proof of how much their exploitation and slaughter have been standardized, falling under fallacious appeals to tradition, the "circle of life," the food chain argument, and God, along with absurd assertions that animals are saved within the prisons humans have built for them such as zoos, circuses, and farms. From a Western perspective, the truths arising from speciesism are especially grisly to consider. Billions upon billions of sentient species are imprisoned and slaughtered because Homo sapiens like the way they taste. As omnivores, humans can live without meat, but they choose not to for the most base, selfish reason of preference. Yet even the billions and billions mentioned does not factor in species suffering on fur farms, in laboratories, in people's backyards, and in "entertainment" venues such a horse races, circuses, dog fights, cock fights, and even brothels and pornography. None of these human contrivances have anything to do with the "circle of life" or the food chain. Rather, they are the end game of human mastery from a species unbound and unchecked.

---

63. I turn to Buddhist literature at times because I believe it speaks so well to the human condition.

All of these acts of violence are happening right now, and although there are individuals and organizations calling for cessation of these atrocities, religious institutions remain virtually silent on the issues, barring those few voices attempting to refashion their speciesist belief systems into something worth saving. But no matter how hard they look or how creative they get with their chosen religious texts and traditions, the god(s) and their most powerful henchmen remain silent about the suffering of nonhumans, unless and until it impacts humans in a direct or indirect way. Up to now, deliberate and unapologetic atheist responses to this dilemma have been scant, but if it is true, as I believe, that a secular system of ethics holds the most promise for a less sadistic world, those ethics must include consideration of other species. Otherwise, we maintain the worst elements of religion—hierarchy, us/them dualisms, sanctioned rape and murder—that we claim to disavow as non-believers.

It is not pleasant to see our own culpability in maintaining brutal cultural norms, but it is morally imperative that we look at those grotesque realities, that we interrupt our mental narratives of happy animals living naturally within the enclosures humans have built for them. Within the project of animal liberation, which is also human liberation from the perception of our own supremacy, secularists have an advantage over believers, for we don't have to fit our ethics into a Procrustean bed that ultimately contradicts our hopes and our struggles for a kinder world. What we do have are ourselves and each other to pull at the fingers of religion's stranglehold on morality and ethics. We have unlimited avenues for conceiving of and strategizing for a world without gods, including the gods into which we have made ourselves.

Afterword

Scott Hurley

Religion, especially in the nineteenth, twentieth, and twenty-first centuries, has inspired (and continues to inspire) a wide range of responses to difficult social justice issues. We know, for example, that some Christian denominations were very active in the Civil Rights Movement (1954–68)—we only have to think of Martin Luther King, Jr. to acknowledge the significance of the black church in inspiring protest, direct action, and legal challenges to laws, practices, and institutions that supported and encouraged racism and prejudice, or remember the efforts of Quakers who have always opposed war and advocated for peace during times of conflict. When looking at non-Western traditions, we find a movement called socially engaged Buddhism—a twentieth century development spearheaded by religious figures like Thich Nhat Hanh (a Zen Buddhist teacher and founder of Plum Village), Master Cheng Yen (a Taiwanese Buddhist nun and founder of the Buddhist Compassion Relief Tzu Chi Foundation), and the Dalai Lama (the spiritual leader of Tibetan Buddhism)—that directly addresses social, political, and economic suffering caused by war, exploitation, and environmental degradation. Even in the animal rights movement we see religious thinkers taking a stand against animal abuse and oppression, advocating instead for vegan diets and direct action on behalf of animals being tortured, imprisoned, and murdered. Here I'm thinking of the theologian Andrew Linzey who wrote, among other things, *Animal Theology* (1995);

and of Buddhism-inspired animal activist Norm Phelps, author of *The Great Compassion: Buddhism and Animal Rights* (2004); or such scholar activists as Anthony J. Nocella II and Lisa Kemmerer, editors of *Call to Compassion: Religious Perspectives on Animal Advocacy* (2011). Moreover, we find within the churches and temples of various traditions practices that attempt to recognize the importance of nonhuman animals: the "Blessing of the Animals" ritual found in Catholic and Lutheran traditions or the "Releasing of Life" ceremony (the purchasing and releasing of animals being sold for food and entertainment) in Tibetan and Chinese Buddhist institutions are examples.

Unfortunately, we also know that religions of all kinds have been actively involved in the exploitation of both human and nonhumans for centuries. In the 1960s, there were just as many if not more Christian churches advocating segregation and white superiority as were racial and ethnic equality; Buddhist institutions supporting the Japanese war effort in China, most infamously remembered for the "Rape of Nanjing" (1937), were numerous; and the rape and murder of Hindu and Muslim women and children during the Partition of the Indian subcontinent into India and Pakistan (1947) have been thoroughly documented. Moreover, as Professor Socha has amply noted here, institutional religions have not been friendly to nonhuman animals. In some cases, this has come in the form of unapologetic support for the abuse of nonhuman animals by using scripture to justify the killing and eating of them; in other cases, these traditions have tacitly reinforced exploitation by privileging humans in their soteriological goals—only humans can have a personal relationship with Christ, only humans can attain enlightenment. This is true even of what some might consider the most animal friendly traditions like Jainism and Buddhism—traditions that emphasize compassion for all sentient beings and for the most part advocate vegetarianism.

How do we account for these disparate interpretations (uses) of religious traditions and their various texts, rituals, practices, and ideologies? On the one hand, we can recognize the fluidity of religious scriptural traditions—seeing new interpretations arise in the face of new questions being asked. Until recently, most religions have not had to answer questions about human-nonhuman animal relations or ethical treatment of animals, at least not those that are informed by scholarly studies on animal consciousness, fair play, or nonhuman animal social interactions. Furthermore, they have not had to address social, political, economic, and environmental circumstances that bring the ethical treatment of animals into the foreground; that is, for instance, they haven't had to function in a world facing environmental destruction to the degree that we are now in the twenty-first century. Nor have they had to respond to the kind of animal suffering experienced in Concentrated Animal Feeding Operations or research laboratories. So the recent interpretations that address human-nonhuman animal relations are efforts by religious thinkers to make their traditions relevant to these problems. After all, this is what theology is—the study of how God or ultimate truth relates to the universe. The ethical life is central to this pursuit.

But some questions arise. Are religious texts, ideas, "truths," and practices really relevant to animal rights issues? Are they able to contribute meaningfully to efforts to end nonhuman animal exploitation? Is there a point when we just throw up our hands and say "Enough. There is nothing of value here anymore that can adequately address the kind of suffering experienced by both human and nonhumans in our world today?" When do we say that religion has had its day and now we need to turn to something else? These are the kinds of questions that this book is asking and answering in its efforts to demonstrate how religion has not only failed to overcome injustice, but has contributed to it (and continues to contribute to it), supporting a status quo that perpetuates nonhuman animal oppression. Under such conditions, theological interpretations and reinterpretations that advocate more positive understandings of and actions toward nonhuman animals feel more like mental gymnastics—forcing outdated values and ethics on contemporary issues; hence, we have the Procrustean bed metaphor that serves as the foundation of this book. In Socha's estimation, religion is at best impotent when it comes to providing solutions to human and nonhuman animal exploitation and at worst supportive of a worldview that justifies animal cruelty, suffering, and oppression. However one wishes to answer the above questions, Socha's work is a much needed critique of and challenge to religious traditions and their ethical systems. She has thrown down the gauntlet. I wonder if it is too heavy to be picked up.

Bibliography

Acampora, Ralph R. *Corporal Compassion: Animal Ethics and Philosophy of Body*. Pittsburgh: U of Pittsburgh P, 2006. Print.

Adams, Carol J., Ed. *Ecofeminism and the Sacred*. New York: Continuum, 1993. Print.

Adams, Carol J. "Introduction." *Ecofeminism and the Sacred*. Adams 19–9. Print.

_____. *Sexual Politics of Meat, The: A Feminist-Vegetarian Critical Theory*. New York: Continuum, 1990. Print.

Adams, Carol J., and Josephine Donovan, Eds. *The Feminist Care Tradition in Animal Ethics*. New York: Columbia UP, 2007. Print.

Adams, Carol J., and Margorie Procter-Smith. "Taking Life or 'Taking on Life?'" *Ecofeminism and the Sacred*. Adams 295–310. Print.

Ahmed, Leila. "The Veil Debate Again." *Feminist Theory Reader: Local and Global Perspectives*. McCann and Kim 306–316. Print.

Akers, Keith. *The Lost Religion of Jesus Christ: Simple Living and Nonviolence in Early Christianity*. New York: Lantern, 2000. Print.

Ali, Ayaan Hirsi. *Infidel*. New York: Simon and Schuster, 2008. Print.

"Americans Love the Bible but Don't Read It Much, Poll Shows." *Huff Post: Religion*. HuffingtonPost.com, 4 Apr. 2013. Web. 25 Aug. 2013.

"Animal Experiments: Overview." *Peta.org*. People for the Ethical Treatment of Animals, n.d. Web. 15 Aug. 2013.

Animal Liberation Victoria. "Fish: 99+ Million Tons Killed Each Year." *All-creatures.org*, n.d. Web. 11 July 2013.

Animal Rights Coalition. "Our Mission and Core Values." *Animalrightscoalition.com*, n.d. Web. 27 Apr. 2012.

Angier, Natalie. "Pigs Proven to Be Smart, If Not Vain." *The New York Times*. The New York Times Company, 9 Nov. 2009. Web. 17 July 2013.

Anton, Leonora LaPeter. "A Native American Protests When White People Dress, or Play American Indians." *Tampa Bay Times*. Tampa Bay Times, 15 June 2012. Web. 28 July 2013.

Aquinas, Thomas. *The Summa Theologica of St. Thomas Aquinas*. 1265–74. Trans. Fathers of the English Dominican Province. 2nd ed. *New Advent*, Online Edition, 2008, Kevin Wright. Web. 4 Apr. 2013.

Atheist Community of Austin. "Atheism, Animal Rights, and Ethical Veganism (1/2)." *YouTube*. YouTube, 21 Dec. 2008. Web. 8 Mar. 2013.

_____. "Atheism, Animal Rights, and Ethical Veganism (2/2)." *YouTube*. YouTube, 21 Dec. 2008. Web. 8 Mar. 2013.

Austin-Broos, Diane. "The Anthropology of Conversion: An Introduction." *The Anthropology of Religious Conversion*. Buckser and Glazier 1–12. Print.

Avalos, Hector. *Fighting Words: The Origins of Religious Violence*. Amherst, NY: Prometheus, 2005. Print.

Bailey, Cathryn. "On the Backs of Animals: The Valorization of Reason in Contemporary Animal Ethics." *Feminist Care Tradition*. Adams and Donovan 344–359. Print.

Bailey, Edward I. *Implicit Religion in Contemporary Society*. GA Kampen, The Netherlands: Kok Pharos Publishing House, 1997. Print.

Bailey, Ronald. "Why Do So Many Believers Think Atheists Are Worse Than Rapists?" *Reason.com*. Reason Foundation, 27 Mar. 2012. Web. 23 Jan. 2014.

Balcombe, Jonathan. *Second Nature: The Inner Lives of Animals*. New York: Macmillan, 2010. eBook.

_____. *Pleasurable Kingdom: Animals and the Nature of Feeling Good*. New York: Palgrave Macmillan, 2006. Print.

Barad, Judith. "Catholic Exemplars: Recent Popes, Medieval Saints, and Animal Liberation." *Call to Compassion*. Kemmerer and Nocella 127–136. Print.

Beit-Hallahmi. "Atheists: A Psychological Profile." *The Cambridge Companion to Atheism*. Martin. eBook.

Bekoff, Marc. "Animals Are Conscious and Should Be Treated as Such." *New Scientist: Opinion*. Reed Business Information Ltd., 26 Sept. 2012. Web. 2 Aug. 2013.

Bernstein, Mark. "Contractualism and Animals." *Philosophical Studies: An International Journal for Philosophy in the Analytic Tradition* 86.1 (1997): 49–72. Print.

Blake, Lillie Devereux. "Woman in Paganism and Christianity." *Women without Superstition*. Gaylor 246–251. Print.

Bookchin, Murray. *Social Ecology and Communalism*. Oakland, CA: AK Press, 2007. Print.

Buckser, Andrew, and Stephen D. Glazier, Eds. *The Anthropology of Religious Conversion*. New York: Rowman & Littlefield, 2003. Print.

_____. Preface. *The Anthropology of Religious Conversion*. Buckser and Glazier xi–xviii. Print.

Cabezón, José Ignacio, Ed. *Buddhism, Sexuality, and Gender*. Albany, NY: State U of New York P, 1992. Print.

Caputo, John D. "Atheism, A/theology, and the Postmodern Condition." *The Cambridge Companion to Atheism*. Martin. eBook.

Carus, Felicity. "UN Urges Global Move to Meat and Dairy-free Diet." *Theguardian.com*. Guardian News and Media Limited, 2 June 2010. Web. 22 Aug. 2013.

Catholic Church. *Catechism of the Catholic Church.* 2nd ed. New York: Random House, 2003. Print.

Cavalieri, Paola, and Peter Singer, Eds. *The Great Ape Project: Equality Beyond Humanity.* New York: St. Martins, 1993. Print.

Chapple, Christopher. "Inherent Value without Nostalgia: Animals and the Jaina Tradition." *A Communion of Subjects.* Waldau and Patton 241–249. Print.

Chomsky, Noam. Introduction. *Anarchism.* Guérin vii-xx. Print.

Christian Vegetarian Association. *Would Jesus Eat Meat Today?* Cleveland, OH: CVA, n.d. Print.

Christina, Greta. "Coming Out: How to Do It, How to Help Each Other Do It, and Why?" Minnesota Atheists & American Atheists Regional Conference. 10 Aug. 2013. Presentation.

Cleaver, Kathleen. "Interview: Kathleen Cleaver." *Frontline.* Public Broadcasting Service, n.d. Web. 24 Mar. 2014.

Clough, David L. *On Animals: Volume 1: Systematic Theology.* London: T & T Clark, 2012. Print.

Coetzee, J.M. Foreword. *Second Nature: The Inner Lives of Animals.* By Jonathan Balcombe. New York: Macmillan, 2010. eBook.

Colb, Sherry. "Two Arguments for Eating Animals: It's Natural and Animals Do It." *Free from Harm.* 25 July 2013. Web. 29 Mar. 2014.

Cox, Christopher. *Nietzsche: Naturalism and Interpretation.* Berkeley, CA: U of California P, 1999. Print.

Craig, Winston J., Ann Reed Mangels, and the American Dietetic Association. "Position of the American Dietetic Association: Vegetarian Diets." *Journal of the American Dietetic Association* 109.7 (2009): 1266–82. Print.

Cunningham, Scott. *Wicca: A Guide for the Solitary Practitioner.* Woodbury, MN: Llewellyn Worldwide, 2010. eBook.

Darwin, Charles. *The Descent of Man.* 2nd ed. 1874. *Guttenberg.org.* Project Guttenberg, Aug. 2000. Web. 16 June 2011.

Davis, Kara, and Wendy Lee, Eds. *Defiant Daughters: 21 Women on Art, Activism, Animals, and* The Sexual Politics of Meat. New York: Lantern Books, 2013. Print.

Dawkins, Richard. "Gaps in the Mind." *The Great Ape Project.* Cavalieri and Singer 81–87.

_____. *God Delusion, The.* New York: Houghton Mifflin, 2008. Print.

_____. "Peter Singer—The Genius of Darwin: The Uncut Interviews with Richard Dawkins." *YouTube.* YouTube, 17 Jan. 2013. Web. 2 Aug. 2013.

_____. "Richard Dawkins—Science and the New Atheism." Interview with D.J. Grothe. *Pointofinquiry.org.* Center for Inquiry, 7 Dec. 2007. Web. 18 Aug. 2013. MP3.

_____. *River Out of Eden: A Darwinian View.* 1995. New York: Basic Books, 2008. Print.

Day, Vox. *The Irrational Atheists: Dissecting the Unholy Trinity of Dawkins, Harris, And Hitchens.* Dallas: BenBella, 2013.

De Cleyre, Voltairine. "The Case of Women Versus Orthodoxy." *Women without Superstition*. Gaylor 364–376. Print.

_____. "Crime and Punishment." *Women without Superstition*. Gaylor 376–378. Print.

_____. "Sex Slavery." *Women without Superstition*. Gaylor 362–364. Print.

Dennett, Daniel C. *Breaking the Spell: Religion as a Natural Phenomenon*. New York: Penguin, 2006. Print.

Dominick, Brian A. "Animal Liberation and Social Revolution." 3rd Ed. Syracuse, NY: Critical Mess Media, 1997. Print.

Douglass, Frederick. *The Narrative of the Life of Frederick Douglass*. Madison, WI: Cricket House Books. eBook.

Drum, Kevin. "Secular Ethics Are Doing Just Fine, Thank You Very Much." *Mother Jones*. Mother Jones and the Foundation for National Progress, 22 Dec. 2013. Web. 4 Mar. 2014.

D'Silva, Joyce. "Introduction." *Animals, Ethics, and Trade*. D'Silva and Turner xxi-xxvi. Print.

D'Silva, Joyce, and Jacky Turner, Eds. *Animals, Ethics, and Trade: The Challenge of Animal Sentience*. New York: Routledge, 2012. Print.

DuBois, W.E.B. "The Color Line and the Church." *DuBois on Religion*. Zuckerman 169–171. Print.

Dunayer, Joan. *Speciesism*. Derwood, MD: Ryce, 2004. Print.

Durkheim, Émile. 1912. *The Elementary Forms of Religious Life*. Oxford: Oxford UP, 2001. Print.

Eisler, Riane. *The Chalice and the Blade: Our History, Our Future*. New York: HarperCollins, 2011. Print.

Elise, Travis. "Anti-Capitalism and Abolitionist." *Confronting Animal Exploitation*. Socha and Blum 22–43. Print.

Epstein, Greg. *Good Without God: What a Billion Nonreligious People Do Believe*. New York: HarperCollins, 2010. Print.

Fanon, Frantz. 1963. *The Wretched of the Earth*. Trans. Richard Philcox. New York: Grove Press, 2004. Print.

Federal Bureau of Investigation. "Crime in the United States." *Federal Bureau of Investigation*. U.S. Department of Justice, 2010. Web. 24 Nov. 2013.

fonza, annalise. "Black Women, Atheist Activism, And Human Rights Black Women, Atheist Activism, And Human Rights: Why We Just Cannot Seem To Keep It To Ourselves!" *Cross Currents* 63.2 (2013): 185–197. Print.

Food, Inc. Dir. Robert Kenner. Perf. Eric Schlosser, Richard Lobb, and Vince Edwards. Magnolia Pictures, 2008. Film.

Foer, Jonathan Safran. *Eating Animals*. New York: Back Bay Books, Print.

Francione, Gary. "Ahimsa and Veganism." *Jain Digest* 28.1 (2009): 9–10. *Animal Rights: The Abolitionist Approach*. Blog, Web. 24 Nov. 2013. PDF.

_____. "Jainism's Greatest Gift—Ahimsa." *Faith in Memphis*. Blog, 16 Apr. 2011. Web. 25 Nov. 2013.

_____. "New Atheism, Moral Realism, and Animal Rights: Some Preliminary Reflections." *Animal Rights: The Abolitionist Approach.* Blog, 15 Apr. 2012. Web. 8 Mar. 2013.

_____. "Six Principles of the Abolitionist Approach to Animal Rights, The." *Animal Rights.* Blog, n.d. Web. 27 Oct. 2013.

Freedman, Rory, and Kim Barnouin. *Skinny Bitch.* Philadelphia: Running Press, 2005. Print.

Friend, Tim. *Animal Talk: Breaking the Code of Animal Language.* New York: Simon and Schuster, 2005. Print.

Gaard, Greta, Ed. *Ecofeminism: Women, Animals, Nature.* Philadelphia, Temple UP, 2010. Print.

Gaard, Greta. "Living Interconnections with Animals and Nature." *Ecofeminism.* Gaard 1–12. Print.

Gabriel, Kara I., Brook H. Rutledge, and Cynthia L. Barkley. "Attitudes on Animal Research Predict Acceptance of Genetic Modification Technologies by University Undergraduates." *Society and Animals* 20.4 (2012): 381–400. Print.

Gasque, Thomas J. "The Power of Naming." *University of South Dakota: College of Arts and Sciences.* University of South Dakota Harrington Lecture Series, n.d. Web. 17 July 2013. PDF.

Gaylor, Annie Laurie, Ed. *Women without Superstition: No Gods, No Masters.* Madison, WI: Freedom from Religion Foundation, 1997. Print.

_____. "Introduction." *Women without Superstition.* Gaylor 1–14. Print.

_____. "Mary Wollstonecraft: Revolutionary for Womankind." *Women without Superstition.* Gaylor 17–19. Print.

Gaziano, Joe, and Jacquie Lewis. "All Beings Are Equal but Some Are More Equal Than Others: Buddhism and Vegetarianism in the U.S." *Western Buddhist Review* 6 (2013): 58–77. PDF.

Geertz, Clifford. "Religion as a Cultural System." *Theories of Religions.* Kunin and Miles-Watson 207–228. Print.

Gervais, William M., Azim F. Sharif, Ara Norenzayan. "Do You Believe in Atheists? Distrust Is Central to Anti-Atheist Prejudice." *Journal of Personality and Social Psychology* (unedited proof of manuscript). University of British Colombia, n.d. Web. 23 Jan. 2014. PDF.

Goldman, Emma. "The Failure of Christianity." *Women without Superstition.* Gaylor 384–390. Print.

Graf, Fritz. *Greek Mythology: An Introduction.* Baltimore, MD: JHU Press, 1996. Print.

Guérin, Daniel. *Anarchism.* New York: Monthly Review Press, 1970. Print.

Guérin, Daniel. Foreword. *No Gods, No Masters.* Guérin 1–3. Print.

Guérin, Daniel, Ed. *No Gods, No Masters: An Anthology of Anarchism.* Trans. Paul Sharkey. Oakland, CA: AK Press, 2005. Print.

Guither, Harold D. *Animal Rights: History and Scope of a Radical Social Movement.* Carbondale, IL: SIU Press, 1998. Print.

Halweil, Brian. "Meat Production Continues to Rise." *Vital Signs Online.* Worldwatch Institute, 20 Aug. 2008. Web. 14 Dec. 2013.

Hamad, Ruby. "Halal." *Defiant Daughters*. Davis and Lee 3–17. Print.

Handwerk, Brian. "Shark Facts: Attack Stats, Record Swims, More." *National Geographic News*. National Geographic Society, 13 June 2005. Web. 3 Nov. 2013.

Harris, Angela P. "Should People of Color Support Animal Rights?" *Journal of Animal Law* 5 (2009): 15–32. Print.

Harris, Sam. *The Moral Landscape: How Science Can Determine Human Values*. New York: Simon and Schuster, 2011. Print.

Herzog, Harold A. "'The Movement Is My Life': The Psychology of Animal Rights Activism." *Journal of Social Issues* 49.1 (1993): 103–119. Print.

Hitchens, Christopher. "Cartoon Debate: The Case for Mocking Religion." *Slate.com*. The Slate Group, 4 Feb. 2006. Web. 1 Sept. 2013.

———. *Got Is Not Great: How Religion Poisons Everything*. New York: Random House, 2008. Print.

———. *Portable Atheist, The: Essential Readings for the Non-believer*. Philadelphia: De Capo Press, 2007. Print.

Hitler, Adolf. *Mein Kampf*. 1927. Trans. James Murphy. Scottsdale, AZ: Bottom of the Hill, 2010. Print.

———. *The Speeches of Adolf Hitler, April 1922–August 1939, Vol. 2*. Ed. and Trans. Norman H. Baynes. Oxford: Oxford UP, 1994. Print.

Holy Bible, The: New International Version. Biblica, 2011. *BibleGateway.com*. Web. 23 Apr. 2013.

Howard-Snyder, Daniel. "Introduction: The Evidential Argument from Evil." *The Evidential Argument from Evil*. Howard-Snyder xi-xx. Print.

Howard-Snyder, Daniel, Ed. *The Evidential Argument from Evil*. Bloomington, IN: Indiana UP, 1996. Print.

"How Many Roman Catholics Are There in the World?" *Bbc.co.uk*. British Broadcasting Corporation, 14 March 2013. Web. 3 Oct. 2013.

"How Many Sharks Are Actually Killed Each Year?" *Sharkproject.org*, n.d. Web. 3 Nov. 2013.

"How Often Does Sexual Assault Occur?" *RAINN: Rape, Abuse, & Incest National Network*. RAINN, n.d. Web. 24 Nov. 2013.

Hutchinson, Sikivu. *Godless Americana: Race and Religious Rebels*. Los Angeles: Infidel Books, 2013. Print.

Hyland, J.R. *The Slaughter of Terrified Beasts: A Biblical Basis for the Humane Treatment of Animals*. Sarasota, FL: Viatoris Ministries, 1998. Print.

Hyman, Gavin. "Atheism in Modern History." *The Cambridge Companion to Atheism*. Martin. eBook.

Ingersoll, Robert G. *The Best of Robert Ingersoll: Selections from His Writings and Speeches*. Ed. Roger E. Greeley. Amherst, NY: Prometheus, 1988. Print.

———. "Vivisection." 1890. *The Secular Web*, n.d. Web. 13 Aug. 2013.

"Is Sam Harris Vegan?" *Whyculturedmeat.org*. n.d. Web. 9 Sept. 2013.

"Is Richard Dawkins Vegan?" *Whyculturedmeat.org*. n.d. Web. 2 Oct. 2013.

Jamison, Wesley, V., Casper Wenk, and James Parker. "Every Sparrow That

Falls: Understanding Animal Rights Activism as Functional Religion." *Society and Animals* 8.3 (2000): 305–330. Print.

Jefferson, Thomas. 1902. *The Life and Morals of Jesus of Nazareth (The Jefferson Bible)*. *Sacredtexts.com*, n.d. Web. 11 July 2013.

Jenkins, Stephanie, and Vasile Stănescu. "One Struggle." *Defining Critical Animal Studies*. Nocella, Sorenson, Socha, and Matsuoka 74–85. Print.

Jensen, Robert. *Getting Off: Pornography and the End of Masculinity*. Brooklyn, NY: South End Press, 2007. Print.

Jesus Seminar, The. *The Five Gospels: What Did Jesus Really Say?* Trans. Robert W. Funk, Roy W. Hoover, and The Jesus Seminar. New York: Scribner, 1996. Print.

John Paul, II (Pope). "Address of John Paul II to Members of the Pontifical Academy of Sciences." *Vatican*. 23 Oct. 1982. Web. 4 June 2013.

Johnson, Rob. "Are Atheism and Veganism Related?" *The Abolitionist: Animal Rights Magazine*, 14 Feb. 2012. Web. 7 May 2013.

jones, pattrice. "Afterword: Flower Power." *Confronting Animal Exploitation*. Socha and Blum 263–280. Print.

Jørgensen, Johannes. *Saint Francis of Assisi: A Biography*. Trans. Thomas O'Conor Sloane. London: Longman, Greens, and Co., 1912. eBook.

Kant, Immanuel. "Duties to Animals." Kuhse and Singer 564–565.

Kaufman, Stephen R. *Guided by the Faith of Christ: Seeking to Stop Violence and Scapegoating*. Cleveland: Vegetarian Advocates Press, 2008. Print.

Kaufman, Stephen R., and Nathan Braun. *Good News for All Creatures: Vegetarianism as Christian Stewardship*. Cleveland: Vegetarian Advocates Press, 2004. Print.

Keith, Lierre. *The Vegetarian Myth: Food, Justice, and Sustainability*. Crescent City, CA: Flashpoint Press, 2009.

Kemmerer, Lisa. *Animals and World Religions*. New York: Oxford UP, 2012. Print.

Kemmerer, Lisa, Ed. *Speaking Up for Animals: An Anthology of Women's Voices*. Boulder, CO: Paradigm, 2012. Print.

Kemmerer, Lisa, and Anthony J. Nocella II, Eds. *Call to Compassion: Religious Perspectives on Animal Advocacy*. New York: Lantern Books. 2011. Print.

Keown, Damien. *A Dictionary of Buddhism*. Oxford, UK: Oxford UP, 2003. Print.

Kheel, Marti. "The Liberation of Nature: A Circular Affair." *The Feminist Care Tradition*. Adams and Donovan 39–57. Print.

King, Martin Luther. 1968. "I Have a Dream." *American Rhetoric: Top 100 Speeches*. American Rhetoric, n.d. Web. 4 Apr. 2014.

Komjathy, Louis. "Daoism: From Meat Avoidance to Compassion-Based Vegetarianism." *Call to Compassion*. Kemmerer and Nocella 83–103. Print.

Korsgaard, Christine M. "Facing the Animal You See in the Mirror." *The Harvard Review of Philosophy*. XVI (2009): 3–7. Print.

Kotz, Peter. "How Undercover Animal Rights Activists Are Winning the
    Ag-Gag War." *CityPages*. City Pages, 22 May 2013. Web. 2 June 2013.
Kunin, Seth Daniel, and Jonathan Miles-Watson. *Theories of Religion: A
    Reader*. New Brunswick, NJ: Rutgers UP, 2006. Print.
Kuhse, Helga and Peter Singer, Eds. *Bioethics: An Anthology*. Malden, MA:
    Wiley-Blackwell, 2006. Print.
Lackey, Michael. *African American Atheists and Political Liberation: A
    Study of the Sociocultural Dynamics of Faith*. Gainesville, FL: U Florida P,
    2008. Print.
Lankavatara Sutra, The: A Mahayana Text. Trans. Daisetz Teitaro Suzuki.
    Taipei: SMC Publishing, Inc., 1991. Print.
Laws, Charlotte. "The Jain Center of Southern California: Theory and
    Practice across Continents." *Call to Compassion*. Kemmerer and Nocella
    49–60. Print.
Lehto, Bill. Rev. of *The Moral Landscape: How Science Can Determine
    Human Values*. *The Fourth R* 24.2 (2011): 19. PDF.
Linzey, Andrew. *Creatures of the Same God: Explorations in Animal
    Theology*. New York: Lantern, 2009. Print.
_____. "Is Religion Bad for Animals?" *Huff Post: Religion*. HuffingtonPost.
    com, 27 July 2013. Web. 27 Oct. 2013.
Lovejoy, Arthur O. *The Great Chain of Being*. Cambridge, MA: Harvard
    UP, 1936. Print.
Low, Phillip. "The Cambridge Declaration on Consciousness." Eds. Jaak
    Panksepp, Diana Reiss, David Edelman, Bruno Van, Swinderen, Philip
    Low and Christof Koch. *Fcmconference.org*. 7 July 2012. Web. 18 Aug.
    2013.
MacKinnon, Catharine. "Of Mice and Men: A Fragment on Animal
    Rights." *The Feminist Care Tradition in Animal Ethics*. Adams and
    Donovan 316–332. Print.
Martin, Darnise C. *Beyond Christianity: African Americans in a New
    Thought Church*. New York: NYU P, 2005. Print.
Martin, Michael. "Atheism and Religion." *The Cambridge Companion to
    Atheism*. Martin. eBook.
Martin, Michael, Ed. *The Cambridge Companion to Atheism*. Oxford:
    Cambridge U P, 2006. eBook.
McCance, Dawne. *Critical Animal Studies: An Introduction*. Albany, NY:
    SUNY Press, 2013. Print.
McCann, Carole, and Seung-Kyung Kim. *Feminist Theory Reader: Local
    and Global Perspectives*. 3rd Ed. New York: Routledge, 2013. Print.
McElroy, Wendy. "Religion and American Feminism." *Society* 42.3 (2005):
    28–31. Print.
McFague, Sallie. "An Earthly Theological Agenda." *Ecofeminism and the
    Sacred*. Adams 84–98. Print.
McWilliams, James. "Archive for the 'Vegan Conversion Narratives'
    Category." James-McWilliams.com. 30 May 2012. Web. 19 Dec. 2013.
Mepham, Ben. "The Ethical Matrix as a Decision-making Tool, with
    Specific Reference to Animal Sentience." *Animals, Ethics, and Trade*.
    D'Silva and Turner 134–146. Print.

Mizelle, Brett. *Pig*. London: Reaktion Books, 2012. Print.

"Misogyny and Insults to Women." *The Skeptic's Annotated Bible*. The Skeptics Annotated Bible, n.d. Web. 27 Mar. 2014.

Moore, Heather. "The Fiercest Predators of the Sea." *Speaking Up for Animals*. Kemmerer 95–105. Print.

Morton, Timothy. *The Cambridge Companion to Shelley*. Cambridge, England: Cambridge UP, 2006. Print.

Moseley, Benjamin. *A Treatise on Tropical Diseases: On Military Operations; and on the Climate of the West-Indies*. 3rd ed. London: T. Caldwell, 1792. eBook.

Nasrin, Taslima. "On Islamic Fundamentalism." *Women without Superstition*. Gaylor 615–621. Print.

Nibert, David. Foreword. *Defining Critical Animal Studies: An Intersectional Social Justice Approach for Liberation*. Eds. Anthony J. Nocella II, John Sorenson, Kim Socha, and Atsuko Matsuoka. New York: Peter Lang, 2014. Print.

Nocella, Anthony J. II, John Sorenson, Kim Socha, and Atsuko Matsuoka, Eds. *Defining Critical Animal Studies: An Intersectional Social Justice Approach for Liberation*. New York: Peter Lang, 2014. Print.

NonviolenceUnited.org. "A Life Connected: VEGAN" Online video clip. *YouTube*. YouTube, n.d. Web. 6 Aug. 2013.

Nowatzki, Al. "Conversion Narrative in Veganism." *These Little Piggies Had Tofu*. Blog, 20 Sept. 2012. Web. 17 May 2013.

_____. "Religion and Vegan Advocacy." *These Little Piggies Had Tofu*. Blog, 7 Mar. 2012. Web. 17 May 2013.

_____. "Veganism and Woo." *These Little Piggies Had Tofu*. Blog, 14 Nov. 2012. Web. 17 May 2013.

_____. "Vegan Parenting: Navigating and Negating Speciesist Media." *Confronting Animal Exploitation*. Socha and Blum 89–111. Print.

Nozick, Robert. *Anarchy, State, and Utopia*. New York: Basic Books, 1974. Print.

Oduah, Chika, and Lauren E. Bohn. "Blacks, Mirroring Larger U.S. Trend, 'Come Out' as Non-believers." *The New York Times*. The New York Times Company, 25 May 2014. Web. 27 Mar. 2014.

Onfray, Michel. *Atheist Manifesto: The Case Against Christianity, Judaism, and Islam*. New York: Arcade Publishing, 2001. Print.

Oppenheimer, Mark. "Scholars Explore Christian Perspectives on Animal Rights." *The New York Times*. The New York Times Company, 6 Dec. 2013. Web. 13 Dec. 2013.

Overall, Christine. "Feminism and Atheism." *The Cambridge Companion to Atheism*. Martin. eBook.

Painter, Nell Irvin. *The History of White People*. New York: W.W. Norton, 2011. eBook.

Park, Jin. "The Visible and the Invisible: Rethinking Values and Justice from a Buddhist-Postmodern Perspective." Luther College Religion Forum. Decora, IA. 14 Mar. 2013. Presentation.

Patterson, Charles. *Eternal Treblinka: Our Treatment of Animals and the Holocaust*. New York: Lantern, 2002. Print.

Pedersen, Helena, and Vasile Stănescu. Introduction. *Women, Destruction, and the Avant-Garde*. Socha ix-xi. Print.

Pew Charitable Trusts, The. "The Global Religious Landscape." *Pewtrusts. org*. The Pew Charitable Trusts, 18 Dec. 2012. Web. 7 June 2013.

Phelps, Norm. *The Dominion of Love: Animal Rights According to the Bible*. New York: Lantern, 2002. Print.

"pink cloud." *Urban Dictionary*. Urban Dictionary, n.d. Web. 30 Jan. 2014.

Pluhar, Evelyn B. "Arguing Away Suffering: The Neo-Cartesian Revival." *Between the Species* 9.1 (1993): 27–41. Print.

Pollan, Michael. *The Omnivore's Dilemma: A Natural History of Four Meals*. New York: Penguin, 2006. Print.

Pollard, Stephen. "For Once, Richard Dawkins Is Lost for Words." *Telegraph.co.uk*. Telegraph Media Group Limited, 14 Feb. 2012. Web. 25 Aug. 2013.

Potter, Will. *Green is the New Red*. San Francisco: City Lights, 2011. Print.

"Procrustean bed." *The Free Online Dictionary*. Farlex, Inc., n.d. Web. 4 May 2013.

Quran, English Translation of the Message of The. Trans. Syed Vickar Ahmed. 3rd ed. Lombard, IL: Book of Signs Foundation, 2007. Print.

"Race and the Priesthood." *The Church of Jesus Christ of Latter-Day Saints*. The Church of Jesus Christ of Latter-Day Saints, n.d. Web. 18 Mar. 2014.

Rambo, Lewis R. "Anthropology and the Study of Conversion." *The Anthropology of Religious Conversion*. Buckser and Glazier 211–222. Print.

———. *Understanding Religious Conversion*. New Haven, CT: Yale UP, 1993. Print.

Regan, Tom. *Defending Animal Rights*. Urbana and Chicago: U of Illinois P, 2001. Print.

———. *The Case for Animal Rights*. Berkeley: U of California P, 2004. Print.

"Report: Number of Animals Killed in US Increases in 2010." *FARM.org*. Farm Animal Rights Movement, n.d. Web. 15 Aug. 2013.

Rising, Dallas. "Turning Our Heads: The 'See No Evil' Dilemma." *Confronting Animal Exploitation*. Socha and Blum 11–21. Print.

Rowlands, Mark. *Can Animals Be Moral?* New York: Oxford UP, 2012. Print.

———. "Contractarianism and Animal Rights." *Journal of Applied Philosophy* 14.3 (1997): 235–247. Print.

Russell, Bertrand. "Why I Am Not a Christian." 1927. *Why I Am Not a Christian and Other Essays on Religion and Related Subjects*. Ed. Paul Edwards. New York: Simon and Schuster, 1957. 3–23. Print.

Schweitzer, Albert. *The Animal World of Albert Schweitzer*. Ed. Charles R. Joy. Trans. Charles R. Joy. Hopewell, NJ: The Ecco Press, 1950. Print.

Sciberras, Colette. "Buddhism and Speciesism: On the Misapplication of

Western Concepts to Buddhist Beliefs." *Journal of Buddhist Ethics* 15 (2008): 214–240.

Scully, Matthew. *Dominion: The Power of Man, the Suffering of Animals, and the Call to Mercy.* New York: St. Martin's Press, 2002. Print.

Shah, Bharat S. *An Introduction to Jainism.* 2nd ed. New York: Setubandh Publications, 2002. Print.

Shamsi, Rashid. "Why Islam Forbids Pork?" *The Muslim World League Journal* (October 1999). Islamic-World.net, n.d. Web. 17 June 2013.

Sharma, Vidushi. "Knowing Ignorance." *Defiant Daughters.* Davis and Lee 157–166. Print.

Shelley, Percy Bysshe. 1813. "The Necessity of Atheism." *Secular Web.* Internet Infidels, n.d. Web. 3 Nov. 2013.

Shermer, Michael. "Confessions of a Speciesist." *Scientific American.* January 2014: 88. Print.

Singer, Peter. *Animal Liberation.* 3rd ed. New York: Ecco, 2002. Print.

_____. *How Are We to Live? Ethics in an Age of Self Interest.* Amherst, NY: Prometheus, 1995. Print.

Singer, Peter, and Jim Mason. *The Ethics of What We Eat: Why Our Food Choices Matter.* Emmaus, PA: Rodale, 2006. Print.

Socha, Kim. "'Dreaded Comparisons, The' and Speciesism: Leveling the Hierarchy of Suffering." Socha and Blum 223–240. Print.

_____. "Dumb Animals, Crazy Broads, and Ugly Truths: Rooting for the Avant-Garde." Diss. Indiana University of Pennsylvania, 2010. Print.

_____. "'Just tell the truth': A Polemic on the Value of Radical Activism." *Confronting Animal Exploitation.* Socha and Blum 44–65. Print.

_____. *Women, Destruction, and the Avant-Garde: A Paradigm for Animal Liberation.* Amsterdam: Rodopi, 2011. Print.

Socha, Kim, and Sarahjane Blum, Eds. *Confronting Animal Exploitation: Grassroots Essays on Liberation and Veganism.* Jefferson, NC: McFarland, 2013. Print.

Sponberg, Alan. "Attitudes toward Women and the Feminine in Early Buddhism." *Buddhism, Sexuality, and Gender.* Cabezón 3–36. Print.

Staff at ABS. "8 Black Celebrities Who Don't Believe in Jesus." *AtlantaBlackStar.com.* Atlanta BlackStar, 29 Aug. 2013. Web. 4 Apr. 2014.

Stănescu, James. "Toward a Dark Animal Studies: On Vegetarian Vampires, Beautiful Souls, and Becoming—Vegan." *Journal for Critical Animal Studies* 10.3 (2012): 26–50. PDF.

Stanton, Elizabeth Cady. "The Degraded Status of Women in the Bible." *Women without Superstition.* Gaylor 124–127. Print.

Stearns, Peter N. *Gender in World History.* New York: Routledge, 2006. Print.

Steinfeld, Henning, Pierre Gerber, Tom Wassenaar, Vincent Castel, Muaricio Rosales, and Cees de Haan. "Livestock's Long Shadow: Environmental Issues and Options." (Executive Summary) *Food and Agriculture Organization of the United Nations.* Animal Liberation Front, 2006. Web. 18 Mar. 2014.

Stenger, Victor J. *The New Atheism: Taking a Stand for Science and Reason.* Amherst, NY: Prometheus, 2009. Print.

Suicide Food. Blog, 27 Dec. 2011. Web. 17 Oct. 2013.

Sullivan, Andrew. "There's a New Power in America—Atheism." *The Sunday Times.* Times Newspapers Ltd., 15 Mar. 2009. Web. 26 June 2011.

Sullivan, Mariann. "The Church of Veganism." *Our Hen House.* Our Hen House, 7 Feb. 2013. Web. 26 May 2013.

Sylvan, Diane. "Wiccan Spirituality and Animal Advocacy: Perfect Love and Perfect Trust." *Call to Compassion.* Kemmerer and Nocella 225–232. Print.

"Tatanka: About Bison." *Tatanka: Story of the Bison.* n.d. Web. 28 July 2013.

Thurman, Robert. "Buddha's Wheel of Life." *npr.org.* National Public Radio, n.d. Web. 2 Nov. 2013.

Torpy, Jason. "Why Vegan Priorities Are Humanist Priorities." *Americanhumanist.org.* American Humanist Association, n.d. Web. 1 Sept. 2013.

Torres, Bob. *Making a Killing: The Political Economy of Animal Rights.* Oakland, CA: AK Press, 2007. Print.

Tuttle, Will. *The World Peace Diet: Eating for Spiritual Health and Social Harmony.* New York: Lantern, 2005. Print.

"Veganism, a Definition." *The Vegan Light Bulb.* 20 Apr. 2011. Web. 22 Aug. 2013.

Waldau, Paul. *The Specter of Speciesism: Buddhist and Christian Views of Animals.* Oxford: Oxford UP, 2003. Print.

Waldau, Paul, and Kimberly Christine Patton, Eds. *A Communion of Subjects: Animals in Religion, Science, and Ethics.* New York: Columbia UP, 2006. Print.

Watson, Donald. "Should the Vegetarian Movement Be Reformed?" *The Vegetarian* 1.2 (Spring 1948): 23–27. *The Vegetarian World Forum.* International Vegetarian Union, 6 Apr. 2010. Web. 18 May 2013.

Weber, Max. "Politics as Vocation." *From Max Weber: Essays in Sociology.* Eds. H.H. Gerth and C. Wright Mills. Trans. H.H. Gerth and C. Wright Mills. Abingdon: Routledge, 1991. 77–128. Print.

Weil, Kari. "A Report on the Animal Turn." *differences: A Journal of Feminist Cultural Studies* 21.2 (2010): 1–23. Print.

Weinberg, Steven. "A Designer Universe." *PhysLinks.com.* PhysLinks.com, n.d. Web. 23 Apr. 2013.

Wiesel, Elie. "The Perils of Indifference." 12 Apr 1999. *Americanrhetoric.com.* American Rhetoric, 2011. Web. 18 June 2011.

Wilson, Peter D. 1995. "Secular Ethics and Animal Rights." *Secular Web.* Internet Infidels, 1997. Web. 8 Mar. 2013.

"Wolves of the World." *International Wolf Center: Learn.* International Wolf Center, n.d. Web. 30 July 2013.

Yinger, Milton J. *The Scientific Study of Religion.* New York: Macmillan, 1970. Print.

Zuckerman, Phil, Ed. *DuBois on Religion.* New York: Rowman & Littlefield, 2000. Print.

Index

Acampora, Ralph R., 53, 94
Adams, Carol J., 27, 38, 50, 177
    n. 57
Ali, Ayaan Hirsi, 95 n. 37, 178–179
anarchism, 25, 54
anthropocentrism, definition of, 23
    n. 8
Aquinas, Thomas, 40–42, 51, 80

Bailey, Edward I., 155–156
Balcombe, Jonathan, 114–115
Barad, Judith, 41–42, 80
Bernstein, Mark, 148
Bible, 17–20, 30–31, 34–39,
    44–45, 47, 55–58, 74–75, 120,
    163, 179–180
Bookchin, Murray, 53, 57, 167
Buddha (see Buddhism)
Buddhism, 8–9, 24, 61–66, 180
    n. 58, 183, 191–192
Buddhist (see Buddhism)

Cambridge Declaration on
    Consciousness, 123
Catholicism, 8–9, 40–43, 46, 76,
    92 n. 35, 192
chickens, 14, 16, 58, 110–111, 127
Chomsky, Noam, 25–26
Christian (see Christianity)
Christian Vegetarian Association,
    43–44, 56–57
Christianity, 17–20, 23–24, 37–39,
    48–49, 81, 88, 90, 121, 130,
    146, 172–174

Christina, Greta, 26–27
Cleaver, Kathleen, 172
Clough, David I., 35–37, 57–58,
    76, 116–117
Coetzee, J.M., 114
conversion, 23–24, 142–143, 150–
    154, 161
critical animal studies, 149–150

Darwin, Charles, 9, 11–12, 99–100
Dawkins, Richard, 2, 33, 92–93,
    95–100, 105–106, 114,
    133–136
De Cleyre, Voltairine, 90, 137, 147,
    181–182
Dennett, Daniel, 3, 95, 114
Dominick, Brian, 165–166
Douglass, Frederick, 88
DuBouis, W.E.B., 172
Dunayer, Joan, 60, 89, 137
Durkheim, Émile, 2–3, 143

ecofeminism, 38, 50
Eisler, Riane, 49–50, 52
Elise, Travis, 117, 119
Epstein, Greg, 169

Fanon, Frantz, 171
fish, 30, 35–36, 43–44, 123
fonza, annalise, 37, 141, 160,
    175–177
Francione, Gary, 33, 67–69,
    115–119

Gaard, Greta, 50
Gaylor, Annie Laurie, 54, 95 n. 37,
    131, 176–177
Geertz, Clifford, 3, 143
Goldman, Emma, 24, 38, 90, 146,
    172
Great Chain of Being, 58 n. 19,
    121–123, 126

Hamad, Ruby, 48, 58–59
Harris, Sam, 101–113, 179
Herzog, Harold A., 32, 156
hierarchy, 49–60
Hindu (see Hinduism)
Hinduism, 23 n. 9, 60, 64–66,
    183, 192
Hitchens, Christopher, 10, 23, 76,
    100–101, 179
Hitler, Adolf, 91–92
Hutchinson, Sikivu, 111 n. 43, 116
Hyland, J.R., 19–37, 55, 77, 81

Indigenous traditions, 20, 23 n. 9,
    36, 44. n. 16, 61 n. 22, 71–73,
    81–82
Ingersoll, Robert G., 94–96, 103,
    169
Islam, 47–48, 58–59, 75 n. 27, 76,
    101, 159, 178–181, 192

Jain (see Jainism)
Jainism, 23 n. 9, 60–61, 66–71
Jensen, Robert, 51–53
Jesus Christ, 17–19, 30, 36, 43–46,
    48–49, 57, 81, 156, 180
Jewish (see Judaism)
John Paul II (Pope), 41–42
Johnson, Rob, 132
jones, pattrice, 21–22
Judaism, 55–56, 75, 91, 130

Kant, Immanuel, 168–169
Kaufman, Stephen R., 56, 163–164
Kemmerer, Lisa, 20, 31–32, 47 n.
    18, 55, 58, 63, 65–66, 71, 73,
    81–82, 192
Kheel, Marti, 122

King, Martin Luther, 172, 185,
    191
Korsgaard, Christine, 127, 168–169

Lackey, Michael, 27, 52, 92, 142,
    144, 147–149, 161, 170–171,
    173, 175
Lankavatara Sutra, The, 63–64
Laws, Charlotte, 69–70
liberation theology, 37, 39–40, 43,
    54, 77
Linzey, Andrew, 39, 41, 46, 65, 70,
    81, 118, 191

Mason, James, 7, 128
McFague, Sallie, 38, 54
McWilliams, James, 152–153
Muslim (see Islam)

Nasrin, Taslima, 149, 179
Nibert, David, 52–53
Nowatzki, Al, 68, 80, 90–91,
    157–159
Nozick, Robert, 108–109, 124

Onfray, Michel, 4–5, 90, 119–120
Overall, Christine, 38, 145, 178,
    184

Phelps, Norm, 31, 41–43, 45, 57,
    75, 77, 192
pigs, 44–46, 59, 76–77, 83,
    100–101
plants, ethics of eating, 13–14,
    126–129
Pollan, Michael, 167
Potter, Will, 12, 26
Procrustean bed, definition of, 1–2,
    6–7
progressive revelation, 37–40, 43,
    48, 73–85

Quran, 20, 37, 58, 76, 102 n. 40,
    178–180

Rambo, Lewis R., 3, 23–24, 47,
    142, 151–152, 154

Regan, Tom, 78, 168–169
Rising, Dallas, 124
Rowlands, Mark, 103–104, 148
Russell, Bertrand, 45

Scully, Matthew, 30, 48–49, 120
sharks, 109
Shermer, Michael, 133–134
Singer, Peter, 4–5, 7, 17, 62–63,
   89, 93–94, 98–100, 105,
   112–113, 128–130, 133–136,
   146–147
Skinny Bitch, 76–77
Socha, Kim, 17, 68, 117
speciesism, definitions of, 32 n. 10,
   89
Stănescu, James, 149, 152
Stanton, Elizabeth Cady, 34, 177
Stenger, Victor, 7, 13 n. 5, 33, 52,
   73–74, 92–96, 105, 116, 143,
   146

St. Francis of Assisi, 41, 46, 80
suicide food, 83
Sylvan, Diane, 40, 84

Torpy, Jason, 132–133
Tuttle, Will, 40, 52, 72, 76, 116,
   120, 164, 167

vegan(ism), 7–15, 30, 46, 79–80,
   106, 128–129, 132–133, 149,
   150–170

Watson, Donald, 128–129, 161–
   163, 166
Wicca, 23 n. 9, 83–85
Wilson, Peter D., 118, 124–125,
   128, 136–137, 166
wolves, 80–81

Yinger, Milton J., 155–157

About the Author

Kim Socha, Ph.D., Indiana University of Pennsylvania, is the author of *Women, Destruction, and the Avant-Garde: A Paradigm for Animal Liberation* (Rodopi: 2011) and is a contributing editor to *Confronting Animal Exploitation: Grassroots Essays on Liberation and Veganism* (McFarland Publishing: 2013) and *Defining Critical Animal Studies: A Social Justice Approach for Liberation* (Peter Lang: 2014). She has also published on topics such as Latino/a literature, surrealism, critical animal studies, and composition pedagogy. Kim is an English professor and activist for animal liberation, drug policy reform, and transformative justice.

www.ingramcontent.com/pod-product-compliance
Lightning Source LLC
Jackson TN
JSHW010719100325
80410JS00026B/163